MW01225852

Woodworker's
39 Sure-Fire Projects

Woodworker's
39 Sure-Fire Projects

Editors of
Woodworker's Magazine

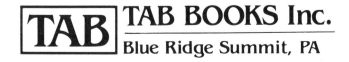

TAB BOOKS Inc.
Blue Ridge Summit, PA

FIRST EDITION
FIRST PRINTING

Copyright © 1989 by Davis Publications, Inc.
Printed in the United States of America

Reproduction or publication of the content in any manner, without express
permission of the publisher, is prohibited. No liability is assumed with respect
to the use of the information herein.

Library of Congress Cataloging-in-Publication Data

Woodworker's 39 sure-fire projects / by the editors of Woodworker
   magazine.
       p.   cm.
   Includes index.
   ISBN 0-8306-9051-4 : ISBN 0-8306-9351-3 (pbk.)
   1. Furniture making—Amateurs' manuals. I. Woodworker (New York,
N.Y. : 1980)   II. Title: Woodworker's thirty-nine sure-fire
projects.
TT195.W66 1989
684.1'042—dc19   88-38533
                                            CIP

TAB BOOKS Inc. offers software for sale. For information
and a catalog, please contact TAB Software Department,
Blue Ridge Summit, PA 17294-0850.

Questions regarding the content of this book
should be addressed to:

   Reader Inquiry Branch
   TAB BOOKS Inc.
   Blue Ridge Summit, PA 17294-0214

Cover photograph courtesy of Davis Publications, Inc.

Contents

Introduction   vii
All-in-One Entertainment Center   1
Banjo Wall Clock   12
Bedside Table   16
Butler's Tray Table   18
Captain's Trundle Bed   25
Charming Pine Rocking Horse   35
Cheese and Wine Cart   45
Chessboard Game Table   52
Child's Footlocker   61
Child's Bookrack/Stool   69
Colonial Desk with Bookrack   72
Classy Contemporary Bar   78
Compact Bar/Cabinet Combo   88
Compact Picnic Group   93
Compact Writing Desk   96
Contemporary Hall Clock   100

Corner Bookcase/Desk   109
Decorative Bookshelf/Table   117
Divider Unit with Desk   123
Dough Box End Table   129
Durable Butcher Block Table   132
Foldaway Bed/Storage Unit   138
Functional Occasional Table   146
Handsome Wardrobe   152
Home Office   161
Lightweight Desk   171
Magazine Table   174
Mobile Server   182
Modern Storage Cabinet   192
Sawhorse Toolbox   202
Spice Racks   207
Super Workbench   210
3-in-1 Patio Unit   218
3-in-1 Sports Gear Cabinet   223
Tile-Top Table with Built-In Planter   228
Trestle Desk   236
Trestle Table and Benches   242
Two Shaving Bars   248
Wall-Hung Sewing Center   252
Index   259

Introduction

THIS BOOK CONTAINS AN ASSORTMENT OF fine furniture projects for the beginning and intermediate woodworker. They have been collected by the editors of *Woodworker* Magazine and represent the work of various craftsmen, chief among them John Capotosto. We at TAB BOOKS are proud to bring you this collection and are sure you will find *39 Surefire Projects* to be a source of enjoyment, not only in doing the work you love, but in using the projects in your home as well.

Most of the materials in this book are available at your local lumberyard. Some of the more unusual items—the carvings, clock mechanisms, spindles, finials, and appliques—are also available from Armor Products, P.O. Box 445, East Northport, NY 11731.

All-In-One Entertainment Center

BEFORE YOU START this project, read the instructions carefully to familiarize yourself with what is involved. Check the sizes of the component shelves; your equipment may require more space. Change the dimensions accordingly. You will find it a pleasure to organize your home electronics in these handsome cabinets made of oak veneers. The larger unit holds a TV and VCR and has a storage compartment. To the right, a narrow vertical drawer stores video cassettes, stacked on the shelves so the labels can be easily read.

The TV rests on a pullout shelf which swivels, enabling the screen to be directed toward the viewer. The VCR rests on a pullout platform to accommodate top loading units. The audio equipment unit has four shelves, three of which are adjustable in 1-inch increments to accommodate components of varying heights. The top shelf has a pullout platform for a turntable.

The softly tinted glass doors keep out the dust and add to the appearance of the piece. Special hardware is used, eliminating the need for drilling the glass. A second vertical drawer, on the left, stores

Fig. 1-1. Mark dado sites on story stick. Draw dado lines on board then align dadoes of dadoing square with pencil marks.

Fig. 1-2. Dadoing square is clamped into place then dadoes are cut with router fitted with ¾-inch bit. Clean burr at corners.

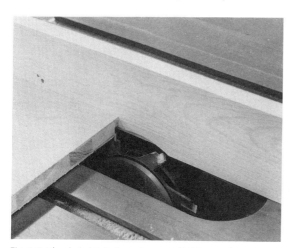

Fig. 1-3. The dado blade is made to cut slightly into the auxiliary wood fence. Set blade and fence to make ¼ × ⅜ rabbet.

Fig. 1-4. Locate shelf support holes then use awl to mark centers for drill bit. Drill ¼-inch shelf support holes ⅜ deep.

audio cassette tapes. The bottom pull-out compartment holds record albums. Five metal dividers hold the records in small easy-to-manage groups.

Two base pieces are used for the speakers, one at each end. Each has a swivel platform to position speakers for the best acoustical results. Except for some solid lumber used for trim, construction is entirely of plywood: ¾ inch for the cabinets and ¼ inch for the rear panels. Oak was used for the project in the photo but other wood species may be substituted. Most joints are dadoed and glued, reducing the number of fasteners used.

Plywood is available in either veneer core or lumber core. You might prefer lumber core because it can be used without edging in some cases. It has a wide center band which can be sanded smooth and will take a finish far superior to the veneer core which must always be edged. For example, the vertical drawer fronts, the album drawer front and the storage

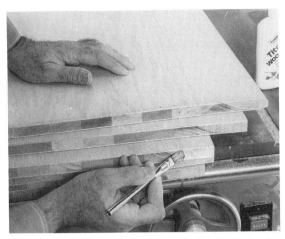

Fig. 1-5. Rough-assemble cabinet parts for fit. Glue sizing the edges of plywood panels with diluted aliphatic resin glue.

Fig. 1-6. Aprons have been fastened with glue and screws, holes counterbored. Final assembly is glued and clamped.

compartment door did not need to be edged.

Regardless of the plywood used, we recommend that your table saw and radial arm saw be fitted with a plywood blade because of the smooth cut it produces. The materials list shows the actual cut sizes of the various parts. The overall measurements will be greater because of the edging which is added after assembly in most cases.

Set the saw fence to rip the 19-inch widths of the sides, top and bottoms, then reset the fence to rip the dividers and fixed shelves which are 18¾ inches wide to allow clearance for the rear panel. The lengths of each piece are then cut to size. If your components require wider shelves, make the necessary adjustments in the measurements at this time.

The dadoes should be cut with a router fitted with a ¾-inch cutter, preferably carbide. To ensure accuracy and to simplify dadoing, make up a dadoing square. This consists of a piece of hard wood with crosspieces fastened at each end. You can also make it with just one crosspiece.

Regardless of the design, the members must be perpendicular. Assemble with glue and screws. After the glue sets, clamp the jig to a piece of scrap and cut a dado into the crosspiece. The depth of cut should be ¼ inch.

Mark the location of each dado on all boards, then position the jig so its dado lines up with the dado marks on the board. Clamp securely then cut the dado. Position clamps at both ends of the jig, but so they won't obstruct the travel of the router.

When all the dadoes have been cut, clean the corners with sandpaper. A 1-inch dowel wrapped with 220-grit paper works fine to remove the burr.

After cutting the dadoes, rabbet the rear edges of the side, top and bottom members. Make the rabbet ¼ inch deep and ⅜ inch wide using a router, or on the table saw using a dado blade. If the table saw is used, clamp a wood auxiliary fence to the saw fence so you can run the dado right up to the fence. Actually, you should let the dado blade bite into the wood fence slightly to assure you of a good clean cut. The divider and side panel of the audio cabinet

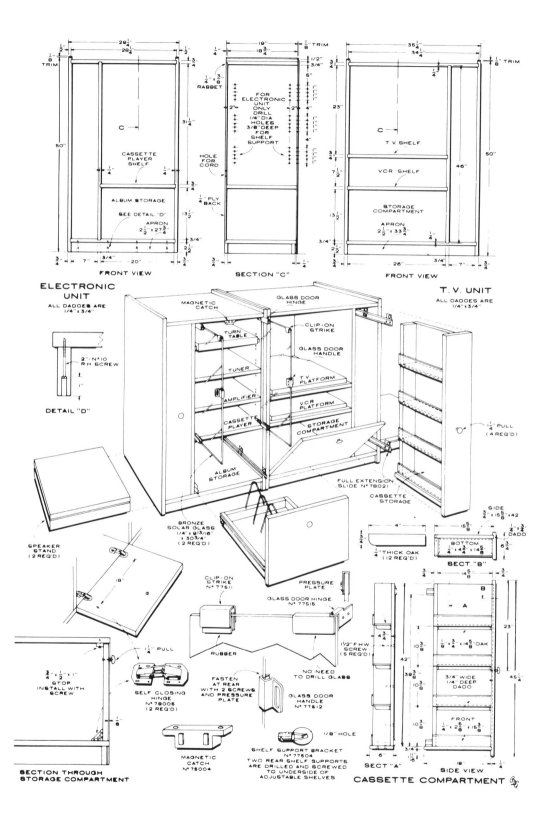

FRONT VIEW

SECTION "C"

FRONT VIEW

ELECTRONIC UNIT
ALL DADOES ARE 1/4" x 3/4"

T. V. UNIT
ALL DADOES ARE 1/4" x 3/4"

DETAIL "D"

SPEAKER STAND (2 REQ'D)

SECTION THROUGH STORAGE COMPARTMENT

SECT "A"

SIDE VIEW

CASSETTE COMPARTMENT

4

are drilled for the shelf peg supports. Locate the ¼-inch holes as indicated in the drawing and drill them ⅜ inch deep.

The main cabinet members can now be assembled. This must be done in stages. The sequence is as follows: 1) shelf (or shelves) to the divider; 2) divider to top and bottom members; 3) sides to top and bottom.

Before assembly, glue-size the edges of the shelves and tops and bottoms. Do this by diluting the glue with water. Brush on and allow to dry (about 15 minutes), then sand lightly. Now apply the glue full-strength and assemble in the sequence outlined above. Use cauls under the clamps to prevent damage to the workpiece. Make sure the pieces are perpendicular after the clamps have been applied. Allow the glue to set then add the next section. The sides are added in the final assembly.

The edging can now be added to the exposed edges of the front and top. Use solid oak that has been dressed to a thickness of ¾ inch. This will require greater accuracy when applying, but it will mean far less work later. If you use ¹³⁄₁₆-inch stock, it will be easier to apply, but then the overhang will have to be trimmed. Take your choice.

Rip the stock to a width of ⅛ inch, on the table saw. Set the fence ⅛ inch away from the blade then lock securely. Push the piece through the saw blade using a push stick. Glue the ⅛-inch trim to the plywood edging using double-pointed brads. To use the nails, grasp them with the pliers and force them into the plywood edges, spaced about 8 inches apart. Push them until about ¹⁄₁₆ inch protrudes.

Starting with the side members, apply glue to the plywood edge and to the undersides of the oak edging. Carefully position the trim over the plywood and press down, allowing the brad points to penetrate the underside of the trim. Add cauls and clamp securely. The shelf members are edged next followed by the divider, then top and bottom and lastly, the other side member. After the front edges are completed, add the two strips to the top edges of the side panels.

The vertical drawers for the cassettes are of simple construction. The front panel is dadoed to take the bottom and side panels. The rear and bottom are fastened with butt joints. When fastening the cassette shelf supports, use two spacer blocks to obtain the proper spacing. Make the blocks 4 × 10⅜ inches and place them at the sides of the opening starting at the bottom. Apply glue to the back of the 14⅝-inch support and, resting it on the blocks, fasten to the panel. Add the 4-inch side pieces then repeat for the next shelf working upward.

The shelves are made of ¼-inch oak plywood. The top of the front members are edged with solid oak. Cut ¼- x -¼-inch strips on the table saw and glue them carefully to the top edge of the shelf fronts. Here the double pointed nails are almost a necessity. You can make a simple clamping jig as shown in the photo. This is far better than trying to use clamps on such a thin piece. The same jig is used to edge the ¼-inch plywood of the turntable bases. Simply insert the glued-up stock against the backboard, then insert the wedges and tap them gently until the joint closes tightly. Do not wipe away any glue that squeezes out. Let it dry then scrape off and sand later.

When assembling the shelves, note that three have the fronts extending from the left and three from the right. This is

Fig. 1-7. Sand cabinet with care. Close-up view of doublepointed nails. For ⅛-inch edging, let point protrude ⅛ inch.

Fig. 1-8. Upper full-extension drawer slide has been installed into cassette compartment. Use slotted holes.

Fig. 1-9. The TV swivel is installed onto fixed shelf and platform is mounted into sides using access holes predrilled.

Fig. 1-10. Locating screw holes in VCR platform with pencil. Use awl to make screw pilot hole. Mount door spring hinge.

Fig. 1-11. Simple gluing jig for the ¼-inch shelves. Saw fence is used as a backstop. Tap wedge to tighten joint. Sand cabinet.

Fig. 1-12. Speaker base swivel is being mounted to underside of swivel top. Remove the swivel top before applying finish.

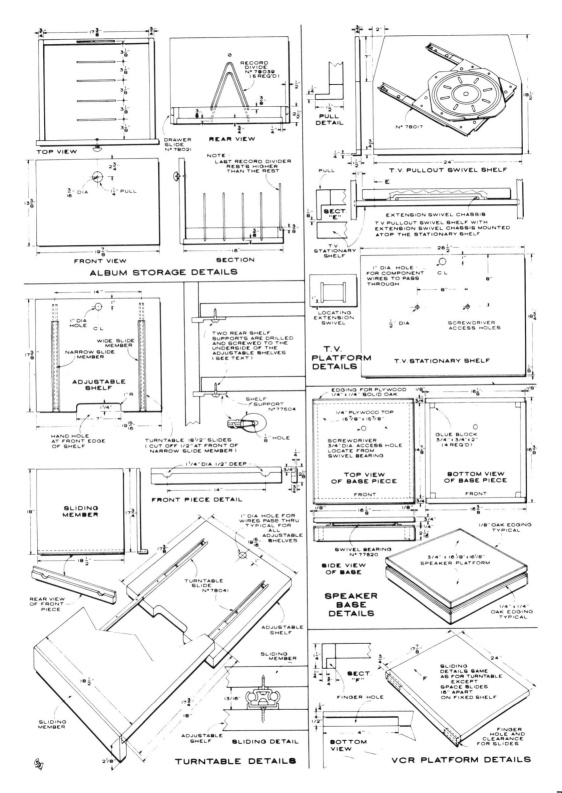

ALBUM STORAGE DETAILS

TOP VIEW

REAR VIEW

RECORD DIVIDER
N° 78039 (6 REQ'D)

DRAWER SLIDE N° 78021

NOTE:
LAST RECORD DIVIDER RESTS HIGHER THAN THE REST

FRONT VIEW

SECTION

3/16" DIA
1/4" PULL

PULL DETAIL

T.V. PULLOUT SWIVEL SHELF

N° 78017

PULL

SECT "E"

EXTENSION SWIVEL CHASSIS

T.V PULLOUT SWIVEL SHELF WITH EXTENSION SWIVEL CHASSIS MOUNTED ATOP THE STATIONARY SHELF

T.V. STATIONARY SHELF

LOCATING EXTENSION SWIVEL

T.V. STATIONARY SHELF

1" DIA. HOLE FOR COMPONENT WIRES TO PASS THROUGH

1/2" DIA

SCREWDRIVER ACCESS HOLES

T.V. PLATFORM DETAILS

ADJUSTABLE SHELF

1" DIA HOLE
WIDE SLIDE MEMBER
NARROW SLIDE MEMBER

TWO REAR SHELF SUPPORTS ARE DRILLED AND SCREWED TO THE UNDERSIDE OF THE ADJUSTABLE SHELVES (SEE TEXT)

SHELF SUPPORT N° 77504

1/8" HOLE

HAND HOLE AT FRONT EDGE OF SHELF

TURNTABLE 18 1/2" SLIDES (CUT OFF 1/2" AT FRONT OF NARROW SLIDE MEMBER)

1 1/4" DIA 1/2" DEEP

FRONT PIECE DETAIL

EDGING FOR PLYWOOD 1/4" x 1/4" SOLID OAK

1/4" PLYWOOD TOP 16 5/8" x 16 5/8"

SCREWDRIVER 3/4" DIA. ACCESS HOLE LOCATE FROM SWIVEL BEARING

TOP VIEW OF BASE PIECE
FRONT

GLUE BLOCK 3/4" x 3/4" x 2" (4 REQ'D)

BOTTOM VIEW OF BASE PIECE
FRONT

SWIVEL BEARING N° 77520

SIDE VIEW OF BASE

1/8" OAK EDGING TYPICAL

3/4" x 16 1/8" x 16 1/8" SPEAKER PLATFORM

SPEAKER BASE DETAILS

1/4" x 1/4" OAK EDGING TYPICAL

SLIDING MEMBER

1" DIA HOLE FOR WIRES PASS THRU TYPICAL FOR ALL ADJUSTABLE SHELVES

TURNTABLE SLIDE N° 78041

ADJUSTABLE SHELF

REAR VIEW OF FRONT PIECE

SLIDING MEMBER

ADJUSTABLE SHELF

SLIDING MEMBER

ADJUSTABLE SHELF

SLIDING DETAIL

TURNTABLE DETAILS

SECT "F"

FINGER HOLE

BOTTOM VIEW

SLIDING DETAILS SAME AS FOR TURNTABLE EXCEPT SPACE SLIDES 16" APART ON FIXED SHELF

FINGER HOLE AND CLEARANCE FOR SLIDES

VCR PLATFORM DETAILS

MATERIALS LIST

Unless otherwise specified all lumber is ¾" oak lumber core plywood. All measurements are in inches.

Purpose	Size	Description	Quantity
TV Unit			
Side	19" × 50"		2
Divider	18¾" × 46"		1
Top	19" × 34¼"		1
Bottom	19" × 34¼"		1
TV shelf	18¾" × 26½"		1
VCR shelf	18¾" × 26½"		1
TV platform	17¾" × 24"		1
TV platform front	¾" × 1½" × 24"	Solid oak	1
VCR platform	17⅞" × 24"		1
VCR platform front	¾" × 1¼" × 24"	Solid oak	1
Apron	2½" × 33½"		1
Rear panel	¼" × 34⅜" × 46"	Plywood	1
VCR compartment front	6¹³⁄₁₆" × 45¼"		1
Compartment side	15⅝" × 42"		1
Compartment rear	4¾" × 42"		1
Compartment bottom	6" × 18"		1
Shelf bottom	¼" × 4¾" × 14⅝"	Plywood	3
Shelf front	¼" × 2⅝" × 15⅜"	Plywood	4
Shelf support	⅛" × ¾" × 14⅝"	Oak	3
Shelf support end	⅛" × ¾" × 4"	Oak	6
Storage compartment door	13¼" × 25⅞"		1
Electronic Unit			
Side	19" × 50"		2
Divider	18¾" × 46"		1
Top	19" × 28¼"		1
Bottom	19" × 28¼"		1
Apron	2½" × 33¾"		1
Rear panel	¼" × 28⅜" × 46"		1
Fixed shelf	19" × 20½"		1
Adjustable shelf	17¾" × 19¹⁵⁄₁₆"		2
Turntable adjustable shelf	17⅜" × 19¹⁵⁄₁₆"		1
Turntable platform	17¾" × 18½"		1
Turntable platform front	¾" × 2⅛" × 18½"	Oak	1
Album storage front	13⅜" × 19⅞"		1
Album storage bottom	16" × 17⅞"		1
Album storage side	2½" × 15¾"		2
Album storage rear	1¾" × 17⅜"		1
Cassette compartment front	6¹³⁄₁₆" × 45¼"		1

Purpose	Size	Description	Quantity
Cassette compartment side	15⅝″ × 42″		1
Cassette compartment rear	4¾″ × 42″		1
Cassette compartment bottom	6″ × 18″		1
Shelf bottom	¼″ × 4¾″ × 14⅝″	Plywood	3
Shelf front	¼″ × 2⅝″ × 15⅜″	Plywood	4
Shelf support	⅛″ × ¾″ × 14⅝″	Oak	3
Shelf support end	⅛″ × ¾″ × 4″		6
Glass door	¼″ × 9¹³⁄₁₆″ × 30¾″		2
Speaker base front	2¹⁄₁₆″ × 16⅛″		2
Speaker base front	2¹⁄₁₆″ × 16⅛″		2
Speaker base side	2¹⁄₁₆″ × 14⅞″		4
Speaker base top	¼″ × 15⅞″ × 15⅞″		2
Speaker platform	16⅛″ × 16⅛″		2
Glue block	¾″ × ¾″ × 2″		8
Solid oak trim	¾″ × 12″ × 8′		1
Miscellaneous			
Glass hinge		No. 77515	4
Glass door handle		No. 77512	2
Clip-on strike plate		No. 77511	2
Magnetic catch		No. 75004	1
Shelf support		No. 78040	6
Pull		No. 78038	4
Record divider		No. 78039	5
Spring loaded hinge		No. 78005	2
Drawer slide		No. 78021	3 sets
Turntable slide		No. 78041	2 sets
TV swivel		No. 78017	1
Swivel bearing		No. 77520	2
Double pointed nail		No. 83007	100
Screw	1½″—8 FH		10
Screw	2″—10 RH		6
Screw (for glass hinges & rear panels)	½″—6 Pan head		62

Note: The miscellaneous hardware items are available from Armor Products. The numbers shown are from the Armor catalog.

because the cassette drawers are mirror opposites. Apply glue to the front edge of the shelves and along the lower part rear of the shelf front. Again, use the double pointed brads and clamp in the jig.

Install the three shelves by gluing them to the shelf supports. Glue the projecting ends of the fronts to the edge of the rear panel. The lower front piece does not have a shelf. It rests on the floor of the drawer. Just use a glue block at the corner opposite the projecting part, and lay a bead of glue along the bottom edge.

The album drawer had a full-size front panel but the sides and rear are only 2½ inches high. This allows easy access to the albums: Cut ¼- × -¾-inch rabbets at the bottom of the front and side panels, then drill the 3⁄16-inch holes for the record dividers. The one set of holes made in the rear panel will make that divider stand higher than the rest. This will have no effect on the storage of the records. If you like, you can drill these holes deeper so the last divider will be even with the rest.

The adjustable shelves are made as shown. The two lower ones for the audio cabinet are identical. Cut them to size then add the ⅛-inch oak trim to the fronts. The notch at the front of the turntable shelf serves as a hand hole. Add ⅛-inch trim at the front edge then round off the corners with the router.

All three shelves should be drilled at the rear with a 1-inch hole. This will allow access for the component cables. The turntable shelf has a 2⅛-inch-deep front to conceal the shelf and slide hardware. Note that two mortises are required at the rear edge of the front piece, allowing clearance for the slide hardware.

The TV platform rests on the pull-out swivel which in turn rests on the fixed shelf. The platform has a 1½-inch oak front which is rabbeted along its length. The rear of the shelf is clipped diagonally to allow clearance for the shelf to turn either in its retracted or extended position. A suitable hole (1 inch diameter) should be drilled into the rear of the fixed TV shelf. This will allow cables to pass through from the VCR. Two screwdriver holes are also drilled into

the fixed shelf as shown. These are needed to install the sliding track.

The VCR platform also pulls out to allow easy access to the top of the VCR. The platform has a ¾- × -1¼-inch oak front with finger grips at each end. These notches also serve as clearance for the movable part of the sliding hardware.

This door is a plain rectangle with the edges exposed. (If you used veneer core plywood, the edges should be trimmed with ⅛-inch oak edging.) Instead of opening sideways, this door drops down. The spring-loaded hinges serve as dropleaf supports and the springs allow it to self-close when it is raised. They eliminate the need for catches. All that is required is a stop block under the VCR shelf. The nice part about using these hinges is that they allow the door to set in ⅛ inch.

The glass doors are installed with the special hinges which eliminate the need to drill the glass.

The speaker bases consist of the base part and the movable top which turns on 12-inch swivels. Make the base sides and ends of plywood and use oak edging for the exposed end pieces. The top is covered with ¼-inch oak plywood with edges trimmed in ¼- × -¼-inch oak. Use the gluing jig to fasten the trim. The tops are made of ¾-inch plywood edged with ⅛-inch oak.

The rear panels are made to fit into the rabbeted parts of the cabinet. Drill the necessary holes for cords and cables then install with screws.

The adjustable shelf support pegs are drilled to take screws. The screws are installed after the shelves are in place. They prevent the shelves from moving toward the glass, but more important, they prevent the turntable platform from tilting when it is extended.

The turntable's movable slide members must be shortened about ¾ inch. Use a hack saw and cut off the front ends. If you cut away one of the screw mounting holes, redrill about 1 inch from the end. Install the slides with wood screws. The TV turntable is mounted with its fixed track 1 inch from the front of the shelf. The access holes are used to fasten the movable track to the underside of the platform.

The storage compartment is mounted with spring-loaded hinges. Support the free end of the door on blocks and butt the bottom edge against the front edge of the cabinet. Center the door from side to side, then position the hinges and mark the hole locations. Use screws only in the slotted holes then try the door. If okay, install the rest of the screws.

The left cassette drawer uses two lefthanded tracks and slides. The right hand door uses the right hand set. The lower set should be installed ⅛ inch above the bottom panel. The fixed track should be placed as far back as possible so the drawer fronts set in ⅛ inch when closed. The album drawer hardware is installed like the cassette drawers, ⅛ inch from the bottom panel.

Install the glass doors with the special hinges. Set the hinges ⅛ inch in from the cabinet frame then mount one in each corner. Insert the pressure plates onto the glass. These have adhesive on one surface. Peel off the protective backing then apply to the glass at the inside corners. The set screws of the hinges are made to bear against these plates. Adjust the glass so that it is properly centered. Install the strike plates at the top of the doors, then install the magnetic catch so that it contacts the back of the strike plates.

The cabinet may be finished by applying a paste wood filler with the desired color (stain) such as a light oak, medium oak or dark oak (Golden Oak). Apply the filler as per the manufacturers instructions then apply suitable sealer and topcoats of lacquer.

Another method of finishing is to use a Danish oil finish. We chose Deftco Danish Oil Finish. Simply brush it on, let stand for 30 minutes, then wipe with clean cloths. The resulting finish is deep, mellow, and long lasting.

Banjo Wall Clock

THIS BANJO CLOCK doesn't play music but the sound of its battery-operated movement is pleasing, and it will keep you well informed of the time. Made of pine, the case is not difficult to build. The moldings are standard and available at lumber yards. The turned finial, decorative eagle, and clock works can also be purchased.

Using a saber saw or jigsaw, cut the outline of the clock, including the rectangular cutout for the movement. Next, shape the edge with a router. If you do not have a router, you can round the edges with sandpaper. A beading cutter was used on the clock shown, but you may prefer another shape. Note that the shaping is interrupted at several points, (see drawing). Add the molding, attaching it with brads and glue.

At the top, allow the ends to protrude, then trim off with a coping saw after the glue has dried. The molding at the neck is mitered. Cut the front piece first, then fit the side sections to it.

To mount the finial, drill a ⅜-inch hole ¾ inch deep into the bottom. Then insert a 1½-inch length of dowel. Drill a corresponding hole into the ¼-inch platform and the top of the case. Also drill a clearance hole at the rear of the case for the hanger.

The eagle was shiny bright when purchased, but it was "antiqued" by spraying it with black paint. Before the

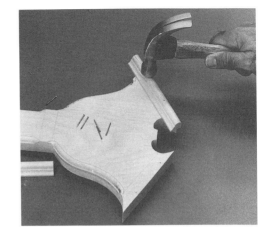

Fig. 2-1. Having cut the case and shaped the edges with a router, attach the molding pieces.

Fig. 2-2. Cut an opening in case to accommodate the clock's battery operated mechanism.

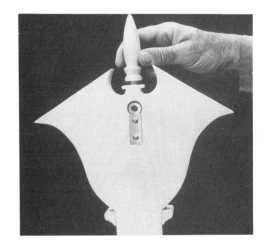

Fig. 2-3. Drill a ⅜-inch hole ¾ inch deep into both finial and case. Attach finial with 1½-inch dowel.

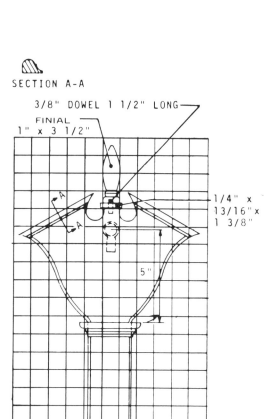

SECTION A-A

3/8" DOWEL 1 1/2" LONG

FINIAL
1" x 3 1/2"

1/4" x
13/16" x
1 3/8"

5"

FRONT VIEW EACH SQUARE
EQUALS= 1"
1 1/8" PINE, CLEAR OR COMMON

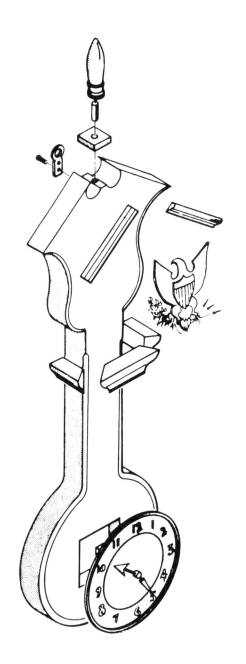

14

MATERIALS LIST

Purpose	Size	Description	Quantity
Basic unit	1⅛″ × 11″ × 23″	Pine	1
Finial platform	¼″ × 1″ × 1½″	Pine	1
Trim	¾″ × 2′	Nose and cove molding	1

Note: You will also need, finial, eagle, dial, clock movement, hardware, etc.

paint has a chance to dry, wipe the surface with a cloth. This will create highlights while the depressions remain dark. To mount the eagle, pierce two tiny holes with a brad, then install with escutcheons. The dial is also mounted with escutcheons.

Bedside Table

WHY MUST A bedside table be boring? They always look alike. Simple and square, often useful, but never interesting.

This table, however, would be an unusual addition to any bedroom. It's made with a handsome curve that's painted a bright color, and includes plenty of tabletop space for phone or bedside lamp. There's also a convenient drawer and even a bin ideally suited for tucking away your telephone directory where it can be found when needed. Drawer and fronts are naturally finished wood, a nice accent to the rest of this colorful table.

It's all made from ¾-inch birch plywood (except for the drawer bottom and slides). See the adjacent Materials List.

To begin construction, cut out the top, bottom, sides, and back as shown. Take the sides, and lay out the cutout. This can be cut with a hole saw for the curves and a table saw for the straight cuts. Or use a saber saw or band saw for everything. Now, assemble the top, bottom, back, and sides with glue and No. 4 finish nails.

The drawer and front are made next, so they fit exactly to the dimensions of the main body of the table. Cut out the drawer pieces as shown in the drawing. Assemble the drawer with No. 4 finish nails through the sides into the front and back of the drawer and glue.

Cut the drawer slides out of a piece of scrap pine and attach them to the inside of the table with glue and No. 17 brads. Use the drawer that you have made to determine the exact position of the slides.

Next, attach the front with glue and No. 4 finish nails through the sides.

To finish the table, start by covering all exposed plywood edges with veneer tape. Set all nails and apply wood putty. Sand unit with No. 80, then with No. 120 sandpaper until smooth enough for finishing.

The drawer and front were finished with a fine natural stain made from 60 percent boiled linseed oil and 40 percent turpentine. The main body of the table was finished with four coats of high gloss latex enamel. Each coat was brushed on and sanded with No. 220 paper between coats.

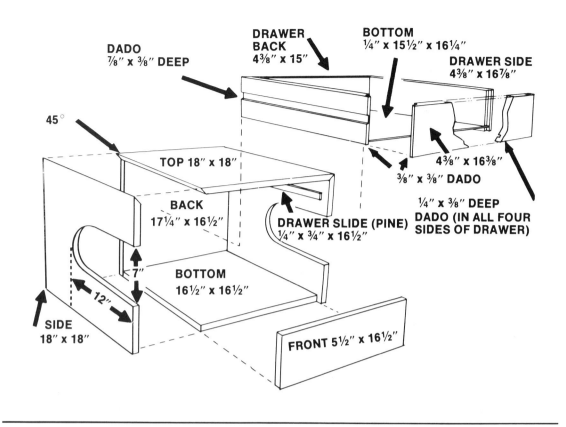

DADO
⅞″ x ⅜″ DEEP

DRAWER BACK
4⅜″ x 15″

BOTTOM
¼″ x 15½″ x 16¼″

DRAWER SIDE
4⅜″ x 16⅞″

45°

TOP 18″ x 18″

4⅜″ x 16⅜″

⅜″ x ⅜″ DADO

¼″ x ⅜″ DEEP
DADO (IN ALL FOUR SIDES OF DRAWER)

BACK
17¼″ x 16½″

DRAWER SLIDE (PINE)
¼″ x ¾″ x 16½″

7″

BOTTOM
16½″ x 16½″

12″

SIDE
18″ x 18″

FRONT 5½″ x 16½″

MATERIALS LIST

Size	Description	Quantity
¾″ × 18″ × 18″	Birch plywood	3
¾″ × 17¼″ × 16½″	Birch plywood	1
¾″ × 16½″ × 16½″	Birch plywood	1
¾″ × 5½″ × 16½″	Birch plywood	1
¾″ × 4⅜″ × 16⅜″	Birch plywood	1
¾″ × 4⅜″ × 15″	Birch plywood	1
¾″ × 4⅜″ × 16⅞″	Birch plywood	2
¼″ × 15½″ × 16¼″	Masonite	1
¼″ × ¾″ × 16½″	Pine board	2
1½″	No. 4 finish nails	
¾″	No. 17 finish nails	
	Veneer tape	
	Contact cement	15′
	White glue	

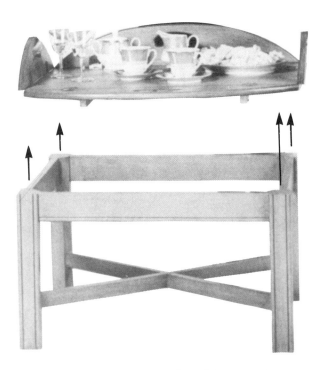

Butler's Tray Table

HERE'S A NEAT woodworking project that you'll be proud of—a butler's tray table. As the name implies, it serves two purposes—a sturdy table and a handsome serving tray. Special butler tray hinges have no projections and are spring loaded so they will hold in any position. A clever self-centering arrangement on the underside of the tray holds it in place on the base so it cannot accidentally slide off. The unit shown was made of lumber-core birch, but other woods may be substituted. For a colonial look, pine may be used.

Start with the base. Cut the squares for the legs to size, then clip the diagonal on the table saw. Be sure to place the fence so the waste will fall away from the blade, otherwise a kickback may result.

The legs are now ready to be grooved. This can be done either on the shaper, if you have one, or with the router. If the router is used, it would be best to mount it inverted on a table, as shown. This converts it to a mini-shaper and makes it much easier to use. Insert a V cutter in the router collet and set the proper depth of cut. The cut should be ⅛ inch deep. A makeshift fence consisting of a small piece of wood and a couple of clamps will do. Set the fence so the cut is ⅜ inch in from the edge of the work. Run the work through, then change cutters and round off the three corners shown. If your cutter has a pilot, you will not require the fence.

Rails for the table are cut to size and drilled to take two ⅜-inch dowels. Dowel transfer points are used to locate the holes. Prop up the work as shown for proper alignment. Center punch the prick marks left by the points, then proceed to drill the holes for the dowels. The depth of the holes should be 1¹⁄₁₆ inch. Insert dowels with glue and assemble the base.

The top board is prepared next. If your table saw fence will not extend far enough, try this: clamp a strip of wood to the

Fig. 4-1. When ripping the diagonal for the legs, it is best to set the fence on the proper side to give you the maximum safety.

Fig. 4-2. The router is being used to groove the legs. The inverted position shown makes it easier working small pieces.

Fig. 4-3. Accuracy makes the drill press ideal for holes. If you use a portable drill, be sure it's straight and square.

Fig. 4-4. Place base on top, center carefully. Mark off the inside edges of the rail, then slowly cut along the guides.

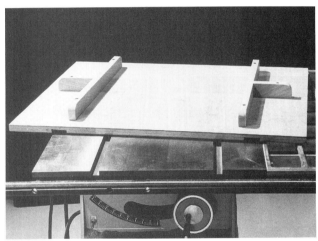

Fig. 4-5. The aligning jig on the underside of the top is made with rounded corners to make the tray "fall" into its place.

Fig. 4-6. Shown here is the easy way to mortise hinges. The plywood jig will give perfect results every time. Note center lines.

20

Fig. 4-7. One hinge is already mounted and the other is ready to be. Remember other types of wood, as pine, may be used.

Fig. 4-8. One advantage of lumber-core plywood is that edges can be sanded easily. Here the table base is ready for finishing.

underside of the work, then use the edge of the table as a guide. Place the assembled base on the tabletop and carefully center it. Next mark off the jig which consists of four cleats, two long and two short. They are cut so they will be a trifle smaller than the inner dimension of the rails. Align and then install.

The curved sides are made next. These can be cut either on the band saw or with a saber saw. After cutting, sand the edges smooth then shape the edge still using the router as a shaper.

Next, mortise the hinges. Some butler hinges have half-round ends while others are square. Regardless of the hinge used, a mortising jig made of ¼-inch plywood can be used advantageously. Simply note the distance from the outside of the cutter to the outside of the router base plate.

Trace the outline of your hinge onto a piece of ¼-inch plywood, then enlarge the outline by adding the dimension obtained from the edge of the cutter to the edge of the base plate. This will give you an outline of your hinge measuring something like 8 × 14 inches. Cut this out, saving the outside part. This is now a guide for the router and if you will make a trial cut on scrap wood, you should find that the hinge will fit perfectly into the mortise.

The butler hinge is unique in that the leaves are not the same thickness. This means that the mortise will have to be made to the deepest part of the hinge. Shims are made to be placed under the thinner part, as shown. Some butler hinges have the same thickness leaves, so it is

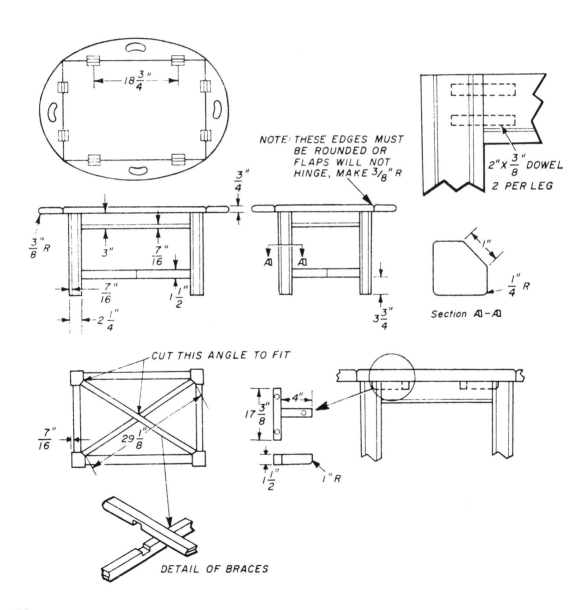

DETAIL OF BRACES

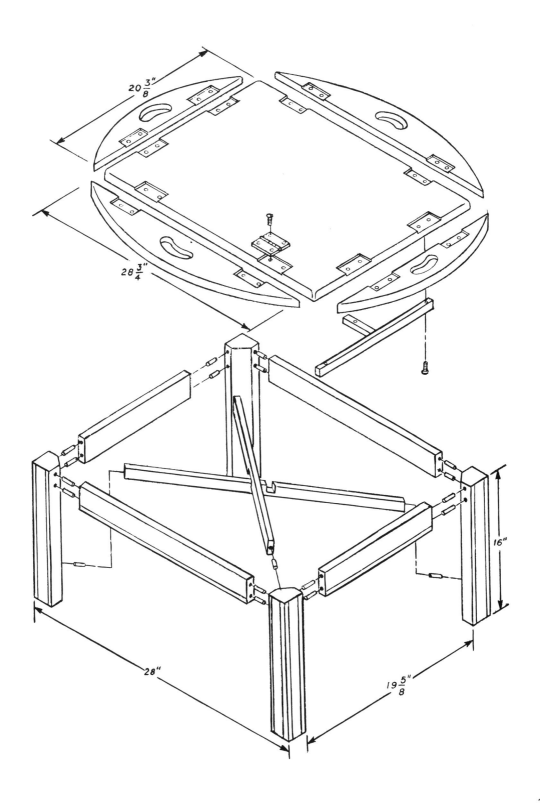

20 3/8"

28 3/4"

16"

28"

19 5/8"

23

Purpose	Size	Description	Quantity
Top	¾″ × 20⅜″ × 28⅞″	Red birch	1
Flaps	¾″ × 4¾″ × 28¾″	Red birch	2
Flaps	¾″ × 4¾″ × 20⅜″	Red birch	2
Rails	¾″ × 3″ × 23½″	Red birch	2
Rails	¾″ × 3″ × 17⅛″	Red birch	2
Legs	2¼″ × 2¼″ × 16″	Red birch	4
Stretcher	¾″ × 1½″ × 29⅛″	Red birch	2
	1½″	No. 8 Round-head screws	as needed
	⅜″ × 2″	Dowels	as needed

Note: You will also need butler tray hinges and finishing materials.

recommended that you not mortise for the hinge until you have it in hand. The dimension for the mortise was purposely left out of the drawing.

When mortising, place both the sides and table top in position and mortise them together.

Stretchers are added to complete the construction. Stretchers are glued in place and held with screws driven diagonally.

To finish the table, remove the hinges and sand all parts thoroughly. Then finish to your liking. Antique red (with the base coat thinned so the rich grain pattern of the red birch would show through) was used on this tray table. Many finishes are possible, and if antiquing is not your cup of tea, try a wood-tone stain topped off with a French polish.

Captain's Trundle Bed

THIS CAPTAIN'S TRUNDLE BED has a lower drawer that rolls out to be used as an extra bed or as a bin for clothes, bedding, toys, or whatever. It is designed so that both upper and lower sections take a 39- × -75-inch mattress (standard twin size). The drawer is mounted on casters and rolls out easily from either side. Prefinished paneling, in the head- and footboards as well as the roll-out bin, simplifies construction and adds to the appearance of this fine furniture. Finish of the solid lumber can be made to match or contrast with the paneling.

Common lumber is used for construction. By carefully choosing and cutting, you can eliminate most knots. The knots are not objectionable however, and some folks prefer them, so take your pick.

Rip the legs from a length of $^8\!/_4$ (2-inch) - × - 12-inch pine. The actual size of the board is $1^{13}\!/_{16} \times 11\frac{1}{4}$ inches. Cut four pieces, each $2\frac{1}{16}$ inches wide. After cutting, use a plane or jointer if you have one and smooth the rough edges left by the saw blade.

Next rip the two side pieces from $^5\!/_4$- × -10-inch stock (actual size $1^3\!/_{16} \times 9\frac{1}{4}$

inches), and trim the ends to make them 7⅜ inches long. Cut the cross members from the same material. Make two pieces each 6 × 39 inches and from the remaining strip, make two pieces each 3 × 39 inches.

Make a pattern for the scroll at the top of the crosspieces. Draw the necessary squares and plot the shape onto the pattern, using wrapping paper or thin cardboard. Cut the curved portion of the pattern, then trace onto the crosspieces. Cut the shape

with a saber saw fitted with a 10-tooth contour blade—this should leave a fairly smooth cut.

The side rails are made next. The offset step can be cut in several ways. You can rip most of the long section, then use a saber saw to finish at the offset. You can also use a band saw, or (although slower), you can cut the entire length with a saber saw. In either case, you will have to smooth out the edge. The best way to do this is to use

Fig. 5-1. Cut the slots for the paneling on a table saw. Notice the tape marks which indicate the start and stop points of blind slots.

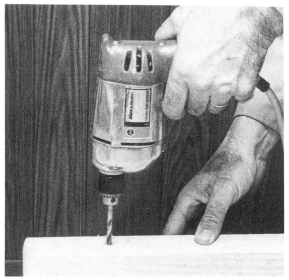

Fig. 5-2. The pilot holes for the screws in the bed posts are drilled as pictured above. The countersunk holes should be drilled first.

the router and template. The template is made only for the offset. A straight edge is then used for the long, straight part. The router is fitted with a flush cutter at least 1¼ inches long. Make the template from a piece of ⅛-inch hardboard. See detailed drawing.

Tack the template in place so that the cutter just bites into the rough saw-cut edge of the board. Nail the template to the inner surface of the side so the holes won't show.

Of course you can finish the edge by using a plane on the straight part and sandpapering the offset. Round the two

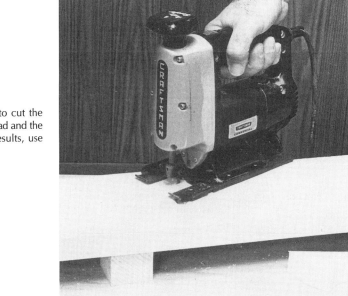

Fig. 5-3. Use a saber saw to cut the shaped edges of both the head and the foot boards. For the best results, use a smooth cutting blade.

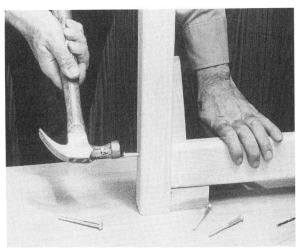

Fig. 5-4. Place a piece of scrap paneling in corners to align posts and cross members. Put scrap wood under crosspiece to position it.

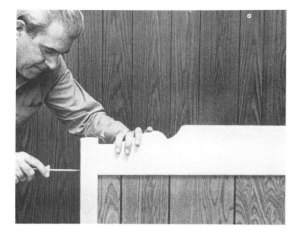

Fig. 5-5. Assemble the head and foot board sections with glue and screws. Countersunk screw heads will be concealed by wood buttons.

Fig. 5-6. Having cut side pieces with a saber saw, you can clean edges using a router and template, or else plane and sandpaper.

Fig. 5-7. The ends of the side pieces are dadoes to receive the bed hooks. Use a side cutter about ⅜ or ½ inch deep and use a guide.

upper edges and outer edge of the lower part of the sides. The cross members are rounded on all four edges.

Cut a groove for the end panels in each of the crosspieces. Note that the groove is centered. Use either a dado blade or make several passes with a regular blade on your table saw. The upper pieces are cut on the lower edge. The top edge is cut in the lower pieces.

Before making the cut in the workpiece, check the width of the cut on a scrap piece. The panel should fit snugly. Make the groove $1\frac{1}{32}$ inch deep.

Reset the fence for the posts, placing the grooves in the center. Note that blind grooves are made. Place masking tape on the saw table and draw starting and stopping lines as shown. Make test cuts on scrap lumber first. Hold the work slightly above the revolving blade with the end of the piece aligned with the pencil mark. Carefully lower the work into the blade and advance until the rear end of the post reaches the mark on the second piece of tape. Grooves (dadoes) should start and stop 3 inches before ends of posts. See detail.

Locate the screw holes in each of the posts. Note that the spacing is different at the tops and bottoms. Drill the $\frac{1}{2}$-inch counterbore hole first. Make it $\frac{3}{8}$ inch deep,

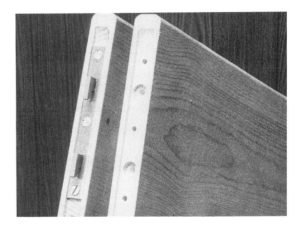

Fig. 5-8. Here we see the side piece ends, one with hooks, the other without. The larger holes are drilled clearance for rear projections.

Fig. 5-9. To locate the mating parts of the hook hardware, match posts to side which are on trundle with ½-inch spacer in between.

then follow with the screw clearance hole.

After the holes have been drilled, round off the edges of the posts and form the slight curve at the top. Do this on a lathe if possible, otherwise use a block of wood wrapped with rough sandpaper and do it by hand. Drill a dowel hole at the top to receive the dowel for the acorn ornament. The ornaments are available at home improvement centers and lumber yards. Some of these have a rather large threaded dowel. To simplify matters, insert the threaded dowel, cut it off at the base, then redrill a ⅜-inch hole to take a regular dowel.

Round off the edges of the posts with a small rounding cutter in your router. A ¼-inch radius cutter is recommended.

Before assembling the parts, sand all pieces carefully. Install a scrap piece of ¼-inch paneling into the corners to align the posts and cross members. Place a piece of 1½-inch wood under the crosspiece to position it on the post. Then mark and drill pilot holes for the screws into the ends of the cross members. Assemble the parts with glue.

The ends of the side pieces are dadoes to receive the bed hooks. Use a side cutter about ⅜ or ½ inch deep. Nail a guide strip on the inner surface of the rail. Place it so the depth of cut will match the thickness of the hardware.

For the hooks shown, the depth is ⅛ inch. Make the cut just a trifle deeper. At the rear end of the side rail, the dado is blind. At the front, only the top need be blind. The bottom can run off the edge. See detailed drawing. You will have to file the back of the hook to match the curve of the

Fig. 5-10. The casters shown here are a special type made for the trundle beds. They can be installed quite easily with just three screws.

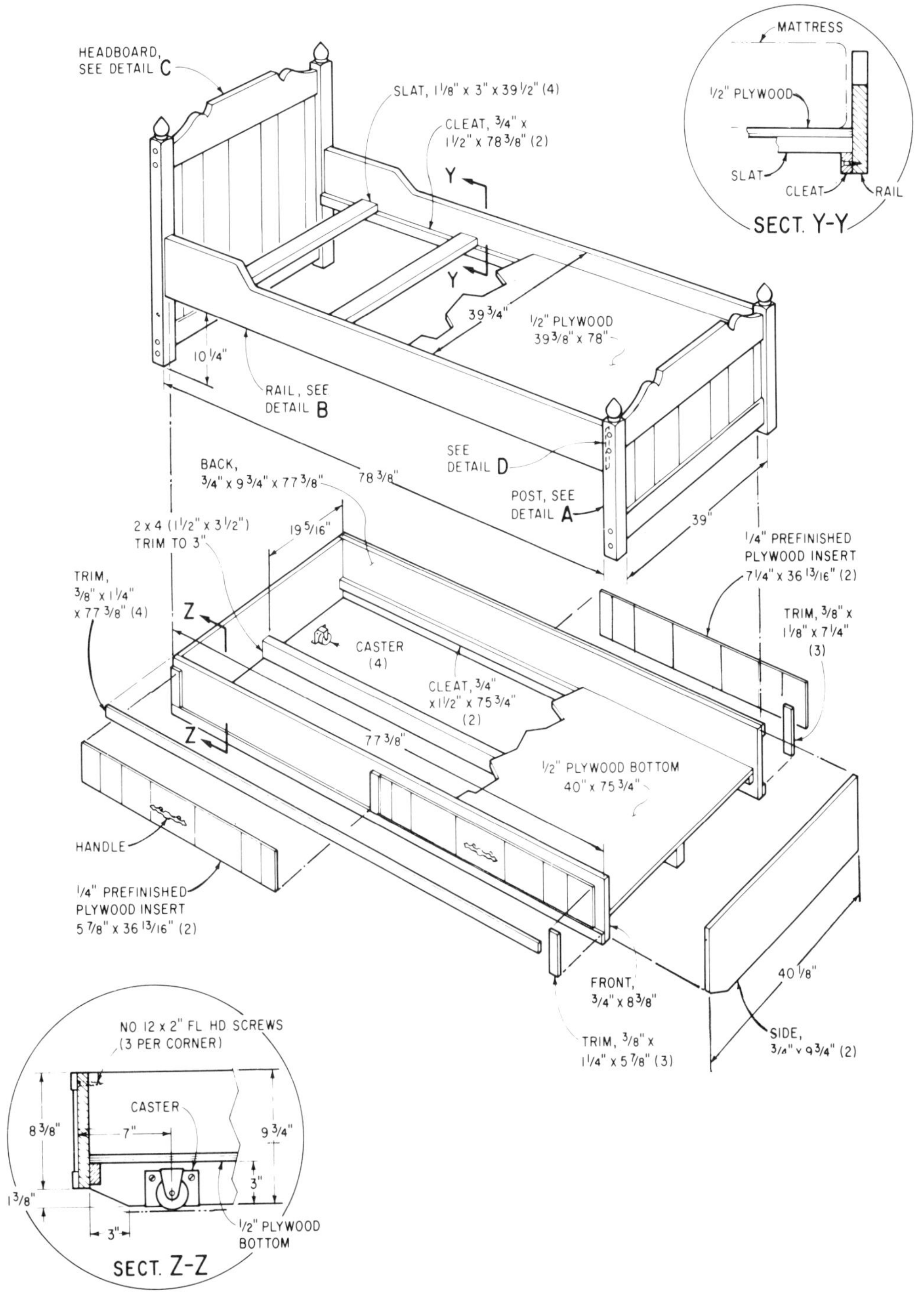

HEADBOARD, SEE DETAIL C
SLAT, 1 1/8" x 3" x 39 1/2" (4)
CLEAT, 3/4" x 1 1/2" x 78 3/8" (2)
Y
Y
39 3/4"
1/2" PLYWOOD 39 3/8" x 78"
10 1/4"
RAIL, SEE DETAIL B
SEE DETAIL D
78 3/8"
POST, SEE DETAIL A
39"
MATTRESS
1/2" PLYWOOD
SLAT
CLEAT
RAIL
SECT. Y-Y
BACK, 3/4" x 9 3/4" x 77 3/8"
2 x 4 (1 1/2" x 3 1/2") TRIM TO 3"
19 5/16"
TRIM, 3/8" x 1 1/4" x 77 3/8" (4)
Z
Z
CASTER (4)
CLEAT, 3/4" x 1 1/2" x 75 3/4" (2)
77 3/8"
1/4" PREFINISHED PLYWOOD INSERT 7 1/4" x 36 13/16" (2)
TRIM, 3/8" x 1 1/8" x 7 1/4" (3)
1/2" PLYWOOD BOTTOM 40" x 75 3/4"
HANDLE
1/4" PREFINISHED PLYWOOD INSERT 5 7/8" x 36 13/16" (2)
FRONT, 3/4" x 8 3/8"
TRIM, 3/8" x 1 1/4" x 5 7/8" (3)
40 1/8"
SIDE, 3/4" x 9 3/4" (2)
NO 12 x 2" FL HD SCREWS (3 PER CORNER)
CASTER
8 3/8"
7"
9 3/4"
3"
1 3/8"
3"
1/2" PLYWOOD BOTTOM
SECT. Z-Z

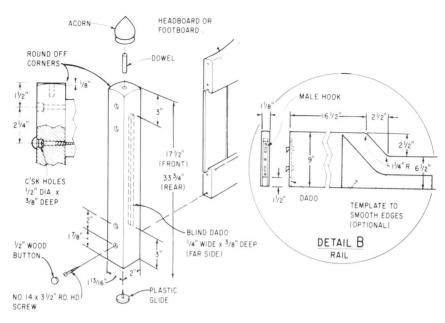

ACORN

HEADBOARD OR FOOTBOARD

DOWEL

ROUND OFF CORNERS

1/8"

1 1/2"

2 1/4"

3"

17 1/2" (FRONT)

33 3/4" (REAR)

C'SK HOLES 1/2" DIA. x 3/8" DEEP

1/2" WOOD BUTTON

2"

1 7/8"

3"

2"

1 13/16"

NO. 14 x 3 1/2" RD. HD. SCREW

PLASTIC GLIDE

BLIND DADO 1/4" WIDE x 3/8" DEEP (FAR SIDE)

MALE HOOK

1/8"

16 1/2"

2 1/2"

2 1/2"

9"

1/4" R. 6 1/2"

1/2"

DADO

TEMPLATE TO SMOOTH EDGES (OPTIONAL)

DETAIL B
RAIL

DETAIL A
POST ASSEMBLY

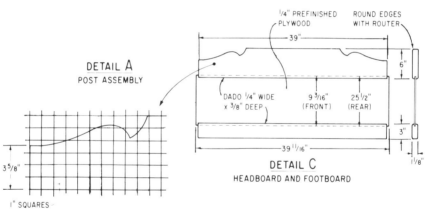

3 5/8"

1" SQUARES

1/4" PREFINISHED PLYWOOD

ROUND EDGES WITH ROUTER

39"

6"

DADO 1/4" WIDE x 3/8" DEEP

9 3/16" (FRONT)

25 1/2" (REAR)

3"

39 11/16"

1/8"

DETAIL C
HEADBOARD AND FOOTBOARD

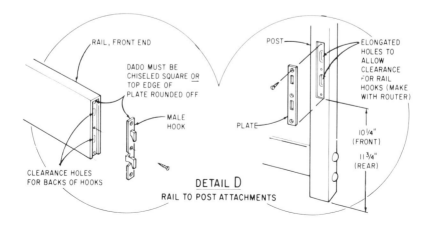

RAIL, FRONT END

DADO MUST BE CHISELED SQUARE OR TOP EDGE OF PLATE ROUNDED OFF

MALE HOOK

CLEARANCE HOLES FOR BACKS OF HOOKS

POST

ELONGATED HOLES TO ALLOW CLEARANCE FOR RAIL HOOKS (MAKE WITH ROUTER)

PLATE

10 1/4" (FRONT)

11 3/4" (REAR)

DETAIL D
RAIL TO POST ATTACHMENTS

32

Purpose	Size	Quantity
Bed		
Post, rear	$1\tfrac{13}{16}'' \times 2'' \times 33\tfrac{3}{4}''$	2
Post, front	$1\tfrac{13}{16}'' \times 2'' \times 17\tfrac{1}{2}''$	2
Header rail	$1\tfrac{3}{16}'' \times 6'' \times 39''$	2
Bottom rail	$1\tfrac{3}{16}'' \times 6'' \times 39''$	2
Side	$1\tfrac{3}{16}'' \times 9'' \times 78\tfrac{3}{8}''$	2
Front panel	$\tfrac{1}{4}'' \times 9\tfrac{3}{16}'' \times 39\tfrac{11}{16}''$	1
Rear panel	$\tfrac{1}{4}'' \times 25\tfrac{1}{2}'' \times 39\tfrac{11}{16}''$	2
Cleats	$\tfrac{3}{4}'' \times 1\tfrac{1}{2}'' \times 78\tfrac{3}{8}''$	1
Slats	$1\tfrac{13}{16}'' \times 3'' \times 39\tfrac{5}{8}''$	6
Bed hooks	$\tfrac{3}{4}'' \times 8''$ FH screws	4 sets
Acorns		4
Buttons (to conceal screws)		16
Plywood	$\tfrac{1}{2}'' \times 39\tfrac{3}{8}'' \times 78''$	1
Glides		4
Screws	$3\tfrac{1}{2}''$-14 RH	16
Trundle		
Front and rear	$\tfrac{3}{4}'' \times 8\tfrac{3}{8}'' \times 77\tfrac{3}{8}''$	2
Sides	$\tfrac{3}{4}'' \times 9\tfrac{3}{4}'' \times 40\tfrac{1}{8}''$	2
Plywood	$\tfrac{1}{2}'' \times 40'' \times 75\tfrac{3}{4}''$	1
Cleat	$\tfrac{3}{4}'' \times 1\tfrac{1}{2}'' \times 75\tfrac{3}{4}''$	2
Center support	$1\tfrac{1}{2}'' \times 3'' \times 75\tfrac{3}{4}''$	1
Trim	$\tfrac{3}{8}'' \times 1\tfrac{1}{4}'' \times 34'$	
Panel insert	$\tfrac{1}{4}'' \times 5\tfrac{7}{8}'' \times 36\tfrac{13}{16}''$	4
Casters		4
Screws	$2''$—12 FH	12

Note: If you cannot locate the bed hooks or casters locally, write to J.C. Armor, P.O. Box 290, Deer Park, N.Y. 11729.

blind dado, or you can chisel out the corner so the hardware will fit.

You will also have to make two passes with the router to obtain the correct width for the hook. Drill out clearances for the protrusions at the rear of the male hooks, then attach with FH screws.

Note that the female plate is not symmetrical. The slots are closer to one end than the other. Orient them properly, then mate with the male. Stand the bed up with props and with trundle in place, lay a ½-inch spacer on the trundle, then rest the rail on it. Carefully mark the posts, indicating the location of the plate vertically.

Now place the post assembly on the work table and draw the exact position for the plate. Route with an end cutter, then clean out the corners with a chisel. Also, chisel out the clearance for the male sections. Install the plate with FH screws.

To make the trundle, rip four pieces of pine. Make two of them 8⅜ inches wide × 77⅜ inches long and two pieces 9¾ × 40⅛ inches. Bevel one corner of each of the 40⅛-inch pieces as shown. Assemble these with nails and glue, using two nails in each side. After the piece has been assembled and squared, add a few screws as shown.

Add two long cleats with their top edge 6⅜ inches from the top of the frame.

Apply glue and nail from the inside, using 1½-inch nails, slanting them slightly. Add a piece of 1½- × -3-inch stock to the center. Be sure its top edge is level with the two cleats.

Add trim to the front and rear as shown, then cut the inserts to size and install with glue. Drill holes for the pulls centering the pulls in each panel.

Finish the piece as you desire. Place masking tape on the paneling to simplify the finishing. Then remove carefully.

Charming Pine Rocking Horse

THE ROCKING HORSE has long been a favorite toy in America. Colonial children played on crude log horses made by their fathers using the most basic of tools. As the rocking horse grew in popularity, skilled carpenters started to make them to order. They were well made and many were passed on from generation to generation as family heirlooms and collectors' items. The rocking horse made from our plan is also sturdily built and designed to last a long time. Hopefully, it too will become a family heirloom while giving your youngsters many hours of joy.

Be sure to read all instructions carefully before starting actual construction.

The horse is constructed of pine and stands 37½ inches tall. The runners are 58½ inches long. The body and runners are cut from ⁵⁄₄-inch stock (1⅛inch actual size). The supports are ⁴⁄₄-inch stock (¾ inch actual size). The "saddle" is padded with foam for greater seating comfort.

The head and body are joined at the neck for two reasons. One is that the lumber is not readily available in widths over 12 inches and secondly, that the grain

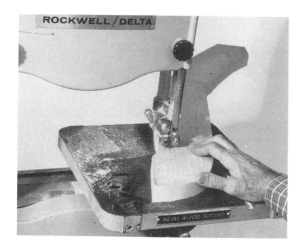

Fig. 6-1. Rocker member is being cut on the band saw. A saber or jigsaw can be used. Rocker is held in a jig for cutting ends.

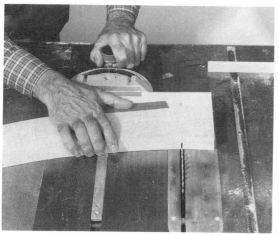

Fig. 6-2. After the end is trimmed, the jig is moved 2½ inches and the first cut of the half-lap is made with lowered saw blade.

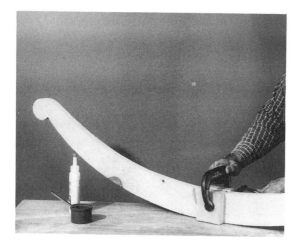

Fig. 6-3. Runner sections are joined at the half-lap to make full runner. Apply glue and clamp securely. Scrap wood protects.

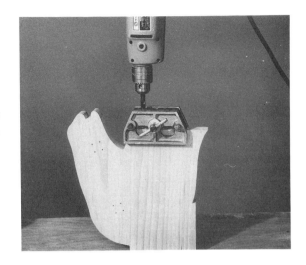

Fig. 6-4. Drilling the dowel holes in the neck. Jig assures accuracy. If done by hand, make hole straight. Insert dowels, then glue.

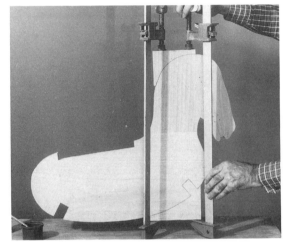

Fig. 6-5. Clamps are applied to join the head and body. The lugs will be sawed away later. Spacer block is then inserted.

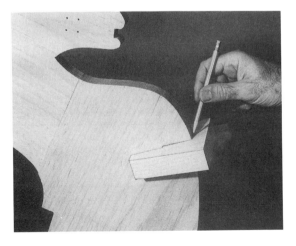

Fig. 6-6. Spacer block inserted and marked so it can be beveled to match body contour. Jig holds it at angle for screw holes.

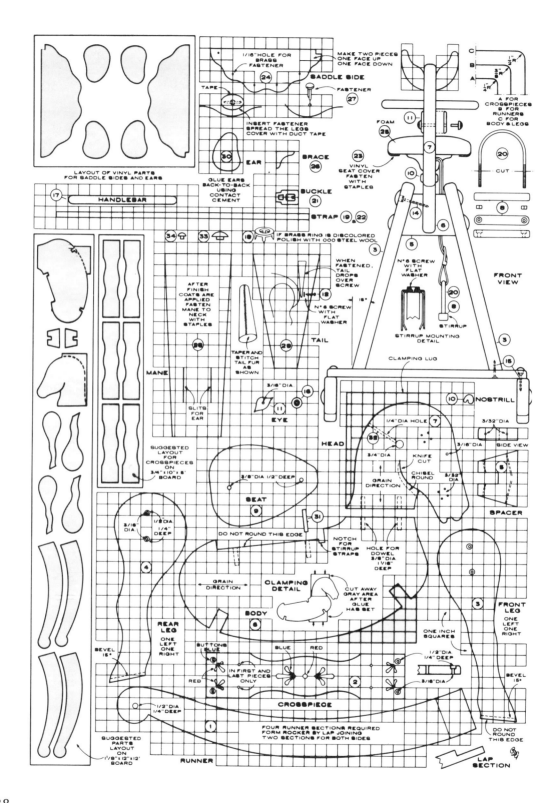

LAYOUT OF VINYL PARTS
FOR SADDLE SIDES AND EARS

1/16" HOLE FOR BRASS FASTENER ②④

MAKE TWO PIECES ONE FACE UP ONE FACE DOWN

SADDLE SIDE

TAPE

FASTENER ②⑦

INSERT FASTENER SPREAD THE LEGS COVER WITH DUCT TAPE

EAR ③⓪

BRACE ②⑧

GLUE EARS BACK-TO-BACK USING CONTACT CEMENT

BUCKLE ②①

STRAP ⑲ ②②

③④ ㉝ ⑱ IF BRASS RING IS DISCOLORED POLISH WITH 000 STEEL WOOL

⑰ HANDLEBAR

WHEN FASTENED, TAIL DROPS OVER SCREW

AFTER FINISH COATS ARE APPLIED FASTEN MANE TO NECK WITH STAPLES

N° 6 SCREW WITH FLAT WASHER

⑱
TAIL ②⑥

TAPER AND STITCH TAIL FUR AS SHOWN

MANE

SLITS FOR EAR

3/16" DIA ⑯
⑪

EYE

SUGGESTED LAYOUT FOR CROSSPIECES ON 3/4"×10"×5' BOARD

SEAT ⑨

3/8" DIA 1/2" DEEP

DO NOT ROUND THIS EDGE

NOTCH FOR STIRRUP STRAPS

HOLE FOR DOWEL 3/8" DIA 1 1/16" DEEP

3/16" DIA
1/2" DIA 1/4" DEEP

④

GRAIN DIRECTION

BODY ⑥

CLAMPING DETAIL

CUT AWAY GRAY AREA AFTER GLUE HAS SET

REAR LEG ONE LEFT ONE RIGHT

BEVEL 15°

BUTTONS BLUE

RED

BLUE RED

IN FIRST AND LAST PIECES ONLY

CROSSPIECE

1/2" DIA 1/4" DEEP

1/2"DIA 1/4" DEEP

3/16" DIA

BEVEL 15°

SUGGESTED PARTS LAYOUT ON 1 1/8"×12"×12' BOARD

RUNNER

① FOUR RUNNER SECTIONS REQUIRED FORM ROCKER BY LAP JOINING TWO SECTIONS FOR BOTH SIDES

DO NOT ROUND THIS EDGE

LAP SECTION

FOAM ㉕
⑪
⑦
⑩
⑭
⑥
⑤
③

②③ VINYL SEAT COVER FASTEN WITH STAPLES

N° 6 SCREW WITH FLAT WASHER

②⓪
⑨
STIRRUP
STIRRUP MOUNTING DETAIL

CLAMPING LUG

15°

FRONT VIEW

③

⑮

⑩ NOSTRILL

1/4" DIA HOLE ⑦

㉟

3/4" DIA

KNIFE CUT

GRAIN DIRECTION

CHISEL ROUND

3/32" DIA

HEAD

3/16" DIA SIDE VIEW

⑤

SPACER

③
FRONT LEG ONE LEFT ONE RIGHT

A
B
C

1"
3/8"
1/4"

A FOR CROSSPIECES
B FOR RUNNERS
C FOR BODY & LEGS

②⓪ CUT

⑧

ONE INCH SQUARES

②

3/32" DIA

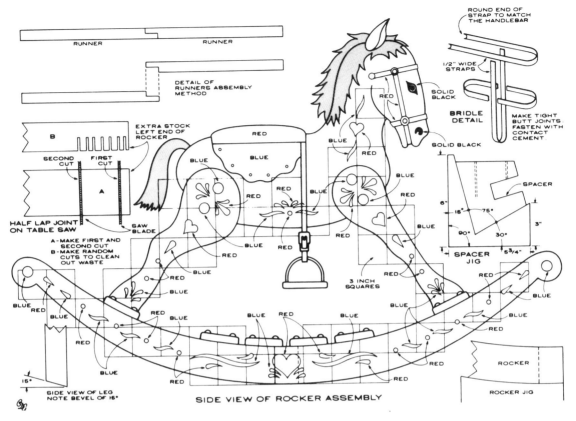

DETAIL OF RUNNERS ASSEMBLY METHOD

RUNNER   RUNNER

ROUND END OF STRAP TO MATCH THE HANDLEBAR

1/2" WIDE STRAPS

BRIDLE DETAIL

MAKE TIGHT BUTT JOINTS. FASTEN WITH CONTACT CEMENT.

SOLID BLACK

SOLID BLACK

RED

RED

RED

RED

BLUE

EXTRA STOCK LEFT END OF ROCKER

SECOND CUT   FIRST CUT

HALF LAP JOINT ON TABLE SAW

SAW BLADE

A—MAKE FIRST AND SECOND CUT
B—MAKE RANDOM CUTS TO CLEAN OUT WASTE

SPACER

SPACER JIG

6"   18°   75°
90°   30°
3"   5³⁄₄"

3 INCH SQUARES

SIDE VIEW OF LEG NOTE BEVEL OF 15°

15°

ROCKER

ROCKER JIG

SIDE VIEW OF ROCKER ASSEMBLY

direction of the head and body should be perpendicular to each other for strength. The runners are also made in two sections because of their size and grain direction.

In the illustrations, each square equals 1 inch of the full-size plan. It's best to make a full-size pattern for each piece. When the layouts are complete, cut the wood pieces to shape using a jigsaw, band saw or saber saw.

Next, drill the holes in the face and legs. The two clusters of four $3/32$-inch holes are for the harness rings and should be drilled through the stock. The two $3/16$-inch screw clearance holes in each leg are drilled through the stock, but the larger ½-inch counterbored holes must be drilled from the outer surface of the legs.

legs are mounted from opposite sides, the holes must be drilled accordingly, one set faceup and the other facedown.

Before joining the head to the body, drill the two $3/8$-inch dowel holes into the mating surfaces. Make the holes $1\frac{1}{16}$ inches deep. Locate the holes accurately by using a doweling jig or dowel centers.

Because the bottom of the head is end grain, you will have to glue size the surface before joining the parts. To size the end grain, thin your glue with an equal amount of water, then brush onto the surface and allow to air dry. The parts can now be glued in the normal manner using the glue full-strength. Insert the dowels and clamp securely.

The clamping lugs, indicated by the

gray areas on the head and body, allow a perpendicular surface for the clamps thus ensuring a good tight joint. After the glue has set, cut away the gray areas. Insert the ¾-inch dowel for the handlebar temporarily, then drill the ¼-inch hole through the head and into the handlebar. Let the drill bit penetrate the dowel about ¼ inch.

After the parts have been cut, round the corners with the router. Do not round the bottom corners of the hoofs where they join the crosspieces or the area where the seat is to be installed.

The spacer blocks are notched to interlock with those in the lower part of the body. They should fit snugly. The pilot hole for the screws should be drilled perpendicular to the edge. The use of a holding jig will ensure accuracy. Cut the jig from a piece of scrap wood.

The rockers are made by cutting four identical half-sections, which are joined with half-lap joints, all cut from the same side. Note that the ½-inch holes for the decorative buttons at the ends are not drilled from the same side; two must be placed on the opposite side so that when the rockers are glued up, all four ½-inch holes will be on the outside.

The half lap must be made carefully to ensure a clean glue line. There are several ways to do this; choose the method you are most comfortable with. Make the half lap one-half the thickness of the lumber and 2½ inches wide. If the joint is made by hand, use a back saw and cut close to the line, then finish with a chisel. Check the mating pieces frequently and try not to undercut them. If you do, you will have to use shims to correct the joint. When properly done, the outside surfaces should be flush.

The band saw can also be used to make this joint. It replaces the hand saw and the same precautions must be taken. The table saw is well suited to make this joint. If you choose this method, be sure to leave a little extra stock at the lap end of the rocker sections.

The sawing jig shown in the photo is used to locate and hold the rockers when making the end, lap, and intermediate cuts. The jig holds the work at the proper angle so the first and last cuts will be parallel to each other. In use, the jig and work are taped to prevent them from creeping laterally.

Set the saw blade slightly higher than the wood and line up the end of the jig with the edge of the saw tooth. Tape the jig to the miter gauge. Now place the work against the jig and align the end line on the runner with the end of the jig. Tape the work to the jig then make the cut to trim the runner to its proper length. Repeat for all four runners.

Now lower the saw blade so its height is exactly one-half the thickness of the runner stock. Reposition the jig, moving it exactly 2½ inches closer to the saw blade then again tape it to the miter gauge. Align the end of the runner with the end of the jig as was done for the first cut, then saw again.

The following cuts need not be measured. Make a series of cuts between the original cuts to clear out the waste. Make the kerf cuts close to each other to achieve the same effect as if you were using a dado blade. An alternate to this method is to use the dado blade to clean out the waste after the first and second cuts are made. Check that the parts fit together okay, then proceed to glue the half sections to make up the full length runners. Apply glue and clamp securely. Be sure to use wood pads under the clamps to prevent damaging the work.

The six crosspieces are identical except that the first and last pieces have extra holes for mounting the horse's hoofs. After the holes are drilled use the router to round off the top corners.

Round the ends of the ¾-inch handlebar which was previously drilled. Do this with a rasp and sandpaper or you can use the router with a ⁵⁄₁₆-inch rounding bit. If the router is utilized, mount it upside down and use as a shaper. Feed the dowel into the cutter then slowly rotate the dowel. Be sure to wear protective goggles.

Cut the rest of the parts. The seat is cut from a piece of ¾-inch thick plywood, which is far stronger than a piece of solid lumber. Drill the two ⅜-inch holes spaced to match the two drilled into the horse's back. The eye pieces and nostrils are cut from ¼-inch stock. Round the edges of these with sandpaper.

After all pieces have been cut and rounded, they must be sanded for a superb finish. Two important areas when sanding are the joints at the halfflaps on the rockers and the butt joint where the head is joined to the body. These must be sanded to remove the "step" if one exists between the two surfaces. Start sanding with 100-grit paper then work down to the finer grits of 120, 220, then 320. Pay particular attention to the end grain. The smoother the end grain, the finer the finish.

Start assembling by placing the rockers on a flat surface with the ends of the rockers aligned. The rockers should be spaced 16¼ inches apart. To simplify assembly, you may wish to cut two pieces of wood 16¼ inches long for use as temporary spacers. Place these spacers between the rockers

and clamp lightly. Now position the four crosspieces onto the runners, centering them from side to side. Space the crosspieces ½ inch apart, then use an awl to locate the screw holes from the crosspieces to the runners. Drill ³⁄₃₂-inch screw pilot holes, then apply glue and screw the crosspieces into place.

Apply glue to the notched spacers then slide them into place on the horse's body. Next add the legs but do not glue them to the spacers yet. The two end crosspieces are now fastened to the hoofs of the assembled horse. Use screws but no glue.

Place the subassembly (the horse with the two crosspieces attached) onto the runners. Center it from end to end, then mark the screw locations, drill pilots, and assemble with screws. If okay, disassemble the legs, hoofs and crosspieces, add glue then reassemble permanently.

The "saddle" is made by sandwiching a 1-inch-thick piece of urethane foam between the plywood and the vinyl. Trim the foam to the outline of the seat then squeeze the sandwich tightly using a clamp as shown. Pull the material taut and staple. When the clamp is removed, the foam will expand, leaving a nicely upholstered seat without wrinkles.

Note that the seat, flaps, mane, and so on should be installed after the finish has been applied to the wood.

Cut the saddle flaps with wavey outline as shown. Make one piece faceup and the other facedown as they are not symmetrical. Punch the holes either with a hole punch or with a nail with the point ground flat. Place the vinyl onto a piece of end-grain hardwood and strike with a hammer for a cleanly punched hole. Add the paper fasteners then spread the legs and cover them with a small piece of tape.

The fasteners can be eliminated and decorative nails substituted. These would be driven into the body of the horse. The fasteners allow the saddle flap to hang loosely for a pleasing effect.

Make the stirrup as shown. The U-bolt is shortened by cutting away the threads as indicated in the drawing. Before installing it you may want to spray it with bronze paint so it matches the buckle. If so, rub the bolt with fine steel wool before spraying or painting.

The stirrup straps are nonadjustable. They are fixed at the height shown which has been determined to be the average height for this size horse. After the stirrups are looped through the buckle, coat them on the back sides with contact cement and join, eliminating the space between the two straps This is a safety precaution, eliminating the possibility of a child placing his head between the straps, a potential hazard.   For this reason we do not recommend the use of reins.

Fasten the saddle flaps with staples along the top edge then install the stirrup straps using No. 6 screws and flat washers. Follow by adding the seat which is positioned with the two dowels. Press the seat down as far as it will go then secure it with the metal brackets. The seat is not glued because of the gathered vinyl on the underside.

The mane and tail are cut from a piece of 6-inch-wide fur. Before installing the mane, install the handlebar and pin it in place with the ¼-inch dowel. Install the mane with staples along its edges. Pull the hair away and staple only through the backing material. Use your fingers to "comb" the fur after it is installed.

The ears are made of vinyl. Cut the pieces as shown then apply contact cement and join them back-to-back. This will give the ears a finished vinyl surface on both sides. Install the ear flaps with screws and flat washers, placed slightly forward of center. Then fold the ear in half and cement the bottom to conceal the screw. Use vinyl cement or epoxy for this.

The tail is sewed along the seam into a cone shape. It is then fastened with a screw and flat washer. See detail.

Fasten the bridle straps with contact cement. Install the longer pieces first. The strap detail drawing shows a space between the various pieces. This was done only for clarity. Cut the parts so they butt against each other snugly.

After the bridle is in place install the rings. They are made of hardened steel which has been brass plated. Some may have a tarnished appearance. If so, rub lightly with steel wool to restore the color. A little clear nail polish will maintain the bright color. The best way to install the rings is to squeeze them on using a clamp. Place the four rings into the holes provided, then use a clamp to seat them. Be sure to position the clamp jaws so the rings seat squarely and not at an angle.

Finish the horse as desired. It may be stained, left natural, or painted as shown, If stained or left natural, it should be given a coat of sealer followed by several coats of brushing or spraying lacquer.

If you prefer to stencil the horse as shown here, give the entire project a coat of white undercoat followed by two coats of white semigloss lacquer or paint. The stencils are applied after the white coats have dried thoroughly. The acrylic colors used for stenciling are easy to use and dry fast.

You may wish to create your own stencils or use the shapes shown. These

MATERIALS LIST

Except where noted, lumber is pine. All measurements are in inches.

Purpose	Size	Description	Quantity
Runner	1⅛″ × 8″ × 32″		4
Crosspiece	¾″ × 4″ × 18″		6
Front leg	1⅛″ × 5¾″ × 17″		2
Rear leg	1⅛″ × 7″ × 17″		2
Leg spacer	1⅛″ × 3½″ × 4⅞″		2
Body	1⅛″ × 10½″ × 22½″		1
Head	1⅛″ × 11¼″ × 12″		1
Stirrup	⅝″ × 13/16″ × 5″	Oak	2
Seat	¾″ × 7″ × 9½″	Plywood	1
Nostril	¼″ × ¾″ × 1″		2
Eye base	¼″ × 1″ × 2″		2
Screw	No. 6″ × 1″ RH		3
Screw	No. 10″ × 3″ FH		4
Screw	No. 10″ × 2½″ FH		4
Screw	No. 10″ × 1½″ FH		32
Eye	¾″ dia.		2
Handlebar	¾″ × 9″		1
Ring	⅞″ dia.		4
Bridle strap	½″ × 24″		2
U-Bolt	5/16″ × 4″		2
Buckle, Western			2
Stirrup strap	½″ × 24″		2
Seat, vinyl	10″ × 12″		1
Saddle flap, vinyl	12″ × 12″		1
Foam	1″ × 7″ × 9½″		1
Brace	1½″ × 1½″		2
Paper fastener		Brass	10
Mane, long pile	6″ × 16″		1
Tail, long pile	6″ × 10″		1
Ear, vinyl	2½″ × 3½″		2
Dowel	⅜″ × 2″		4
Dowel	¼″ × 3¼″		1
Button	1¼″ dia. × ½″	Tenon	12
Button	⅝″ dia. × ½″	Tenon	24
Staple	9/16″		1 box

Note: Altogether, you will need one piece of 5/4″ × 12″ × 12′ pine, one piece of 1″ × 10″ × 5′ pine, and one piece of ¾″ × 7″ × 9″ fir plywood.

may be cut from various materials, such as file folder stock, acetate, polyester or even tracing paper. The acetate and mylar should have a matte surface which will take pencil. We recommend the acetate and polyester as they are translucent and durable.

Lay out the designs selected onto the stencil material, then cut with a sharp knife. We used an Exacto with a No. 11 blade.

Errors can be minimized by coating the stencil back with adhesive. We used a spray adhesive (3M Company) which has a low tack when sprayed on only one surface. Allow the adhesive to dry five minutes before using the stencil.

Position the stencil on the work then use a stencil brush to apply the color to the work. In stenciling, it is very important to remember that the brush should be almost dry. Dip just the tip of the brush into the jar of paint, and no more than $1/16$ inch deep, then rub it on paper towels to remove most of the paint. Rub in 2-inch circles. Repeat several times. Now you can apply it to the work. Dab the brush onto the stencil. Keep on dabbing until the desired shade is achieved.

Note that some of our patterns consist of lefts and rights. You can use one pattern for both, but you will have to clean the stencil of paint and adhesive before reusing it. It may be simpler to just make new stencils. Just trace one set faceup and the other facedown.

The bridle and stirrup straps are available only in light brown. To match your stenciling colors, first give them a base coat of white then apply the desired color.

A full-size plan for building this rocking horse is available from *Armor Products* (see Introduction for address).

Cheese and Wine Cart

HOME CRAFTSMEN are often discouraged from making a rolling cart on wheels because they don't have a lathe for the spokes. This elegant cart was designed and built without a lathe. The turnings are ready-made and available at most lumberyards and home-improvement centers. Even the wheel hubs and rims are made with conventional tools: a router and saber saw.

The cart is made of ¾-, 1⅛-, and 1⅜-inch pine stock (nominal sizes, 1, 1¼, and 1½ inches). It measures 18 × 29 × 29 inches and has a roomy drawer for storing odds and ends. Most rolling carts have a movable hand grip, which must be dropped out of the way to permit the drawer to open. We used a fixed hand grip

and simply made the drawer open from the front. It looks better and is more practical.

Make the top of the cart of 1⅜-inch pine. Glue up four boards, each 5 inches wide, to obtain the necessary width. Note that the Materials List shows the lengths to be 3 inches longer than the finished size. You will trim away the excess after gluing. Dowel pins are necessary to ensure a good, permanent glue line. To prevent warping, invert the first and third boards so the annular rings will alternate. Use four dowels in each section, locating them carefully. If you have a doweling jig, you will be able to center the dowel holes automatically. If you do not have a jig, drill the holes in the first board, then use dowel centers to transfer the location of the holes

Fig. 7-1. Top panel is made by doweling and gluing several boards together. When the glue dries, trim the excess at the ends of the panel.

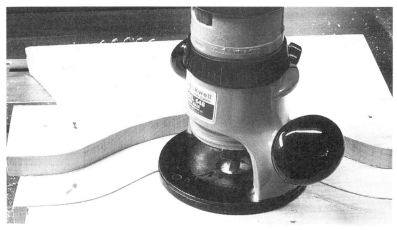

Fig. 7-2. Make the decorative bead on the end panels with a router. Make a wooden template (see diagram) for the router base to follow.

to the mating board. Repeat for the four boards, then apply glue and clamp. After the glue sets, trim the ends to size.

If the surface joints are uneven, use a belt sander to even the surface. Belt sanders cut fast, especially on pine, so use care when sanding. Start with a medium-grit belt, followed by fine.

Make the upper rails of 1⅛-inch stock. After ripping the pieces to width, run a groove along the lower edge using the router fitted with a V-shaped cutter. Tack a wood strip to the rail to guide the cutter.

You will need two side rails and one rear rail. The front is left open for the drawer.

Make the lower side rails in a similar manner, but narrower. The front and rear rails are a bit more tricky to make.

The upper edge must be contoured. In addition, the upper edge is contour grooved. This process requires that you use a shaped wood template to guide the router. Trace the contour of the end panel onto a piece of scrap about 2 inches longer than the panel. Use a narrow piece of wood for the template strip and nail it to the base

Fig. 7-3. Using ready-made legs saves a lot of work. Cut the legs to size and join to the apron with glue and dowels. Use the block to protect the legs.

Fig. 7-4. The rims for wheels are made in four sections. When cutting curved rims, leave end tabs for later assembly. Predrill for spokes.

piece. To contour-cut it parallel to the shape of the panel, you need to use a marking gauge to draw the shape of the template. (To set the gauge, measure the radius of the router base, then add ½ inch.) Trace the shape onto the guide strip and cut with a saber saw. Fasten the strip to the base with a couple of nails, then place the panel into the shaped base. Hold it securely with a stop on the table or with a clamp.

Cut the ⅜-inch deep groove in the rail pieces. They are for the top fasteners. Locate the groove ½-inch from the top edge. The width of the saw kerf is not important. Cut the lower shelf to size, but do not notch the corners yet.

The legs are standard 3- x -32-inch turnings available at your lumberyards. Since the finished length required is 24½ inches, you will need to trim the lengths to size. The square block at the top should measure 5 inches and the lower one 6 inches. (See drawing.) *Note:* If you have a lathe, simply make a template on kraft paper, then turn in the usual manner.

Use the doweling jig to locate and drill the ⅜-inch-diameter holes at the ends of

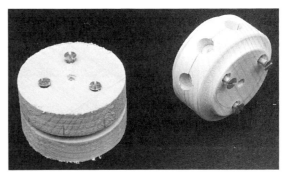

Fig. 7-5. Cut hubs from ¾-inch stock, then saw in half. Reassemble with wood screws and drill for spokes. Hubs are cross-grain for strength.

Fig. 7-6. Separate hub halves, insert spokes, glue, and rejoin hubs with screws. Make the spokes from ready-made spindles cut in half.

Fig. 7-7. Attach the wheel shaft to the hub with three screws. The metal stem will snap into the socket that is placed in the leg.

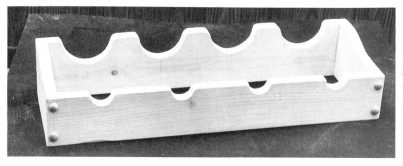

Fig. 7-8. The wine rack is removable. Cut the bottle rests so that bottles lie with necks down. Add wood buttons for looks.

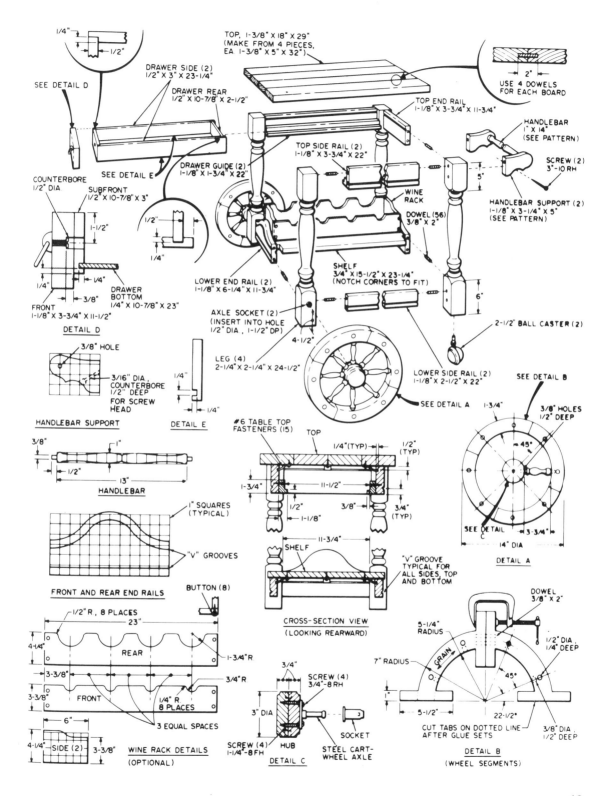

1/4"
1/2"

SEE DETAIL D

TOP, 1-3/8" X 18" X 29"
(MAKE FROM 4 PIECES,
EA 1-3/8" X 5" X 32")

2"

USE 4 DOWELS
FOR EACH BOARD

DRAWER SIDE (2)
1/2" X 3" X 23-1/4"

DRAWER REAR
1/2" X 10-7/8" X 2-1/2"

TOP END RAIL
1-1/8" X 3-3/4" X 11-3/4"

HANDLEBAR
1" X 14"
(SEE PATTERN)

SEE DETAIL E

DRAWER GUIDE (2)
1-1/8" X 1-3/4" X 22"

TOP SIDE RAIL (2)
1-1/8" X 3-3/4" X 22"

SCREW (2)
3"-10 RH

COUNTERBORE
1/2" DIA.

SUBFRONT
1/2" X 10-7/8" X 3"

1/2"

1/4"

WINE
RACK

DOWEL (56)
3/8" X 2"

HANDLEBAR SUPPORT (2)
1-1/8" X 3-1/4" X 5"
(SEE PATTERN)

1-1/2"

5"

1/4"

DRAWER
BOTTOM
1/4" X 10-7/8" X 23"

3/8"

FRONT
1-1/8" X 3-3/4" X 11-1/2"

DETAIL D

SHELF
3/4" X 15-1/2" X 23-1/4"
(NOTCH CORNERS TO FIT)

LOWER END RAIL (2)
1-1/8" X 6-1/4" X 11-3/4"

AXLE SOCKET (2)
(INSERT INTO HOLE
1/2" DIA., 1-1/2" DP)

4-1/2"

6"

2-1/2" BALL CASTER (2)

3/8" HOLE

3/16" DIA.
COUNTERBORE
1/2" DEEP
FOR SCREW
HEAD

1/4"

1/4"

LEG (4)
2-1/4" X 2-1/4" X 24-1/2"

LOWER SIDE RAIL (2)
1-1/8" X 2-1/2" X 22"

SEE DETAIL A

SEE DETAIL B

1-3/4"

3/8" HOLES
1/2" DEEP

HANDLEBAR SUPPORT

DETAIL E

3/8"

1"

45°

1/2"

13"

HANDLEBAR

#6 TABLE TOP
FASTENERS (15)

TOP

1/4" (TYP)

1/2"
(TYP)

SEE DETAIL
C

3-3/4"

14" DIA

DETAIL A

1-3/4"

11-1/2"

1/2"

3/8"

3/4"
(TYP)

1" SQUARES
(TYPICAL)

1-1/8"

"V" GROOVES

11-3/4"

SHELF

"V" GROOVE
TYPICAL FOR
ALL SIDES, TOP
AND BOTTOM

FRONT AND REAR END RAILS

CROSS-SECTION VIEW
(LOOKING REARWARD)

DOWEL
3/8" X 2"

BUTTON (8)

1/2" R, 8 PLACES

23"

4-1/4"

REAR

1-3/4" R

3-3/8"

3/4" R

5-1/4"
RADIUS

1/2" DIA
1/4" DEEP

7" RADIUS

GRAIN

45°

3-3/8"

FRONT

1/4" R
8 PLACES

3/4"

SCREW (4)
3/4"-8 RH

1"

5-1/2"

22-1/2"

3/8" DIA
1/2" DEEP

6"

4-1/4"

SIDE (2)

3-3/8"

WINE RACK DETAILS
(OPTIONAL)

3 EQUAL SPACES

3" DIA

SCREW (4)
1-1/4"-8 FH

HUB

SOCKET

STEEL CART-
WHEEL AXLE

DETAIL C

CUT TABS ON DOTTED LINE
AFTER GLUE SETS

DETAIL B
(WHEEL SEGMENTS)

49

MATERIALS LIST

Purpose	Size	Description	Quantity
Top	1⅜″ × 18″ × 29″ (Make from 4 pieces, ea. 1⅜″ × 5″ × 32″)	Pine	1
Side rail (top)	1⅛″ × 3¾″ × 22″	Pine	2
End rail (top)	1⅛″ × 3¾″ × 11¾″	Pine	1
Handlebar support	1⅛″ × 3¼″ × 5″	Pine	2
Handlebar	1″ × 14″	Pine	1
Leg	2¼″ × 2¼″ × 24½″	Pine	4
Shelf	¾″ × 15½″ × 23¼″	Pine	1
Side rail (lower)	1⅛″ × 2½″ × 22″	Pine	2
End rail (lower)	1⅛″ × 6¼″ × 11¾″	Pine	2
Drawer front	1⅛″ × 3¾″ × 11½″	Pine	1
Drawer side	½″ × 3″ × 23¼	Pine	2
Drawer subfront	½″ × 10⅞″ × 3″	Pine	1
Drawer rear	½″ × 10⅞″ × 2½″	Pine	1
Drawer guide	1⅛″ × 1¾″ × 22″	Pine	2
Wheel segment	1⅛″ × 5″ × 12½″	Pine	8
Wheel hub	¾″ × 2¾″ dia.	Pine	4
Spoke	¾″ × 4¾″	Pine	16
Buttons	½″ × ⅝″	Pine	32
Wine rack front	3⅜″ × 23″	Pine	1
Wine rack rear	4¼″ × 23″	Pine	1
Wine rack side	4¼″ × 6″	Pine	2
		Ornament	3
	2½″	Ball casters	2
	#6	Table top fasteners	15
		Wheel axle assembly	2
	⅜″ × 2″	Dowels	56

Note: You should be able to purchase the necessary turnings and related parts at your local lumber dealer. Should you have difficulty in this respect, write to Armor Products, Box 290, Deer Park, N.Y. 11729. Ask for Cart Price List.

---

the rail pieces. The holes should be 1 inch deep. You can also drill the holes for the caster and wheel sockets into the legs at this time.

Use dowel centers to transfer the dowel holes from the rail ends to the legs. Drill the holes carefully to ensure that they are straight.

Fasten the legs to the side (long) rails with dowels as shown. Use care when applying glue to the rail ends and use it sparingly. Clamp the sections. When the glue has set, remove the clamps and fasten these sections to the end (short) rails. To keep the unit square while clamping, nail a temporary cleat across the upper front.

Next, install the top and lower shelf. Use tabletop brackets to fasten them. You must notch the lower shelf at the corners before installation. Place the shelf in position and, with a pencil, mark exactly where the cuts are to be made. Cut and fit the shelf into place, then fasten with the brackets. Next cut and install the drawer runners, then make the drawer as shown.

To make the wheels, cut eight curved pieces with tabs as indicated. You will use the tabs as an aid to gluing and remove them when the glue has set. Drill the dowel holes in each section. Also drill the spoke holes by supporting the segments in a scrap of wood cut to the same contour as the segment. Drill the $\frac{3}{8}$-inch-diameter holes $\frac{1}{2}$ inch deep.

After the holes are drilled, glue up pairs of segments to make half rims. Insert the dowels, glue, and then clamp. When the glue has set, glue up the half sections to complete the rims. Use a saber saw or table jigsaw to cut away the tabs. You will now have a rim with 8 spoke holes on the inside diameter.

Make a curved sanding block and smoothen the rim until all saw marks are removed. Drill the eight $\frac{1}{2}$-inch- diameter button holes around the face of each rim and drill four holes on the back side.

Cut the spokes from 11-inch spindles. Each spindle will yield two spokes. Cut the spindles in half and then with a sharp knife shape the ends to form the $\frac{3}{8}$-inch tenon. Fit these into the rim without glue.

Now make the hub. Screw two 4-inch-square pieces of $\frac{3}{4}$-inch pine together and be sure to cross the grain of each at right angles to each other. Do not glue at this time. Lay out a $13\frac{3}{4}$-inch circle on the lay-up and cut with a saber saw. Sand the disc until it is perfectly smooth, then shape the outer edge with a router. Next, drill eight $\frac{3}{8}$-inch-diameter, equally spaced holes around the circumference of the disc. The holes must be centered on the parting line.

Remove the screws from the hub to disassemble it. Place the spokes into the sockets formed by drilling, then apply glue to the inner hub surface. Add the second half of the hub and rescrew. Add buttons to complete the wheel.

A special wheel shaft with socket is available. (See Materials List.) Fasten it to the wheel with three round-head screws. Simply force the socket part into the holes previously drilled into the legs. Insert the ball casters into the holes made at the bottom of the rear legs in the same manner.

Add the ornaments to complete the piece. The wine rack is optional. Finish as desired. We used Sapolin stain and three coats of clear gloss lacquer.

Chessboard Game Table

PRIMARILY A GAME TABLE which can be used for playing numerous games, this table features a solid-block chessboard made of light-and-dark-colored squares, glued together and easily made. The roomy drawer will hold plenty of games and other supplies. Leatherette panels at each side of the chessboard add to its elegant appearance.

In the game of chess, the board is placed so that each player has a white square at his right hand. The table shown is for end seating, however if you desire, you can position the board so the players sit at the long sides. The pull-out trays will hold your favorite drink or snack.

Construction of this table is simplified by making use of ready-made legs. These are available at most lumberyards and department stores and they come in various styles and sizes. For this game table, a tapered Italian provincial design 28 inches tall was selected. For the ambitious woodworker, the legs can be made without difficulty, using the table saw for cutting the tapers and the router for fluting.

Assuming you are using the ready-made legs, check the lengths carefully, for although they are made by machine and should be uniform in length, there is sometimes a variation of ⅛ inch between units. If you find this so, recut the legs to make them all equal. Break all sharp edges with fine sandpaper, then set the legs aside.

The aprons are cut to size from a straight piece of poplar or maple. The two end pieces are then notched along the top edge to allow clearance for the sliding trays. The depth of the notch depends on the thickness of the lumber you use. For example, 1-inch-thick stock will be either ¾-inch thick or ¹³⁄₁₆ inch. Most pine purchased at the lumberyards will be ¾-inch thick but the hardwoods, in most cases will be ¹³⁄₁₆ inch. For our purpose, we

Fig. 8-1. To make the chessboard, begin by cutting strips of ash and mahogany for the light and dark colored squares.

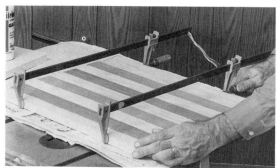

Fig. 8-2. Assemble and clamp the strips in an alternating pattern. It is important that this is done on a flat surface.

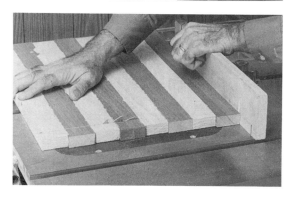

Fig. 8-3. The next step is to true-up the assembled block. Here, a miter gauge is being used to make these cuts.

want the notch to be $\frac{1}{16}$ inch deeper than the thickness of the trays so that it will slide without binding.

The notch can be cut in several ways, but the method shown is preferable as it results in straight smooth cuts. Lower the blade of your table saw until the teeth are below the table surface. Set the fence to the desired width of cut, then position the work against the fence. Holding it firmly, turn the power on and raise the blade. A mark on the fence is used as a guide for the

start of the cut. Slowly feed the work until the length of the notch is cut and use the miter gauge to cut the ends of the notch.

The decorative groove along the bottom edge of the apron is cut next. Use the router with a V cutter for this operation.

The legs are held to the apron with round-head screws. To locate the diagonal screw holes accurately, make a drilling jig with two pieces of scrap wood. Hold the jig tightly when using and drill two holes in the ends of the three apron sections. The

Fig. 8-4. Having cut out the blocks, you will then have to prepare for the assembly and gluing step. Because all of the gluing in this operation will be with cross grains, it will be necessary to first size all of the edges with thinned-out glue.

Fig. 8-5. Set the fence to recut the block so that each square measures $1\frac{7}{8} \times 1\frac{7}{8}$ inch. Use a mark on fence as guide.

Fig. 8-6. When the application of thinned-out glue has dried, you can assemble, glue, and clamp the blocks together. By reversing every other block, you will obtain the checkerboard pattern. Make certain you are again working on a flat surface.

front drawer support is also assembled at this time. Use screws and glue at all joints.

The trays are made of the same stock as the apron. Cleats attached to the rear serve as stops to keep the trays from being pulled out too far. Two cleats screwed to the underside of the top limit the closing travel of the trays so that the front edge of the tray closes flush with the apron.

Runners for the tray prevent sidewise swaying. The drawer runners are assembled, then screwed to the lower part of the side aprons.

The chessboard is made up of alternating light- and dark-colored wood squares, in ash and mahogany. Rip four strips each of the ash and mahogany woods to exactly $1\frac{7}{8}$ inch wide, then glue these

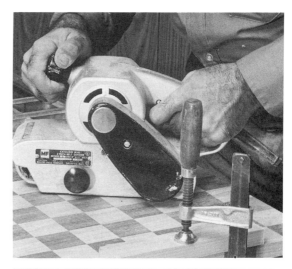

Fig. 8-7. After the glue has set, sand the surface of the chessboard to produce a flat, even surface. A belt sander is best.

Fig. 8-8. Note the dowels used in assembling the tabletop sections. You should do ends first, and then the long sides.

alternating dark and light strips as you go. If you have trouble getting the ash, any other light-colored wood, such as poplar or maple, may be substituted.

When the glue has set, cut apart the striped block to 1⅞-inch widths. Remove all splinters or burrs with fine sandpaper. Next, glue to form the chessboard pattern and since all gluing in this operation will be cross-grain, be sure to size the edges using thinned down glue. Apply with brush to all edges and allow to dry about twenty minutes. Then apply glue full strength as it comes from the container, and clamp firmly.

The table saw is a good place to work as the surface is flat. Protect the top with newspaper when clamping. When the glue

Fig. 8-9. The apron is attached to the tabletop with round head screws which angle in through the pre-drilled holes.

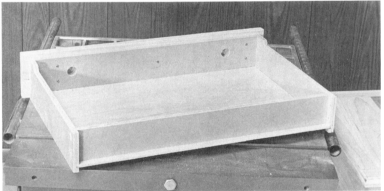

Fig. 8-10. Drawer is of simple construction, using a double front. Screws in front panel can be removed after glue sets.

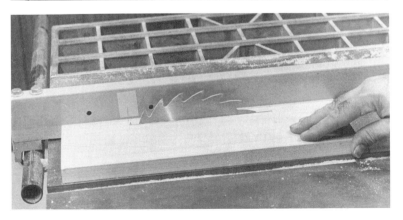

Fig. 8-11. The notching for the end panel trays is done by raising the saw blade as the work is held in stationary position.

Fig. 8-12. This view shows the trays in closed position. Cleats will limit their travel to keep fronts flush with the apron.

Fig. 8-13. Pictured is the completed table before the finish is applied. Lion head pulls are on drawer; knobs go on the trays.

has set, sand the surface flat using a belt sander. Start with an 80-grit belt then work up to 120 and finally finish with a finishing sander and 220 paper.

Add the trim of dark wood all around. The leatherette panel is mounted independently of the ends. The reason for this is the bevel at the top edge of this panel. The small bevel is made before the panel is installed. Use a router fitted with the V cutter and make the bevel cut about $1/16 \times 1/16$ inch. This bevel will allow the

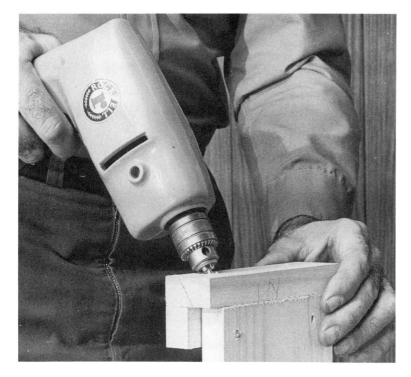

Fig. 8-14. A simple jig is used to drill the diagonal pilot holes for the screws. Make it from available scrap wood.

edge of the leatherette to be protected. It also gives the appearance that the surface below is padded. Assemble with dowels.

Add the ends and sides, then shape the edge with the router fitted with a suitable cutter.

Again using the drilling jig, make the necessary pilot holes for mounting the top.

The drawer is easily made using a double front. The face piece matches the apron; sides, front, and rear are ½-inch plywood and the bottom is ¼-inch plywood. Make rabbet cuts for the rear and bottom section. Drill clearance holes for the pull screws in the front inner panel. Assemble the drawer with glue and 1½-inch finishing nails.

The leatherette panels are cut to size but are not installed until the table has been stained and lacquered. If spraying

equipment is used, mask off both the panel and checkerboard areas. Masking can best be done with kraft paper and masking tape. If you use a brush, you can eliminate the kraft masking over the checkerboard area—however, the edges should be taped anyway to prevent color from running into clear areas.

After color finish is completed, remove masking from chessboard area and apply clear lacquer or varnish over the entire table. When dry, remove the mask from the panel area and cement the leatherette. Spray adhesive works best for this. Apply to leatherette and when the adhesive becomes tacky, apply leatherette to the table surface. Work the edges into the beveled edges.

This completes the table. Add the hardware and get out the chessmen.

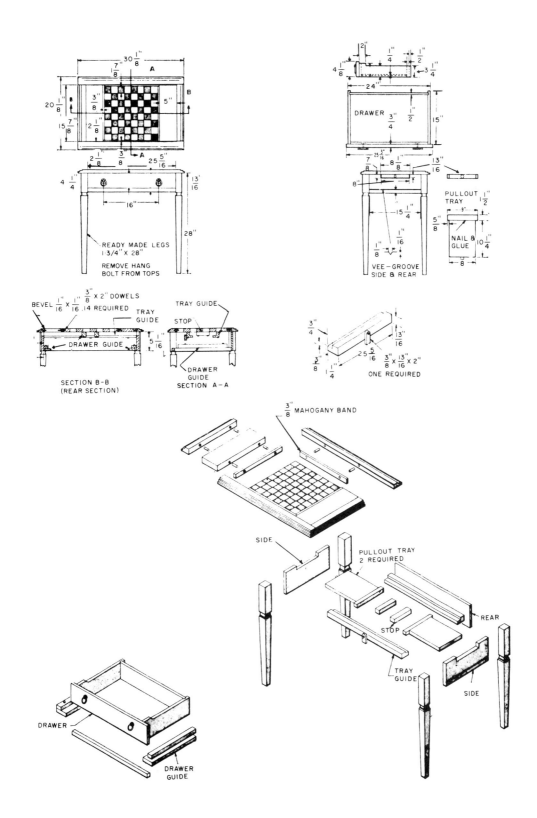

READY MADE LEGS
1·3/4" X 28"

REMOVE HANG
BOLT FROM TOPS

DRAWER

PULLOUT
TRAY

NAIL &
GLUE

VEE—GROOVE
SIDE & REAR

BEVEL $\frac{1}{16}$" X $\frac{1}{16}$" $\frac{3}{8}$" X 2" DOWELS
.14 REQUIRED

TRAY GUIDE

STOP

TRAY
GUIDE

DRAWER GUIDE

SECTION B-B
(REAR SECTION)

DRAWER
GUIDE
SECTION A—A

$\frac{3}{8}$" X $\frac{13}{16}$" X 2"
ONE REQUIRED

$\frac{3}{8}$" MAHOGANY BAND

SIDE

PULLOUT TRAY
2 REQUIRED

STOP

REAR

TRAY
GUIDE

SIDE

DRAWER

DRAWER
GUIDE

MATERIALS LIST

Purpose	Size	Description	Quantity
Apron sides	$^{13}/_{16}$" $\times$ $5^{1}/_{16}$" $\times$ $15^{1}/_{4}$"	Poplar	2
Apron rear	$^{13}/_{16}$" $\times$ $5^{1}/_{16}$" $\times$ $25^{5}/_{16}$"	Poplar	1
Top front and rear ends	$^{13}/_{16}$" $\times$ $2^{1}/_{8}$" $\times$ $30^{1}/_{8}$"	Poplar	2
Top side ends	$^{13}/_{16}$" $\times$ $2^{1}/_{8}$" $\times$ $15^{3}/_{4}$"	Poplar	2
Top panel	$^{3}/_{16}$" $\times$ 5" $\times$ $15^{3}/_{4}$"	Poplar	2
Band end	$^{3}/_{8}$" $\times$ $^{13}/_{16}$" $\times$ 15"	Mahogany	2
Band end	$^{3}/_{8}$" $\times$ $^{13}/_{16}$" $\times$ $15^{3}/_{4}$"	Mahogany	2
Strip	$^{13}/_{16}$" $\times$ $1^{7}/_{8}$" $\times$ 15"	Mahogany	4
Strip	$^{13}/_{16}$" $\times$ $1^{7}/_{8}$" $\times$ 15"	Poplar or Ash	4
Tray	$^{13}/_{16}$" $\times$ 8" $\times$ $10^{1}/_{4}$"	Poplar	2
Tray rear	$^{13}/_{16}$" $\times$ $1^{1}/_{2}$" $\times$ 9"	Poplar	2
Tray guide	$^{13}/_{16}$" $\times$ $1^{1}/_{4}$" $\times$ $25^{5}/_{16}$"	Poplar	2
Tray stop	$^{13}/_{16}$" $\times$ $1^{1}/_{8}$" $\times$ 8"	Poplar	2
Drawer stop	$^{3}/_{8}$" $\times$ $^{13}/_{16}$" $\times$ 2"	Poplar	1
Drawer runner	$^{13}/_{16}$" $\times$ $1^{3}/_{4}$" $\times$ $14^{1}/_{4}$"	Poplar	2
Drawer guide	$^{13}/_{16}$" $\times$ $1^{1}/_{8}$" $\times$ $14^{1}/_{4}$"	Poplar	2
Drawer front	$^{13}/_{16}$" $\times$ $4^{1}/_{8}$" $\times$ $25^{3}/_{16}$"	Poplar	1
Drawer subfront	$^{1}/_{2}$" $\times$ $3^{3}/_{4}$" $\times$ 23"	Poplar	1
Drawer sides	$^{1}/_{2}$" $\times$ $3^{3}/_{4}$" $\times$ 15"	Poplar	2
Drawer rear	$^{1}/_{2}$" $\times$ $2^{3}/_{4}$" $\times$ $23^{1}/_{2}$"	Poplar	1
Drawer bottom	$^{1}/_{4}$" $\times$ $14^{3}/_{4}$" $\times$ $23^{1}/_{2}$"	Plywood	1
Drawer support	$^{13}/_{16}$" $\times$ $2^{3}/_{4}$" $\times$ $25^{5}/_{16}$"	Poplar	1
Legs	$1^{3}/_{4}$" $\times$ $1^{3}/_{4}$" $\times$ 28"	Poplar	4
	$^{3}/_{8}$" $\times$ 2"	Dowels	12
Panels	5" $\times$ $15^{3}/_{4}$"	Leatherette	2
	No. 8 $1^{1}/_{2}$"	Round-head screws	as needed
	No. 8 $2^{1}/_{2}$"	Round-head screws	as needed

Note: You will also need lion pulls, brass pulls, glue, spray adhesive, stain and lacquer.

Child's Footlocker

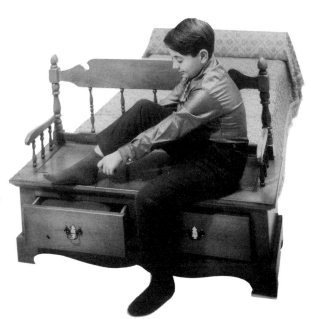

YOU don't need a lathe or other specialized tools to make this attractive child's footlocker. The spindles are assembled from stock items and, except for a few scroll cuts made with a saber saw, every bit of the construction can be done with ordinary hand tools.

The combination of solid lumber and plywood used in construction eliminates the problems that often confront the home craftsman. Wide flat boards are hard to come by in solid lumber except perhaps for knotty pine which is not suitable in this case. Our solution was to use plywood which is available in many types of wood and in several thicknesses. Birch was selected for the child's footlocker illustrated as it has a lovely grain and is smooth, close grained, and easy to finish.

The problem with using plywood, however, is the edge grain which is unsightly and difficult to finish. We decided to use solid lumber to edge the plywood thus eliminating the second problem. A good wood to use for edge work is poplar. It, too, has an excellent grain pattern, is close-grained and is easy to work.

Assembly is accomplished with screws, dowels, nails and glue. Cut all sections to size, check for proper fit, then assemble as shown in the photographs. The edging for the seat section is mitered and assembled with dowel pins. If you cut the miters by hand be sure they are straight and square. Plywood is also used for the end panels. Cut the pieces so the grain runs vertically.

The front framing is cut from poplar and dowelled as shown. Before assembling, lay pieces on a flat table and sand until the joints are flat and smooth. Assemble to the side panels with glue and a couple of nails. Place the nails at the ends where they will be hidden by the base and upper moldings. For added strength, use corner glue blocks on the inside corners.

The turned corner posts are made up by combining two ready-made turnings and square maple blocks as shown. The

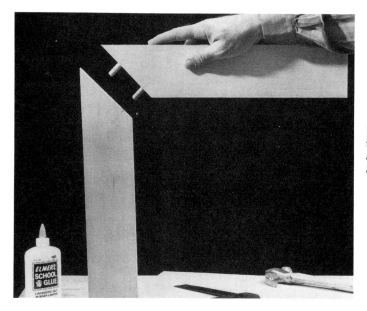

Fig. 9-1. The frame of the footlocker seat is cut from ¾-inch poplar. First miter the corners, then assemble with the aid of both dowels and glue, as pictured in this photograph.

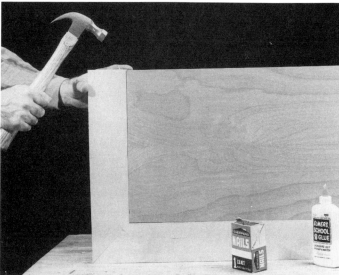

Fig. 9-2. As shown here, nails and dowels are used to attach the poplar frame to the birch plywood seat. If they are readily available, clamps will prove to be very helpful, also.

squares are cut from a length of maple base block. The ends are rounded by using a file and following up with sandpaper. Assemble with dowels and white glue. Ordinary dowels may be used, but grooved dowel pins are best as they will retain the glue better.

The spindles for the seat back and arm rests are also stock items. For the arm rests,

the spindles are cut in half. The cut end of the spindles will have to be whittled so they will fit the holes drilled into the seat. Refer to the drawing.

The drawers are made of ½-inch lumber with ¼-inch plywood bottoms. Three-quarter-inch false fronts are added to the drawers. This greatly simplifies construction and eliminates the need for

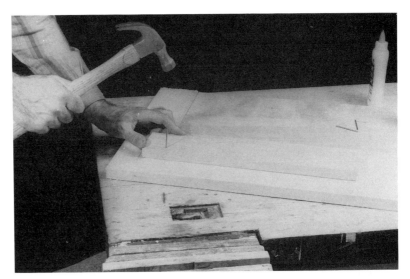

Fig. 9-3. The cleats are attached to the underside of the footlocker seat with the aid of both nails and glue. Note the dimensions for same as listed in the adjacent Materials List.

Fig. 9-4. The poplar front framing is doweled as pictured here. Before beginning the assembly, lay all the pieces on a flat table and sand the joints until they are flat and smooth.

shaping and undercutting. Single track drawer hardware is recommended. The type used here was Knape-Vogt No. 1175.

The base is cut to shape then assembled by means of screws from the inside.

Likewise, the seat is assembled to the side, rear and front by means of cleats and round-head screws.

After assembly, sand smooth then stain and finish as desired.

Fig. 9-5. The base section is fastened to the main section with the aid of screws. Note the single track drawer slide hardware. Knape-Vogt No. 1175 was selected for use in this project.

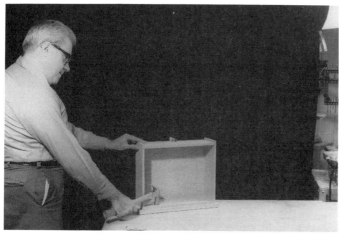

Fig. 9-6. Drawer construction is greatly simplified by the use of false fronts which also eliminate need for shaping, undercutting. Drawer's completed first, then false front added.

Fig. 9-7. No lathe is needed—corner posts are made up by combining two ready-made turnings with square maple blocks. Ends are rounded by a file, sandpaper.

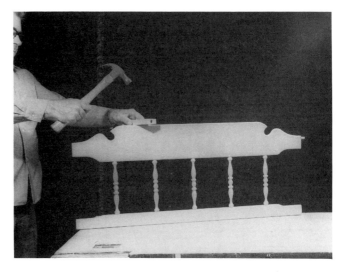

Fig. 9-8. The back piece is drilled to accept the spindles. The scrap under the hammer serves to prevent any damage. Seat back and arm rest spindles are both stock items.

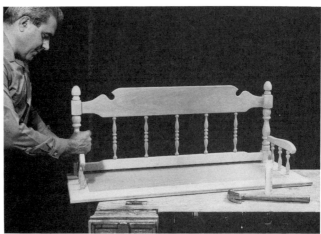

Fig. 9-9. For the two poplar arm rests, the 5$\frac{7}{16}$-inch-long side spindles are cut in half. You will have to whittle their cut ends so as to fit the holes drilled into the seat, as shown here. For further information, refer to the drawing.

Fig. 9-10. The drawers are made of $\frac{1}{2}$-inch lumber with $\frac{1}{4}$-inch plywood bottoms and must be made with the proper allowance for the drawer hardware that is to be used. Therefore, you should obtain the necessary hardware before you actually make the drawers.

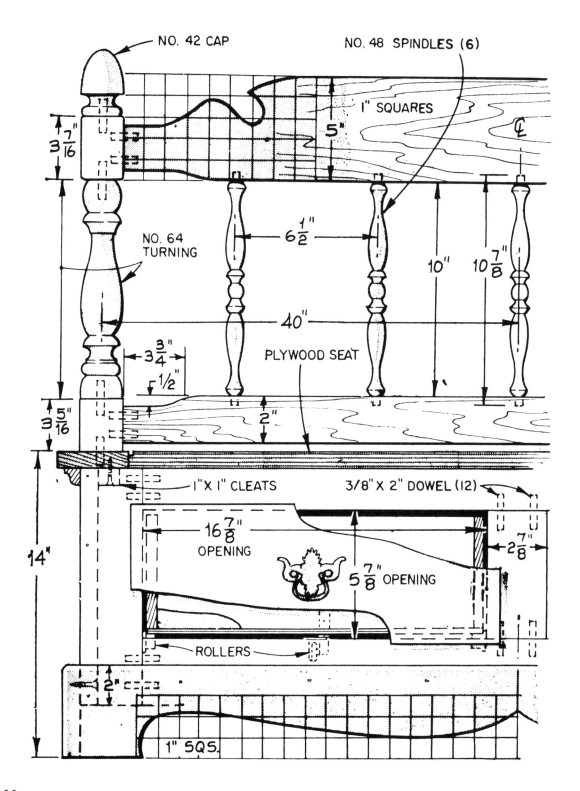

NO. 42 CAP

NO. 48 SPINDLES (6)

1" SQUARES

5"

$3\frac{7}{16}$"

NO. 64
TURNING

$6\frac{1}{2}$"

10"

$10\frac{7}{8}$"

40"

$3\frac{3}{4}$"

$\frac{1}{2}$"

PLYWOOD SEAT

$3\frac{5}{16}$"

2"

1"X 1" CLEATS

3/8"X 2" DOWEL (12)

$16\frac{7}{8}$"
OPENING

$2\frac{7}{8}$"

$5\frac{7}{8}$" OPENING

14"

ROLLERS

2"

1" SQS.

66

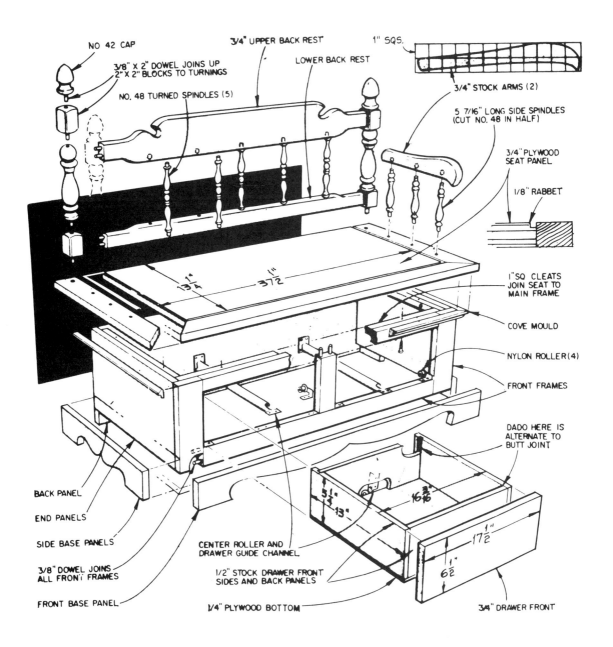

NO 42 CAP

3/8" X 2" DOWEL JOINS UP
2" X 2" BLOCKS TO TURNINGS

NO. 48 TURNED SPINDLES (5)

3/4" UPPER BACK REST

LOWER BACK REST

1" SQS.

3/4" STOCK ARMS (2)

5 7/16" LONG SIDE SPINDLES
(CUT NO. 48 IN HALF)

3/4" PLYWOOD
SEAT PANEL

1/8" RABBET

1 3/4"

37 1/2"

1" SQ CLEATS
JOIN SEAT TO
MAIN FRAME

COVE MOULD

NYLON ROLLER(4)

FRONT FRAMES

DADO HERE IS
ALTERNATE TO
BUTT JOINT

BACK PANEL

END PANELS

SIDE BASE PANELS

3/8" DOWEL JOINS
ALL FRONT FRAMES

FRONT BASE PANEL

CENTER ROLLER AND
DRAWER GUIDE CHANNEL

1/2" STOCK DRAWER FRONT
SIDES AND BACK PANELS

1/4" PLYWOOD BOTTOM

5 1/4"
5 3/4"
13"

16 3/16"

17 1/2"

6 1/2"
1 1/2"

3/4" DRAWER FRONT

MATERIALS LIST

Purpose	Size	Description	Quantity
Upper backrest	¾″ × 5″ × 38″	Poplar	1
Lower backrest	¾″ × 2″ × 38″	Poplar	1
Armrests	¾″ × 2″ × 12″	Poplar	2
	5⁷⁄₁₆″ long	Side spindles	6
	10⁷⁄₈″ long	Rear spindles	5
	Corner post assembly (see drawing)		2
Seat sides	¾″ × 3½″ × 16¾″	Poplar	2
Seat front	¾″ × 3½″ × 44½″	Poplar	1
Seat	¾″ × 13¼″ × 37½″	Lumber core birch	1
Ends	¾″ × 11″ × 15″	Lumber core birch	2
Front frame ends	¾″ × 3″ × 11″	Poplar	2
Front frame center divider	¾″ × 2⁷⁄₈″ × 5⁷⁄₈″	Poplar	1
Front frame top	¾″ × 2″ × 35¾″	Poplar	1
Front frame bottom	¾″ × 3⅛″ × 35¾″	Poplar	1
Front base	¾″ × 4¼″ × 43¼″	Poplar	1
Side base	¾″ × 4¼″ × 15¾″	Poplar	2
Back	¾″ × 13³⁄₁₆″ × 40¼″	Plywood	1
Drawer front	¾″ × 6½″ × 17¼″	Poplar	2
Drawer panels	½″ × 5¼″ × 15³⁄₁₆″	Poplar	4
Drawer panels	½″ × 5¼″ × 13″	Poplar	4
Drawer bottom	¼″ × 13″ × 16³⁄₁₆″	Plywood	2

Note: You will also need ⅜″ × 2″ dowels, ¾″ × 1″ cleats, glue, nails, screws, pulls, and drawer slides (Knape-Vogt No. 1175).

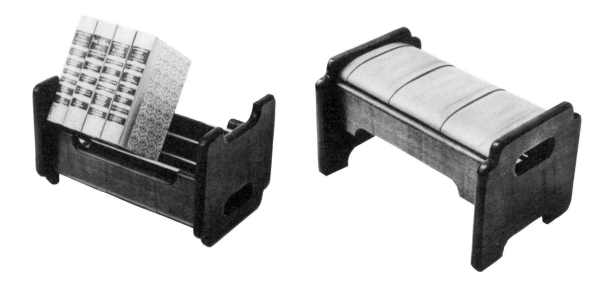

Child's Bookrack and Stool

THIS DOUBLE-DUTY PIECE of furniture should be welcome in any home by both parents and children alike. Standing upright, it is a neat upholstered footstool. Turn it upside down and it becomes a handy bookrack. You can build it for your youngsters for use as a bookrack in their room or as a stool for viewing television in the living-room.

Measuring $9\frac{3}{8} \times 13$ inches, the stool stands 8 inches off the ground. The wood stock used is walnut and a thick layer of foam provides the necessary padding for the cushion, with the polished brass tubing on the opposite side serving as the bookrest. Construction is very easy, with all the dimensions shown on the plans. (See materials list for size of all com-

ponents.) The basic tools needed are a saw, electric drill and a Thermogrip electric glue gun. All bonding is done with the latter, a pistol-shaped tool which uses a polyethylene-based glue that provides a strong, waterproof bond in approximately one minute without the use of clamps, simplifying assembly.

Start by cutting the parts as indicated in the drawings and photos and accurately drill the dowel holes in the mating pieces. The holes for the brass tubing should be drilled slightly oversize to facilitate assembling. All the edges of the wood should be heavily sanded and all joints dowelled for added strength and rigidity. Next bond with the Thermogrip gun. There is no need to wait while the glue sets—just apply glue,

Fig. 10-1. A thin line of hot-melt glue from the Thermogrip electric gun provides an effective bonding agent in the construction of the combination bookrack-stool. The glue dries in approximately 60 seconds.

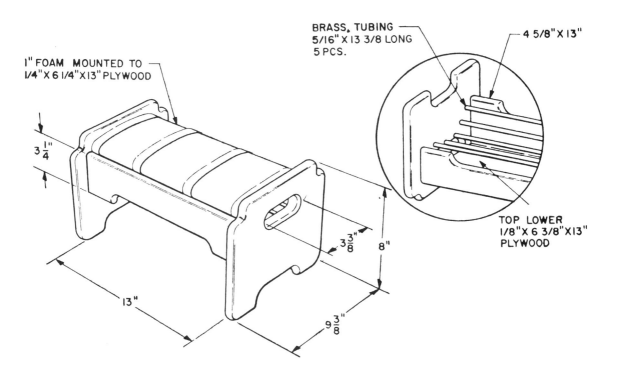

BRASS, TUBING
5/16" X 13 3/8 LONG
5 PCS.

4 5/8" X 13"

1" FOAM MOUNTED TO
1/4" X 6 1/4" X 13" PLYWOOD

$3\frac{1}{4}$"

$3\frac{3}{8}$"

8"

13"

$9\frac{3}{8}$"

TOP LOWER
1/8" X 6 3/8" X 13"
PLYWOOD

MATERIALS LIST

Purpose	Size	Description	Quantity
Ends	8″ × 9⅜″	Walnut	2
Front	3¼″ × 13″		
Rear	4⅝″ × 13″		
Top upper	¼″ × 6¼″ × 13″	Plywood	
Top lower	⅛″ × 6⅜″ × 13″	Plywood	
Brass tubing	⁵⁄₁₆″ × 13⅜″	1-inch foam	5
	½″ dia.	Dowel rod	
		Cushion cover material	

press the parts together for twenty seconds and the project is completed.

If you have a router or shaper available, break all the corners with a quarter round cutter. Otherwise, sand first with a coarse paper, then fine and finally an extra fine grade. Use a paste wood filler to seal the pores. For finishing use a thin wash coat of shellac; apply coat of shellac or varnish.

Colonial Desk with Bookrack

THIS ATTRACTIVE DESK will enhance any room in your home. The single pedestal is an offshoot of the more common double pedestal, which was very popular in colonial days. It has four roomy drawers, with the largest one at the bottom made to hold letter-size folders. The pedestal support serves as a bookrack to hold a good supply of reading materials.

As shown in the drawing, cleats are used extensively. They greatly simplify construction and assembly, as well as eliminate the need to drive nails or screws through the top surface of the desk. Some nails are driven through the side members, but they can be replaced with nails or screws driven from the inside of the cabinet.

The pedestal and bookrack are cut from 1⅛-inch white pine. We used common lumber because it costs about one-half as much as clear. Colonial furniture should have knots, but by carefully selecting your lumber you can eliminate the really bad ones.

You will note that fake tenons are used on the bookshelf members. The final effect looks like the real thing, but the fake method shown is easier and perhaps a little stronger.

The tools required for this project are a table saw, saber saw, router, and drill. In addition, you will need the usual hand tools, such as a hammer, screwdriver, and wrench.

Select flat boards for the top and sides. Cut the pieces to size and shape the bottom edges as shown in the drawing. After cutting the scallop design, use a router with a rounding-off cutter to round off the outside face of the cut. Do not rout the inside face.

Place the top board face down onto a flat surface. (The top of a table saw is ideal because it is exceptionally flat.) Next cut and install the cleats as indicated, using glue and 1¼-inch brads. Rabbet the rear cleats to accept the ¼-inch back panel. Make the rabbet either on the table saw or with the router. Note that the front cleat is

Fig. 11-1. In assembling the colonial desk, cleats are used extensively as in most fine furniture construction. Attach with glue and nails.

Fig. 11-2. An exception is a temporary cleat in the base of the cabinet. Attach it with nails only. Remove it when you install the bottom panel.

Fig. 11-3. Installing the bottom board. Note the two blocks that are aids to positioning. Remove them after you have nailed the bottom board in the proper position.

Fig. 11-4. Use lag screws to join shaped pedestal and base sections, as well as the top section to the pedestal. Use washers under screw heads.

1 inch in from the front. Side cleats are 1¾ inch from the edge.

Next, prepare the side panels. Rabbet the rear edge of both, but note that the left upright is rabbeted at two places near the top. The smaller rabbet is to accept the rear panel of the wide drawer compartment.

To ensure proper alignment in assembly, make up a couple of temporary cleats. At this time also cut the bottom panel for the drawer compartment. Install the temporary cleats so that the bottom panel rests on them as shown. Glue up the section and nail it in place, using a square to make sure the sections are perpendicular. If necessary, nail a diagonal to hold the sections while the glue sets. Add the drawer compartment cleats and install the single drawer compartment, using a temporary spacer block to support the bottom board while nailing.

Cut the 1⅛-inch lumber for the book-rack section to size and round the edges with the router. This time round both sides to obtain a half-round effect.

Make the base piece for the upright by gluing up two pieces of ¾-inch stock. After shaping, assemble to the upright with two 3-inch lag screws.

To align the shelves, drill the dowel holes in the end piece and place it right up to the center upright. Center it and then transfer the hole centers using a pencil. Next locate and drill matching holes in the shelves, then assemble using dowels and screws. Drive the dowels so they protrude ½ inch from the outside.

Make up two fake tenons and assemble with glue.

Drawers are made with double fronts.

Fig. 11-5. Attaching the scalloped base to the backup board at the front of the desk. Glue with nails only at the sides.

Fig. 11-6. Nail and glue the drawer stops to the rear of each compartment. Place them so the drawer fronts protrude ⅜ inch.

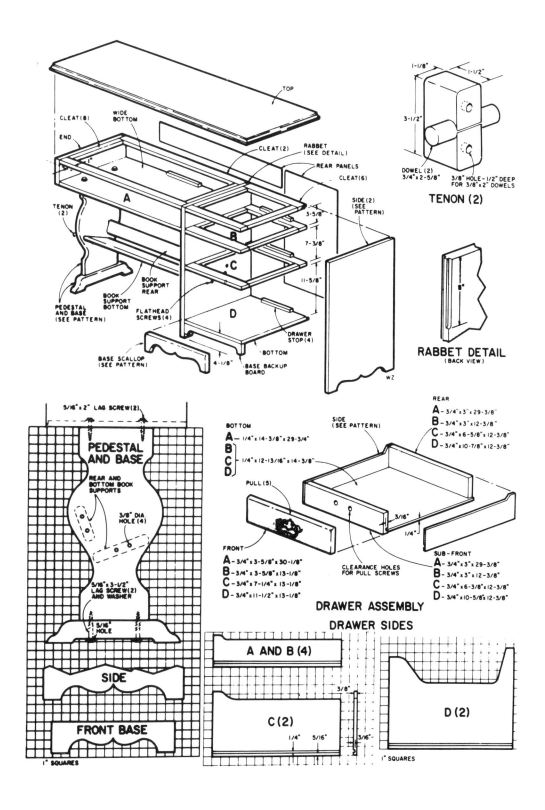

TOP

CLEAT(8)

WIDE BOTTOM

END

CLEAT(2)

RABBET (SEE DETAIL)

REAR PANELS

CLEAT(6)

REAR PANELS

TENON (2)

SIDE(2) (SEE PATTERN)

3-5/8"

7-3/8"

11-5/8"

BOOK SUPPORT REAR

BOOK SUPPORT BOTTOM

PEDESTAL AND BASE (SEE PATTERN)

FLATHEAD SCREWS(4)

DRAWER STOP(4)

BASE SCALLOP (SEE PATTERN)

BOTTOM

4-1/8"

BASE BACKUP BOARD

A

B

C

D

1-1/8"

1-1/2"

3-1/2"

DOWEL (2) 3/4" x 2-5/8"

3/8" HOLE - 1/2" DEEP FOR 3/8" x 2" DOWELS

TENON (2)

8"

RABBET DETAIL (BACK VIEW)

WZ

5/16" x 2" LAG SCREW(2)

PEDESTAL AND BASE

REAR AND BOTTOM BOOK SUPPORTS

3/8" DIA. HOLE (4)

5/16" x 3-1/2" LAG SCREW(2) AND WASHER

5/16" HOLE

SIDE

FRONT BASE

1" SQUARES

BOTTOM

A - 1/4" x 14-3/8" x 29-3/4"
B
C
D

1/4" x 12-13/16" x 14-3/8"

PULL(5)

FRONT

A - 3/4" x 3-5/8" x 30-1/8"
B - 3/4" x 3-5/8" x 13-1/8"
C - 3/4" x 7-1/4" x 13-1/8"
D - 3/4" x 11-1/2" x 13-1/8"

CLEARANCE HOLES FOR PULL SCREWS

SIDE (SEE PATTERN)

REAR

A - 3/4" x 3" x 29-3/8"
B - 3/4" x 3" x 12-3/8"
C - 3/4" x 6-5/8" x 12-3/8"
D - 3/4" x 10-7/8" x 12-3/8"

3/16"

1/4"

SUB-FRONT

A - 3/4" x 3" x 29-3/8"
B - 3/4" x 3" x 12-3/8"
C - 3/4" x 6-3/8" x 12-3/8"
D - 3/4" x 10-5/8" x 12-3/8"

DRAWER ASSEMBLY

DRAWER SIDES

A AND B (4)

C (2)

3/8"

1/4"   5/16"

3/16"

D (2)

1" SQUARES

MATERIALS LIST

Purpose	Size	Description	Quantity
Top	¾″ × 17¼″ × 48″	Pine	1
Side	¾″ × 16⅛″ × 29¼″	Pine	2
End	¾″ × 5¼″ × 16⅛″	Pine	1
Bottom	¾″ × 13¼″ × 16⅛″	Pine	1
Wide bottom	¾″ × 16⅛″ × 30¾″	Pine	1
Base scallop	¾″ × 3½″ × 14¼″	Pine	1
Base backup board	¾″ × 3″ × 13¼″	Pine	1
Cleat	¾″ × 1″ × 11⅞″	Pine	8
Cleat	¾″ × 2″ × 13¼″	Pine	6
Cleat	¾″ × 2″ × 30¼″	Pine	2
Drawer, front	¾″ × 3⅝″ × 30⅛″	Pine	1
Drawer, front	¾″ × 3⅝″ × 13⅛″	Pine	1
Drawer, front	¾″ × 7¼″ × 13⅛″	Pine	1
Drawer, front	¾″ × 11½″ × 13⅛″	Pine	1
Drawer, subfront	¾″ × 3″ × 29⅜″	Pine	1
Drawer, subfront	¾″ × 3″ × 12⅜″	Pine	1
Drawer, subfront	¾″ × 6⅜″ × 12⅜″	Pine	1
Drawer, subfront	¾″ × 10⅝″ × 12⅜″	Pine	1
Drawer, rear	¾″ × 3″ × 29⅜″	Pine	1
Drawer, rear	¾″ × 3″ × 12⅜″	Pine	1
Drawer, rear	¾″ × 6⅝″ × 12⅜″	Pine	1
Drawer, rear	¾″ × 10⅞″ × 12⅜″	Pine	1
Drawer, side	⅜″ × 3⅝″ × 15″	Plywood	4
Drawer, side	⅜″ × 7¼″ × 15″	Plywood	2
Drawer, side	⅜″ × 11½″ × 15″	Plywood	2
Drawer, bottom	¼″ × 14⅜″ × 29¾″	Plywood	1
Drawer, bottom	¼″ × 12¹³⁄₁₆″ × 14⅜″	Plywood	3
Drawer stop	⅜″ × ¾″ × 8″	Pine	4
Rear panel	¼″ × 4½″ × 30¾″	Plywood	1
Rear panel	¼″ × 14³⁄₁₆″ × 25″	Plywood	1
Pedestal	1⅛″ × 10¾″ × 21⅝″	Pine	1
Pedestal base	1¾″ × 2½″ × 15⁷⁄₁₆″	Pine	1
Book support, rear	1⅛″ × 4″ × 27⅜″	Pine	1
Book support, bottom	1⅛″ × 6¾″ × 27⅜″	Pine	1
Tenon	1⅛″ × 1½″ × 3½″	Pine	2
Tenon dowel	¾″ × 2⅝″	Maple	2
Lag screws	⁵⁄₁₆″ × 3½″		2
Lag screws	⁵⁄₁₆″ × 2″		2
Flat washers for screws			4
Dowels	⅜″ × 2″		4
Screws	#8x2½″ FH		4
Pulls	3″ centers		5

Note: Pulls are available from Armor Products.

Sides are ⅜-inch plywood; fronts and rear are ¾-inch pine; and bottoms are ¼-inch plywood. In order to keep drawers level when they are extended, make the side panels to rise at the rear.

Cut the drawer sections to size, then dado the bottoms to accept the ¼-inch bottom panels. Drill clearance holes in the subfront panels and assemble the section with nails and glue. Do not install the front yet. Sand the edges of the ¼-inch bottom panels and slide the panels into place. A little glue in the groove will keep the bottom from rattling.

To install the fronts, center it over the drawer from side to side, raising the front ¹⁄₁₆ inch above the bottom of the drawer. This ¹⁄₁₆-inch offset at the bottom will center the front panel in the compartment opening.

Before permanently mounting the panel, tack it into place with a couple of nails and check the fit. If it is okay, apply glue and mount permanently.

The unit shown was finished in antique olive using a prepared kit. The process is simple. Apply a base color to the work. After drying, brush a glaze coat on and then wipe it off. Wiping can be done with paper, cheesecloth, or even a dry brush. You can add highlights to give the piece an authentic antique appearance.

Classy Contemporary Bar

THIS ELEGANT BAR is fashioned similar to a deluxe commercial model costing over $700. We have added a few extra features which should make this all the more outstanding. For example: the pull-out extensions increase the capacity of the top to provide more working space. Also included is a large compartmented drawer—one section for glassware, and the other for utensils. Heavy-duty drawer slides permit full extension of the drawer for easy accessibility to its contents. A pair of wine racks are included to keep the bottles tilted at the proper storage angle.

The bar top, extensions, and drawer bottom are covered with plastic laminate for ease of maintenance and durability.

The piece has been designed so anyone with a basic knowledge of woodworking can easily build it. Except for the mitered moldings, all joints are butted. No tricky joints to slow you down. The moldings are made with the table saw and router.

Cherry lumber was used for this bar. A bit expensive, but well worth the extra

cost. It is hard, has a beautiful grain pattern, and is very easy to finish.

Because the piece is rather large, concealed casters are recommended for mobility.

To add strength to the joints, dowels must be used.

Rip 6-inch stock to true edges, and if necessary, plane them. Lay out the pieces for the most pleasing grain arrangement. The length of the pieces should be about 27 inches. The ends will be trimmed later after gluing.

Mark the dowel locations using a straight edge. Use four dowels per piece spacing them as shown. Identify each piece with a matching numeral or letter.

The dowels must be straight and centered on the edge of the stock. A doweling jig as shown in the photo is recommended. It can be used with a portable drill or on the drill press. If you use a portable drill, place a tape marker on the drill to serve as a depth gauge. Drill the holes to a depth of $1\frac{1}{16}$ inch in each mating part. Apply a little glue to the dowels then

Fig. 12-1. As shown here, special doweling jig aids in the drilling of holes for the dowels. Note all the alignment marks.

Fig. 12-2. Apply the wood glue to the lower half of the dowel and then drive home with the aid of a hammer. Use spiral dowels.

Fig. 12-3. To facilitate assembly, it's best to remove the glue that accumulates around base of dowel. A stiff brush is ideal.

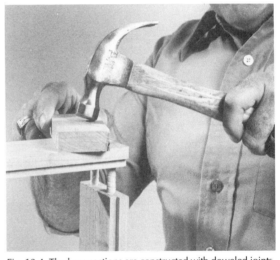

Fig. 12-4. The base sections are constructed with doweled joints. Use a block under the hammer to prevent marring the work.

insert into the holes. Drive the dowel with a hammer until it seats fully. Wipe away any glue squeeze-out. A stiff bristle brush is excellent for removing the excess glue.

Apply glue to both edges of each intermediate piece then assemble and clamp securely. Do not wipe glue squeeze-out. Allow to dry then remove excess with a chisel. If you wipe away the glue while

still wet, discoloration in the joint area will occur, especially if the piece is later stained.

Trimming the ends of the side pieces can be tricky because of the width (over 20 inches). The conventional radial arm saw or table saws do not have the capacity for such a piece. The solution to this vexing problem is easily handled with a saber saw

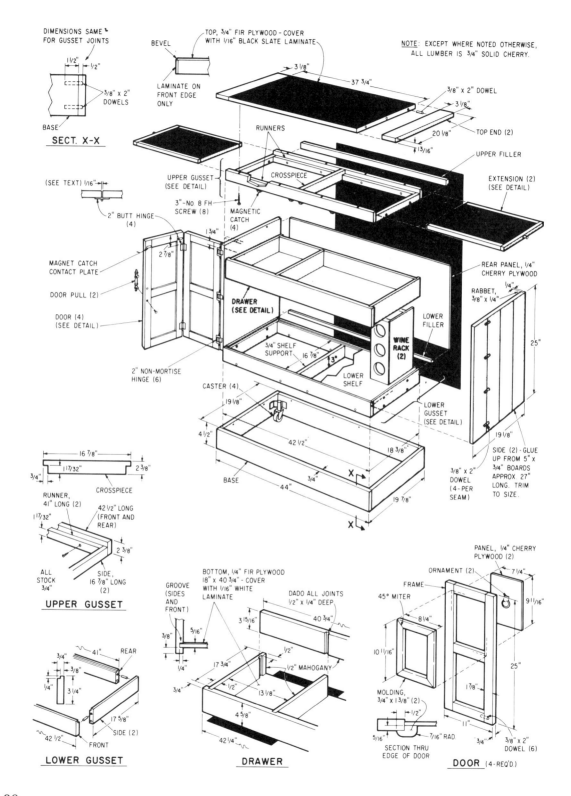

DIMENSIONS SAME
FOR GUSSET JOINTS

1 1/2"   1/2"

3/8" x 2"
DOWELS

BASE

SECT. X-X

BEVEL

LAMINATE ON
FRONT EDGE
ONLY

TOP, 3/4" FIR PLYWOOD - COVER
WITH 1/16" BLACK SLATE LAMINATE

3 1/8"

37 3/4"

NOTE: EXCEPT WHERE NOTED OTHERWISE,
ALL LUMBER IS 3/4" SOLID CHERRY.

3/8" x 2" DOWEL

3 1/8"

20 1/8"   TOP END (2)

13/16"

RUNNERS

UPPER FILLER

(SEE TEXT) 1/16"

UPPER GUSSET
(SEE DETAIL)

CROSSPIECE

EXTENSION (2)
(SEE DETAIL)

2" BUTT HINGE
(4)

3"-No. 8 FH
SCREW (8)

MAGNETIC
CATCH
(4)

1 3/4"

MAGNET CATCH
CONTACT PLATE

2 7/8"

DOOR PULL (2)

DOOR (4)
(SEE DETAIL)

DRAWER
(SEE DETAIL)

REAR PANEL, 1/4"
CHERRY PLYWOOD

RABBET,
3/8" x 1/4"

1/4"

LOWER
FILLER

WINE
RACK
(2)

25"

2" NON-MORTISE
HINGE (6)

CASTER (4)

3/4" SHELF
SUPPORT

16 7/8"

3"

LOWER
SHELF

19 1/8"

SIDE (2) - GLUE
UP FROM 5" x
3/4" BOARDS
APPROX 27"
LONG. TRIM
TO SIZE.

19 1/8"

4 1/2"

42 1/2"

18 3/8"

LOWER
GUSSET
(SEE DETAIL)

3/8" x 2"
DOWEL
(4 - PER
SEAM)

BASE

3/4"

X

44"

19 7/8"

X

16 7/8"

1 17/32"

2 3/8"

3/4"

CROSSPIECE

RUNNER,
41" LONG (2)

42 1/2" LONG
(FRONT AND
REAR)

1 17/32"

2 3/8"

ALL
STOCK
3/4"

SIDE,
16 7/8" LONG
(2)

UPPER GUSSET

3/4"   41"   REAR

3/8"

1/4"   3 1/4"

17 5/8"

42 1/2"   SIDE (2)

FRONT

LOWER GUSSET

BOTTOM, 1/4" FIR PLYWOOD
18" x 40 3/4" - COVER
WITH 1/16" WHITE
LAMINATE

GROOVE
(SIDES
AND
FRONT)

DADO ALL JOINTS
1/2" x 1/4" DEEP

3 15/16"

40 3/4"

3/8"

5/16"

1/2"

1/4"

17 3/4"

1/2" MAHOGANY

1/2"

13 1/8"

3/4"

4 5/8"

42 1/4"

DRAWER

PANEL, 1/4" CHERRY
PLYWOOD (2)

ORNAMENT (2)

7 1/4"

FRAME

45° MITER

9 11/16"

8 1/4"

10 11/16"

25"

1 7/8"

MOLDING,
3/4" x 1 3/8" (2)

1/2"

11"

7/16" RAD.

5/16"

SECTION THRU
EDGE OF DOOR

3/4"

3/8" x 2"
DOWEL (6)

DOOR (4 - REQ'D.)

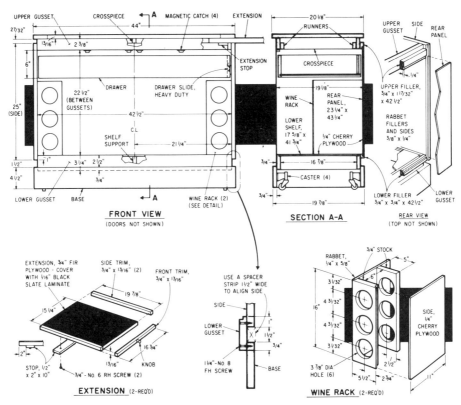

UPPER GUSSET CROSSPIECE A MAGNETIC CATCH (4) EXTENSION
44"
27/32"
1 3/16" 2 3/8"
6"
22 1/2" DRAWER DRAWER SLIDE,
(BETWEEN HEAVY DUTY
GUSSETS)
25" 42 1/2"
(SIDE) C L
SHELF 21 1/4"
SUPPORT
1 1/2" 1" 3/4" 2 1/2"
4 1/2" 3/4"
LOWER GUSSET BASE A WINE RACK (2)
(SEE DETAIL)

FRONT VIEW
(DOORS NOT SHOWN)

EXTENSION
STOP

20 1/8"
RUNNERS
CROSSPIECE
19 1/8"
WINE REAR
RACK PANEL,
23 1/4" x
43 3/4"
LOWER
SHELF,
17 5/8" x
41 3/4" 1/4" CHERRY
PLYWOOD
3/4" 16 7/8"
CASTER (4)
3/4" 19 7/8"

SECTION A-A

UPPER SIDE REAR
GUSSET PANEL
1/4"
UPPER FILLER,
3/4" x 1 17/32"
x 42 1/2"
RABBET
FILLERS
AND SIDES
3/8" x 1/4"
LOWER FILLER LOWER
3/4" x 3/4" x 42 1/2" GUSSET

REAR VIEW
(TOP NOT SHOWN)

EXTENSION, 3/4" FIR SIDE TRIM,
PLYWOOD - COVER 3/4" x 1 3/16" (2) FRONT TRIM,
WITH 1/16" BLACK 3/4" x 1 3/16"
SLATE LAMINATE
19 7/8"
15 1/4"
16 3/4"
2" 1 3/16" KNOB
STOP, 1/2" 3/4" - No 6 RH SCREW (2)
x 2" x 10"

EXTENSION (2-REQ'D)

USE A SPACER
STRIP 1 1/2" WIDE
TO ALIGN SIDE
SIDE
LOWER
GUSSET
X 1 1/2"
3/4"
1 1/4" - No 8 BASE
FH SCREW

RABBET, 3/4" STOCK
1/4" x 5/8" 5"
6"
3 1/32"
4 31/32" SIDE,
16" 1/4"
CHERRY
4 31/32" PLYWOOD
3 1/32"
2 1/2"
3 7/8" DIA 2 3/4" 11"
HOLE (6) 5 1/2"

WINE RACK (2-REQ'D)

(or portable saw) and a router. The saw is used to trim the piece to size, then the router fitted with a straight bit is used to produce a finished smooth edge. Clamp a router guide to the work or, if you prefer, nail the strip to the inside surface. Place the strip so the router will remove only enough stock to smoothen the saw cut.

Rabbet the rear edges of both end pieces to take the 1/4-inch rear panel. Make the rabbet 1/4 × 3/8 inch. Set the panels aside for now.

The base is made with solid stock. To keep costs down, the rear piece can be made of common lumber. The sides and ends are cherry. Butt joints with dowels are used. Note that the front piece overlaps the sides and the sides in turn overlap the rear piece. The dowels penetrate 1 1/2 inch into the end grain and 1/2 inch into the side

grain. See drawing.

Install the dowels and coat the end grain lightly with glue. Allow the glue to set, then apply more and assemble the pieces. Do the rear section first. Install clamps and be sure the assembly is square. When the glue has set, remove the clamps and glue the front to the end pieces, following the same procedure as above.

The lower gussets are made after the base is assembled, in the same manner as the base. After cutting the pieces, drill the 11/64-inch-diameter holes for the 1 1/4-inch—8 FH screws. Next, rabbet one edge of the lower gusset pieces to receive the 1/4-inch bottom panel. Make the rabbet 1/4 inch deep × 3/8 inch wide. Be sure to keep the better surface outward.

After the gusset is assembled sand the surfaces, paying special attention to the end grain of the front piece. Check the fit and if necessary, sand until the gusset telescopes into the base snugly. Let the gusset protrude into the base ⅞ inch then screw securely. Glue is not necessary.

The upper gusset differs from the lower as shown in the drawings. Note that the front and rear pieces are the same length. Cut the various pieces to size, drill the dowel and screw holes, then carefully assemble. Note that the end pieces are narrower than the front and rear sections. Be sure the frame is square as the glue sets. Use temporary diagonal cleats if needed. After the glue has set, remove the clamps and install the runners. These are mounted

Fig. 12-5. Base pieces must fit snugly. Check the fit and if necessary, sand until the gusset telescopes into the base securely, as shown.

Fig. 12-6. The bar end panels are assembled with screws and glue. The spacer at the end (not visible here) assures alignment.

Fig. 12-7. The self-aligned concealed caster is installed with the aid of round head screws. Tabs will provide the proper clearance.

Fig. 12-8. The drawer slides are triple-track type and drawer can be fully extended for easy accessibility to any of the contents.

Fig. 12-9. The drawer bottom is white laminate (added after pieces are cut) on plywood. Sink all the nail heads and fill.

Fig. 12-10. Installing the extensions covered with plastic laminate for easy maintenance. The stop is installed on the underside.

Fig. 12-11. Installing door moldings. Simply apply glue, then force the pieces into the frame. The snug fit will eliminate the need for any clamps.

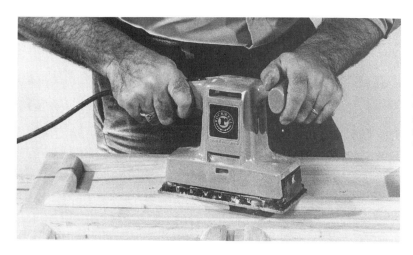

Fig. 12-12. The door moldings are removed as a frame (do not apply glue to the rabbet) so the corners can be sanded. They are sanded first with a medium grit paper, then fine. Reinstall with glue.

along the front and rear gussets. The setback edge should line up with the narrower end pieces. Use a scrap spacer block to assure accuracy.

The base, ends and upper sections are now ready to be assembled. Cut a strip of wood 1½ inch wide and use it as a spacer to locate the sides on the lower gusset. Drill pilot holes for the screws then assemble. The front edge of the side panel should line up with the front edge of the gusset. At the rear, install filler strips at the top and bottom. These will support the rear panel.

Cut and install the rear panel. Drill screw holes through the panel around the perimeter and install with ½—6 RH screws.

Rip the strips for the door stiles and rails from solid stock. Make these 1⅞ inch wide then cut the lengths. Cut eight stiles 25 inches long and make the twelve rails to a length of 7¼ inch.

Drill the ⅜-inch dowel holes 1¹⁄₁₆ inch deep into the ends of each rail. Drill

Fig. 12-13. Back view of the folding doors. The upper butt hinge must clear magnetic catch plate. Note the non-mortise hinges at the corner. Designed for this type of cabinet, they are easily installed.

matching holes into the stiles (three holes per stile). If you use the dowel jig, simply mark the surface of the rails and stiles with the centerline of the dowel. Align the jig with these marks and drill. The holes will be perfectly centered.

Coat the end grain surfaces of the rails with glue and allow to dry. Insert dowels then apply glue again and assemble the parts. Clamp securely to be sure the frames are square before tightening the clamps.

After the door frames are glued, sand the surfaces until all joints are smooth. A belt sander works best for this. Start with 60-grit paper then work down to 120, then 220. Use a finishing sander for the 220 paper.

Next, cut the 1¼-inch strips for the

moldings. Round off the top edge then cut the rabbet. The rabbet can be made with the table saw or router. The rounding off is done with the router.

After the moldings have been cut, measure and miter the ends to fit into the door openings. If a good snug fit is made, the joints can be glued and held without the need for clamps. Simply apply glue, then force the pieces into the frame. Do not apply glue to the rabbet. The moldings can then be removed (as a frame) so the corners can be sanded. Reinstall with glue.

Cut the door panels from a piece of ¼-inch plywood of the same species as the frame. Drill the hole for the decorative pull then sand all edges as well as the front and rear surfaces. Apply a thin bead of glue on

85

MATERIALS LIST

Note: Except where noted, all lumber is ¾″ solid cherry.

Purpose	Size	Description	Quantity
Base front	¾″ × 4½″ × 44″		1
Base side	¾″ × 4½″ × 19⅛″		2
Base rear	¾″ × 4½″ × 42½″		1
Lower shelf support	¾″ × 3″ × 16⅞″		1
Lower gusset front	¾″ × 3¼″ × 42½″		1
Lower gusset side	¾″ × 3¼″ × 17⅝″		2
Lower gusset rear	¾″ × 3¼″ × 41″		1
Lower filler rear	¾″ × ¾″ × 42½″		1
Side panel	¾″ × 19⅛″ × 25″		2
Upper gusset (front)	¾″ × 2⅜″ × 42½″		1
Side gusset	¾″ × 1¹⁷/₃₂″ × 16⅞″		2
Rear gusset	¾″ × 2⅜″ × 42½″		1
Rear filler (upper)	¾″ × 1¹⁷/₃₂″ × 42½″		1
Runner	¾″ × 1¹⁷/₃₂″ × 41″		2
Upper crosspiece	¾″ × 2⅜″ × 16⅞″		1
Extension	¾″ × 15¼″ × 19⅞″	Fir plywood	2
Extension side trim	¾″ × ¹³/₁₆″ × 19⅞″		4
Extension front trim	¾″ × ¹³/₁₆″ × 16¾″		2
Extension stop	½″ × 2″ × 10″		2
Top	¾″ × 20⅛″ × 37¾″	Fir plywood	1
Top end	¹³/₁₆″ × 3⅛″ × 20¹³/₁₆″		2
Rear panel	¼″ × 23¼″ × 43¼″	Cherry plywood	1
Shelf	¼″ × 17⅝″ × 41¾″		1
Door stile	¾″ × 1⅞″ × 25″		8
Door rail	¾″ × 1⅞″ × 7¼″		12
Door panel	¼″ × 7¼″ × 9¹¹/₁₆″	Cherry plywood	8
Door molding	¾″ × 1⅜″ × 7′		(per door)
Drawer front	¾″ × 4⅝″ × 42¼″		1
Drawer side	½″ × 4⅝″ × 18″	Mahogany	2
Drawer rear	½″ × 3¹⁵/₁₆″ × 40¾″	Mahogany	1
Drawer divider	½″ × 3¹⁵/₁₆″ × 17¾″	Mahogany	1
Drawer bottom	¼″ × 18″ × 40¾″	Fir plywood	1
Wine rack (side)	¼″ × 11″ × 16″	Cherry plywood	4
Wine rack (front)	¾″ × 5½″ × 16″		2
Wine rack (rear)	¾″ × 5″ × 16″		2
Dowels	⅜″ × 2″		4 doz.
Screws	1¼″—8 FH		26
Screws	3″—8 FH		8
Screws	¾″—6 RH		4
Screws	½″—6 RH		16
Hinges	2″	Non-mortise	6
Hinges	2″	Butt	4

Purpose	Size	Description	Quantity
Pull			2
Magnetic catch			4
Door ornament			8
Drawer slide, heavy duty			1 pair
Casters, concealed			4
Extension knob			2
Plastic laminate, (black slate)			6'
Plastic laminate, (white)			4'

Note: If you have difficulty in locating the special hardware, write to J. C. Armor Co., Box 290, Deer Park, N.Y. 11729, for their catalog. If you are interested in the special slides, ask for slide 525.

the back side of the frame then install the panels and clamp until the glue sets. A clamping block of wood cut to fit within the panel area will facilitate the clamping.

The doors are installed with non-mortise hinges and butt hinges. The non-mortise type are especially designed for this type of cabinet. They are easily installed without the need for mortising. The butt hinges are used where the doors fold. Install them with the doors butted against each other, then remove the hinges and plane about 1/32 inch of stock off the butting edges. This will then produce the 1/16-inch space between the doors. If necessary, remove a little stock where the center doors meet.

The laminate is added to the tops and drawer after those pieces have been cut to size. Install with contact cement and be sure to work out-of-doors if you use the flammable cement. Follow the manufacturer's recommendations carefully. For the top, apply the front edging first, then trim with the router. Follow with the top piece. Trim the edges flush with a straight cutter then bevel the top front edge either with a file or with a special bevel cutter fitted to the router.

The drawer is made with cherry and mahogany. Cut the pieces to size and assemble as per the drawing. Assemble with nails and glue.

The drawer mounting is not detailed, as various slides may be used. These are usually sold with the mounting instructions included.

Cut and assemble the wine racks as per the drawing.

Finish the wood as desired. A dark pine stain followed with two coats of low gloss Satinlac works well.

Compact Bar/Cabinet Combo

THIS ATTRACTIVE BAR/CABINET features a revolving door with racks for glasses and a detachable front panel that doubles as a serving tray. The use of prefinished panels for all exposed surfaces eliminates the need for finishing and gives the completed piece a swank professional appearance.

The well-proportioned bar has ample storage space for bottles, glassware, ice bucket and the like. The compartment to the left also has a small shelf near the top which is ideal for storing recipes, stirrers, tongs, etc. This shelf is placed high enough to clear the bottles stored below it.

To add further to the appearance, prefinished cove molding is used to edge the lid and base, thus solving the problem of what to do with exposed edges. When carefully cut and applied, the molding looks like it was cut from the panel with a shaper or router. Miters must be cut with a sharp blade; otherwise, the wood will tend to splinter resulting in an unsightly appearance.

Care must also be exercised when cutting the panels as the prefinished surface has a degree of brittleness which makes it prone to surface splitting. This is especially apparent when using dull tools.

The best blade for a table or radial-arm saw when working with prefinished panels is a plywood blade. These are hollow ground and cut very smoothly.

Prefinished panels come in a wide variety of styles and woods. Some are solid panels without grooves while others have random grooves and still others have narrow bands or grooves with wide panels between. Prices vary depending upon

Fig. 13-1. The brackets should be riveted to the revolving door. Then the glass trays are riveted to the brackets as shown here.

Fig. 13-2. Use a hole saw attached to an electric drill to make cutouts for glasses on the serving tray and the revolving racks.

location and quality. The wood selected and the grain pattern have a direct bearing on the price.

Use a nonstaining white glue for assembling all sections and where necessary, use clamps. Clamping will not be practical when working with the cove molding. Here strips of masking tape are recommended to hold the piece while the glue dries.

Both doors are faced with the prefinished material. A framing of ½-inch pine is sandwiched in between to build up the

Fig. 13-3. A headed 2-inch nail serves as a pivot for the revolving door. It was driven fully home after this photograph was taken.

Fig. 13-4. White glue bonds prefinished molding to cabinet. Use masking tape rather than clamps to hold molding while glue dries.

thickness and to prevent warping. The serving tray panel is held in place against the side panels by a friction fit bearing. The overhanging molding on the front edge of the lid also tends to hold the tray-panel securely. When the lid is raised the tray may be removed by pulling it forward slightly to overcome the slight side pressure. If desired, a pair of magnetic catches may be added at the ends.

A pair of knife hinges is used to support the swinging door. These are attached at the top and bottom into a recess cut in the door. The revolving door is affixed by means of a pivot that consists of a pair of 2-inch nails placed as shown. Two

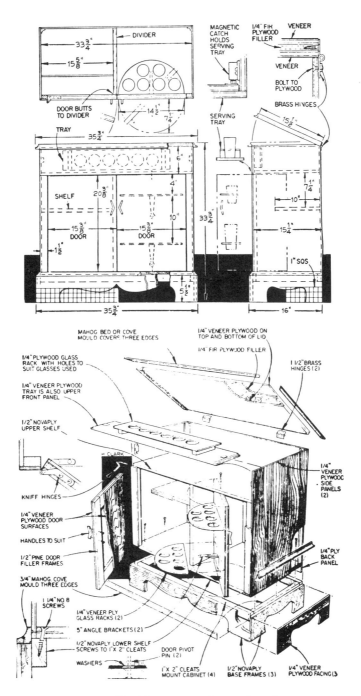

small washers at the bottom will allow the door to revolve freely.

The base is made by gluing the prefinished stock to a piece of ½-inch pine.

Refer to the drawing as to edge treatment. When your bar/cabinet is completely assembled, break all sharp edges with fine sandpaper, then stain the inside if desired.

Purpose	Size	Description	Quantity
Doors			
Door frame	¼" × 15⅜" × 20⅜"	Prefinished	4
Door frame	½" × 2½" × 20⅜"		4
End strips	½" × 2" × 11⅜"		4
End strips, rear	¼" × 1½" × 20⅜"	Prefinished	2
Upper shelf	¾" × 1¼" × 20⅜"	Pine	
Lower shelf	½" × 15" × 33¾"		1
Small shelf	½" × 15" × 33¾"		1
Divider	¾" × 10" × 16"	Pine	1
Sides	¾" × 14" × 20½"	Pine	1
Rear	¼" × 15¼" × 29⅜"	Prefinished	2
Cleats	¼" × 33" × 34¼"	Pine	1
Front base, inner	1' × 1' × 6'		1
Front base, outer	½" × 5½" × 35¼"	Prefinished	1
Side base, inner	¼" × 5½" × 35¾"	Prefinished	1
Side base, outer	½" × 5½" × 15½"		1
Cove molding	¼" × 5½" × 15½"	Prefinished	2
		Prefinished	12'
Lid	¼" × 15½" × 34¼"	Prefinished	2
Lid, inner	7¼" × 14½" × ¼"	Prefinished	2
Glass rack	¼" × 6" × 34¼"	Prefinished	1
Outer serving tray	¼" × 6" × 33¾"	Prefinished	1
Inner serving tray	¼" × 4½" × 24"	Fir plywood	1
Serving tray glass rack		White glue	
		Screws	
	2"	Door pulls	
		Knife hinges	2
		Nails (2) pivot	2
		Washers	2
Shelf brackets	5	Shelf brackets (Stanley)	2
	4' × 8'	Prefinished Fruitwood panel	1 pr.
Lid	1"	Hinges	2

Compact Picnic Group

HERE IS A compact picnic group that is not only easy to move and set up, but which also takes up no more space than a conventional size table of its type. It is particularly suited for families with small children, because there are no benches for youngsters to overturn.

By following the simplified construction plans (see drawings) you can build this outdoor set of furniture with ordinary hand tools and standard materials available at any local lumber yard. Clear redwood lumber was used to construct this group but you can also use a less expensive heart redwood grade for a more rustic look, if you wish. There are approximately one hundred weather-resistant, 3-inch wood screws used for this project. Screw holes should be drilled slightly undersize and

countersunk so screw heads are below the surface of the wood. A pair of screws is used at all points.

The bench arms and the top cleats are cut to size and end trimmed at a 60-degree angle, with all leg pieces cut at 75-degree angles. You should conduct a dry run test to make sure all the parts fit tightly before starting the actual construction.

Begin by assembling the tabletop, leaving approximately ⅜-inch space between the 2- × -6-inch units. The center cleat is screwed flat and the end 2- × -4-inch parts are positioned on edge 14 inches on center from the end of the table. Next turn the top facedown since the unit is easier to assemble in an upside-down position.

Construct the leg units and attach them to the top and cleats. Although easy

Fig. 14-1. Compact picnic table and bench set accommodates between eight and ten adults. Before beginning actual construction on the set, be sure to lay out all the parts to assure a tight fit.

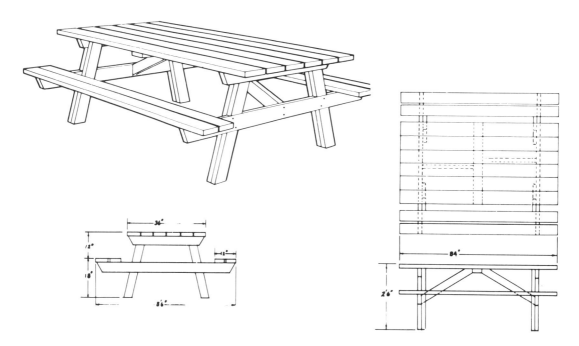

to build, the interlocking legs and bench support with the lapped construction of the double 2- × -4-inch legs will result in an exceptionally sturdy bench and table set. Diagonal braces, cut at a 120-degree angle

are then screwed to the center of the leg units. Finally, right the table to its proper position and fasten the pair of 2- × -6-inch bench boards on each side.

When the group is completely assem-

MATERIALS LIST

Note: All lumber indicated is redwood.

Purpose	Size	Quantity
Top	2″×6″×84″	6
Cleats	2″×4″×35″	3
Bench arms	2″×4″×65″	2
Top & leg braces	2″×4″×40″	2
Legs	2″×4″×34″	4
Leg doubles	2″×4″×14″	4
Leg doubles	2″×4″×10″	4
Bench seats	2″×6″×84″	4
Wood screws (weather resistant)	3-inch	100

bled, round off the tabletop and seat corners to a 2-inch radius, then sand the entire picnic unit smoothly to eliminate any danger of splinters. The redwood set may be left unfinished to weather into a soft pewter color or stained and top coated for additional protection and long life.

Compact Writing Desk

THIS GRACEFUL DESK features a storage well, a drawer, and two bookshelves which run completely through the unit. A modern version of the famous Davenport styling, it is generously proportioned and equally suitable for child or grownup. The lid slopes slightly toward the front, making it far more comfortable than the usual flat-topped desk. A lid support bracket holds the top open so that both hands are free while tidying up, etc. If the desk is to be used by a girl, a mirror may be mounted on the underside of the lid, so the desk can also double as a vanity.

Plywood construction eliminates the need for gluing boards to make up wide panels, and it also does away with bothersome framing. Construction is clean and simple. Judicious use of cleats permits assembling sections without screws or nails on any exposed surfaces. This is the way professional furniture is made.

You can build this desk using hand tools alone, but the work will go much quicker and easier if you have a saber saw, portable drill and sander. Through judicious planning of your cuts, one 4 × 8–foot panel of ¾-inch plywood should be sufficient. You'll need a piano hinge and a 10-inch lid support.

Lay out the sections on the plywood with the grain running the length of the pieces. Inasmuch as the sides are not symmetrical, be sure to lay them out one faceup and the other facedown.

When all sections are laid out, cut them apart with the saber saw. This should be a rough cut close to the line, just to separate the large board into easy-to-handle sections. Curves are cut freehand, but straight lines should be made with the guide wherever possible. Use a new blade and feed the saw slowly to prevent chipping or splintering.

Fig. 15-1. Lay out sections on the plywood and cut apart with saber saw. To make cutouts for bookshelves drill entry hole in one corner.

Fig. 15-2. Judicious use of cleats permits assembling sections without screws or nails on any exposed surfaces—a professional technique.

To make the cutouts for the bookshelves, drill entry holes for the blade near one corner, then proceed to drop out the center. When you near the end of the cut, support the waste to prevent it from falling prematurely, since this could damage the work.

Cut all cleats to size and drill pilot holes for the screws as indicated. A screw pilot bit will make the necessary clearance hole including the countersink for the screw head. Spring clamps are fine for holding the cleats.

Fasten the cleats with glue and screws, then follow by assembling the sections, adding the front panel last. The drawer compartment and lid are added to complete the main construction. The drawer is made

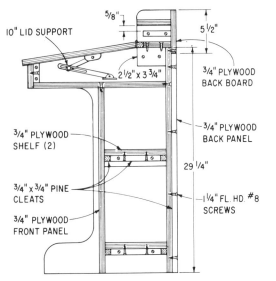

10" LID SUPPORT

5/8"

5 1/2"

2 1/2" x 3 3/4"

3/4" PLYWOOD
BACK BOARD

3/4" PLYWOOD
BACK PANEL

3/4" PLYWOOD
SHELF (2)

29 1/4"

3/4" x 3/4" PINE
CLEATS

1 1/4" FL. HD. #8
SCREWS

3/4" PLYWOOD
FRONT PANEL

CROSS SECTION

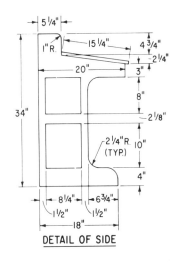

5 1/4"

1" R.

15 1/4"

4 3/4"

2 1/4"

20"

3"

34"

8"

2 1/8"

2 1/4" R.   10"
(TYP.)

4"

8 1/4"

6 3/4"

1 1/2"

1 1/2"

18"

DETAIL OF SIDE

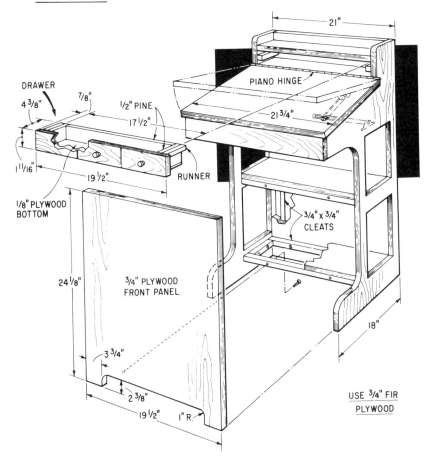

21"

DRAWER

4 3/8"

7/8"

1/2" PINE

17 1/2"

1 11/16"

19 1/2"

RUNNER

1/8" PLYWOOD
BOTTOM

PIANO HINGE

21 3/4"

3/4" x 3/4"
CLEATS

24 1/8"

3/4" PLYWOOD
FRONT PANEL

18"

3 3/4"

2 3/8"

19 1/2"   1" R.

USE 3/4" FIR
PLYWOOD

Fig. 15-3. Curves are cut free hand with a saber saw. One piece construction of the sides saves time spent on separate cuts and assembly.

by dadoing the ends as indicated. Make two parallel cuts ½ inch apart and halfway through the stock, then clean out in between with a chisel. Assemble as shown using a small triangular glue block at the bottom front.

Sand all surfaces thoroughly, first with medium grade paper, followed by fine and extra fine.

Finish as desired. A good treatment consists of two coats of clear brushing lacquer followed with paste wax.

The finished desk will beautify any unused space in your home whether it be the bedroom, living room or entry hall, and its usefulness will more than equal its decorative value.

Contemporary Hall Clock

BUILT OF OAK, this contemporary Scandinavian-style Hall Clock has a rich elegant appearance when finished. With straight simple lines, it is easy to build and features a 10-inch-square dial and a choice of two movements, Bim-Bam or Westminster Chime, imported from West Germany. Both movements are weight-driven and can be purchased with a decorative lyre pendulum.

Basically, the clock case consists of three 62-inch frames. The wider one serves as the door. The others make up the end members. Butt joints are used throughout except for the four base pieces which are mitered. A single dowel is used at each butt joint. This means that you'll have to be more careful when gluing as the pieces could twist. Two dowels at each joint would prevent twisting, but two dowels in a 2-inch-wide piece could be a problem, especially with the rabbets and grooves cut in each edge.

The frame members are 2 inches wide, ripped from wide boards. Some lumber dealers sell 2-inch-wide stock. It may cost a little more than the wider boards, but it does save a lot of ripping and jointing.

Select good flat stock, mark and cut the lengths to 62 inches. If wide boards are being used, rip the widths to 2-inches except for the two front stiles which are ripped to 1¾₁₆ inch widths. Be sure to rip the extra 2-inch pieces for the rails. You will need about 7 feet of 2-inch stock for these.

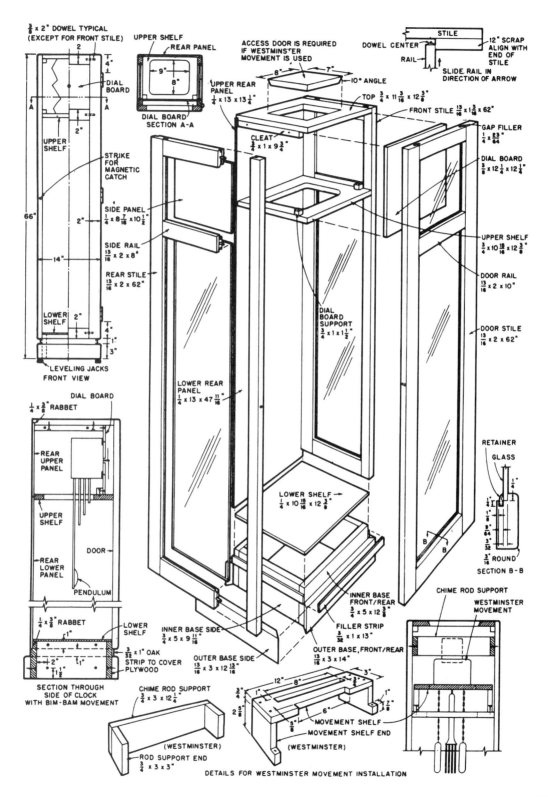

3/8 x 2" DOWEL TYPICAL
(EXCEPT FOR FRONT STILE)

UPPER SHELF

REAR PANEL

9"

8"

DIAL BOARD
SECTION A-A

DIAL BOARD

UPPER SHELF

STRIKE
FOR
MAGNETIC
CATCH

66"

SIDE PANEL
1/4 x 8 7/16 x 10 1/2"

SIDE RAIL
13/16 x 2 x 8"

REAR STILE
13/16 x 2 x 62"

14"

LOWER
SHELF

2"

4 1/4"

1 3/8"

LEVELING JACKS
FRONT VIEW

ACCESS DOOR IS REQUIRED
IF WESTMINSTER
MOVEMENT IS USED

8"

7"

UPPER REAR
PANEL
1/4 x 13 x 13 1/8"

10° ANGLE

TOP 3/4 x 11 3/16 x 12 3/8"

CLEAT
3/4 x 1 x 9 3/4"

STILE

DOWEL CENTER

RAIL

12" SCRAP
ALIGN WITH
END OF
STILE

SLIDE RAIL IN
DIRECTION OF ARROW

FRONT STILE 13/16 x 1 3/4 x 62"

GAP FILLER
1/4 x 23/64"

DIAL BOARD
3/8 x 12 1/4 x 12 1/4"

UPPER SHELF
3/4 x 10 15/16 x 12 3/8"

DOOR RAIL
13/16 x 2 x 10"

DOOR STILE
13/16 x 2 x 62"

DIAL
BOARD
SUPPORT
3/4 x 1 x 1 1/2"

LOWER REAR
PANEL
1/4 x 13 x 47 11/16"

LOWER SHELF
1/4 x 10 15/16 x 12 3/8"

RETAINER

GLASS

1/4"

1/4"

1"

9/64"

3/32"

3/16" ROUND

SECTION B-B

B

B

DIAL BOARD

1/4 x 3/8" RABBET

REAR
UPPER
PANEL

UPPER
SHELF

REAR
LOWER
PANEL

DOOR

PENDULUM

1/4 x 3/8" RABBET

LOWER
SHELF

1"

3/32 x 1" OAK
STRIP TO COVER
PLYWOOD

2"

1"

1 1/2"

SECTION THROUGH
SIDE OF CLOCK
WITH BIM-BAM MOVEMENT

INNER BASE SIDE
3/4 x 5 x 9 11/16"

OUTER BASE SIDE
13/16 x 3 x 12 13/16"

INNER BASE
FRONT/REAR
3/4 x 5 x 12 3/8"

FILLER STRIP
3/32 x 1 x 13"

OUTER BASE, FRONT/REAR
13/16 x 3 x 14"

CHIME ROD SUPPORT

WESTMINSTER
MOVEMENT

CHIME ROD SUPPORT
3/4 x 3 x 12 1/4"

(WESTMINSTER)

ROD SUPPORT END
3/4 x 3 x 3"

12"

8"

4 1/2"

2 1/2"

1"

6"

3/8"

3"

1"

7/8"

MOVEMENT SHELF

MOVEMENT SHELF END

(WESTMINSTER)

DETAILS FOR WESTMINSTER MOVEMENT INSTALLATION

101

Fig. 16-1. Use a backstop to aid accurate transfer of dowel holes from rails to stiles and mark joints for easier assembly later.

Fig. 16-2. Grooves are cut into frame parts to accept insert-type panel retainer. Test each groove to ensure a snug fit.

Fig. 16-3. A table saw is used in cutting rabbets; hold the piece vertically on the first cut and horizontally on the second.

Fig. 16-4. Filler blocks are added to stiles to fill space left by rabbets. Access to dowel holes is cut with a coping saw.

Use a stop gauge to cut the rails to uniform lengths. Make the six end stiles 8 inches long and the three door stiles 10 inches long.

The rails should now be drilled to take ⅜-inch dowels. Make the holes 1¹⁄₁₆-inch deep and center them carefully. A doweling jig is useful for this.

After the holes are drilled in the rails they must be transferred to the stiles. Use dowel centers for this. When locating the

top and bottom rails, place a block of wood at the end of the stile then slide the rail (with a dowel center installed) along the block until the dowel center contacts the stile. The mark will indicate the exact location for the dowel hole. When locating the second rail, use a 12-inch piece of wood to locate the top edge of the rail on the stile. (See sketch).

When all dowel holes are located in the stiles, drill the ⅜-inch-diameter holes,

1-inch deep. The only exceptions are the holes in the front stiles. These holes should be made only ½ inch deep because this stile is narrower than the rest. Also, the dowels for these holes should be cut to 1½-inch lengths.

If you study the drawing you will note that the edge to receive the glass and retainer is grooved and rabbeted. The groove is cut first; it is $\frac{9}{64}$ inch wide and ¼-inch deep. If you have a table saw blade with a $\frac{9}{64}$-inch kerf, use it. Otherwise, you will have to make a couple of passes to obtain the required width.

Make test cuts on scrap wood before cutting the actual stock. Make the first pass in all the pieces including the short rail pieces. When all are grooved, adjust the

Fig. 16-5. Apply a full-strength glue to the walls of the holes, and then drive the ⅜-inch dowels firmly into place.

Fig. 16-6. Clamp the pieces together securely, using scraps of wood in the clamp jaws to avoid damaging surfaces of the work.

Fig. 16-7. Uneven joints in the glued-up frame are leveled with a belt sander, while corners are rounded off with a router.

Fig. 16-8. After drilling the required screw clearance holes, assemble the inner base with both nails and glue.

103

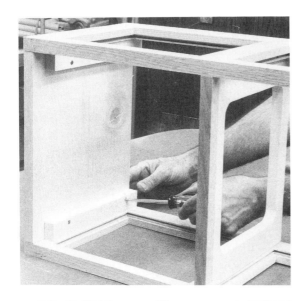

Fig. 16-9. The top is fastened to the side frames with cleats. Note that the cleats are set back to make room for the dial face.

Fig. 16-10. Hanging the door with non-mortise hinges eliminates the need for mortising; three of these hinges are needed.

fence and make the second pass. Follow with the rabbet which is also cut on the table saw. Make the rabbet ¼ inch deep and ²³⁄₆₄-inch wide. Do this in two cuts; first with the work held vertically, then the second pass with the work held horizontally. Be sure to reset the blade height and fence for the second pass. Make test cuts on scrap wood first.

After the grooves and rabbets for the glass panels have been made, you will have to cut the rabbets at the rear of the two rear stiles. This rabbet is made ¼ × ⅜-inch and is needed to receive the plywood panel.

If you butt the rails against the stiles and observe the rear surface, you will note the gap left by the rabbet. This must be plugged or filled before the parts are assembled. Cut small pieces of wood to fit as shown in the drawing. Make six pieces ¼ × 1²³⁄₆₄ × 1½ inches long and twelve pieces ¼ × ²³⁄₆₄ × 1¾ inches long. These must be notched at the ends to match the grooves of the stiles. Since the pieces are

Fig. 16-11. The upper part of the clock case should look like this before putting the dial board and movement in place.

Fig. 16-12. A boxed two-weight movement is fastened to the dial board. Four wood screws should be used to hold it firmly.

small, you won't be able to use the table saw. Instead, use a band saw or coping saw holding the pieces in a vise. The groove is necessary so the panel retainer can be inserted neatly into the center.

Glue the filler pieces into place on the stiles, holding them with a spring clamp or masking tape. When the glue has set, the frames can be assembled. To prevent dry joints, glue size the end grain of the rails using a thin (one part white glue to one part water) coating of glue. Allow to dry about 15 minutes then coat all mating parts with full strength glue. Insert dowels, then join the pieces and clamp securely. Use cauls (scrap strips of wood) under the clamp jaws to prevent marring the work surfaces. The top, shelf pieces and base can be made now while you wait for the glued frame sections to set.

The top is a rectangular board with an access door cut as shown. The door is cut with a jigsaw with the blade set at a 10-degree angle. This will allow the door to drop into place without the need for latches or catches. The angular cut will

MATERIALS LIST

Except as noted all lumber is oak and all measurements are in inches.

Purpose	Size	Description	Quantity
Stile, rear	$^{13}/_{16}'' \times 2'' \times 62''$		2
Stile, front	$^{13}/_{16}'' \times 1^{13}/_{16}'' \times 62''$		2
Side rail	$^{13}/_{16}'' \times 2'' \times 8''$		6
Door stile	$^{13}/_{16}'' \times 2'' \times 62''$		2
Door rail	$^{13}/_{16}'' \times 2'' \times 10''$		3
Gap filler	$^{1}/_{4}'' \times {}^{23}/_{64}'' \times 36''$		1
Top	$^{3}/_{4}'' \times 11^{3}/_{16}'' \times 12^{3}/_{8}''$	Fir plywood	1
Shelf, upper	$^{3}/_{4}'' \times 10^{15}/_{16}'' \times 12^{3}/_{8}''$	Fir plywood	1
Shelf, lower	$^{1}/_{4}'' \times 10^{15}/_{16}'' \times 12^{3}/_{8}''$	Oak plywood	1
Base front/rear, inner	$^{3}/_{4}'' \times 5'' \times 12^{3}/_{8}''$	Fir plywood	2
Base side, inner	$^{3}/_{4}'' \times 5'' \times 9^{11}/_{16}''$	Fir plywood	2
Base front/rear, outer	$^{13}/_{16}'' \times 3'' \times 14''$	Oak	2
Base side	$^{13}/_{16}'' \times 3'' \times 12^{13}/_{16}''$	Oak	2
Filler strip, front	$^{3}/_{32}'' \times 1'' \times 13''$	Oak	1
Filler strip, end	$^{3}/_{32}'' \times 1'' \times 13''$	Oak	2
Side panel	$^{1}/_{4}'' \times 8^{7}/_{16}'' \times 10^{1}/_{2}''$	Oak plywood	2
Rear upper panel	$^{1}/_{4}'' \times 13'' \times 13^{1}/_{4}''$	Oak plywood	1
Rear lower panel	$^{1}/_{4}'' \times 13'' \times 47^{11}/_{16}''$	Oak plywood	1
Cleat	$^{3}/_{4}'' \times 1'' \times 9^{3}/_{4}''$	Pine	2
Dial board support	$^{3}/_{4}'' \times 1'' \times 1^{1}/_{2}''$	Pine	2
Dial board	$^{3}/_{8}'' \times 12^{1}/_{4}'' \times 12^{1}/_{4}''$	Plywood	1
*Movement shelf	$^{3}/_{4}'' \times 3'' \times 12''$	Fir plywood	1
*Movement shelf end	$^{3}/_{4}'' \times 2^{5}/_{8}'' \times 4''$	Fir plywood	2
*Chime rod support	$^{3}/_{4}'' \times 3'' \times 12^{1}/_{4}''$	Fir plywood	1
*Rod support end	$^{3}/_{4}'' \times 3'' \times 3''$	Fir plywood	2
Dowel	$^{3}/_{8}'' \times 2''$		18
Magnetic catch	$^{5}/_{16}''$ dia.		1
Hinge	$2''$	Non-mortise	3
Panel retainer		Insert type	30'
Screw	No. 8—$1^{1}/_{2}''$ FH		34
Screw	No. 8—$^{3}/_{4}''$ FH		4
Screw	No. 5—$^{3}/_{4}''$ FH		22
Leveling jacks	miniature		4
Glass, door upper	Cut to fit		1
Glass, door lower	Cut to fit		1
Glass, side	Cut to fit		2
Dial	$10'' \times 10''$		1
Movement		Bim-Bam or Westminster	1

Note: The items marked with asterisks are required only if Westminster Chime Movement with separate chime rods is used.

Sources of Clock Components:

Craft Products
2200 Dean St.
St. Charles, IL 60174

Emperor Clock Company
Emperor Industrial Park
Fairhope, AL 36532

Klockit
P.O. Box 542
Lake Geneva, WI 53147

Mason & Sullivan Company
86 Higgins Crowell Road
West Yarmouth, MA 02673

permit the door to drop in without any space between the kerf thus keeping out dust.

The upper shelf is made with a cutout to allow chains, weight shells and pendulum to pass through to the waist section.

The base consists of two parts, inner and outer. Plywood is used for the inner base pieces. Cut the parts to size then drill the screw clearance holes before assembling the parts. The outer base pieces are cut to size then mitered.

Assemble the inner base using nails and glue, then add the oak outer pieces fastening them to the inner base with 1½-inch screws as shown. Apply glue to the mitered corners. Do not glue the outer base pieces to the plywood.

Cut three thin strips of oak, ³⁄₃₂ × 1 × 13 inches long. Glue these to the plywood just above the outer base pieces. They serve to conceal the plywood underneath. Cut the end pieces to length, taking the measurements directly from the base piece. Glue these into place, then cut the front to size and install. None is required at the rear as it won't show.

Use a router with a ³⁄₁₆-inch rounding bit to round off all corners of the base.

The glued-up frames should now be ready for work. Remove the clamps and place a frame on a flat surface. Sand the entire surface with a belt sander. Pay particular attention to the joint areas. Sand the front and back of each frame, then use the router to round off the corners as indicated.

The end frames can now be attached to the base and top sections. Cleats are used at the top. Be sure to set the cleats to the rear leaving room at the front ends for the dial board. Screws are used to fasten the cleat to the sides and top. The upper shelf is fastened only with glue, no screws. Be sure to make the cutout in the shelf before installing it.

The door is hung using three non-mortise hinges. A small magnetic catch is used on the door. Drill a ⁵⁄₁₆-inch-diameter hole ⁹⁄₁₆ inch deep into the door stile then install the magnet strike on the front stile. Since a small magnet is used, no door pull is necessary. Simply grasp the stile to open.

The glass should be installed after the finish has been applied. The best way to secure the glass is to use insert type plastic retainer. This material is made to fit into a narrow groove allowing the top or exposed part to hug the glass snugly. It eliminates the need for staples or nails and provides very neat appearance. Another

Fig. 16-13. The Bim-Bam movement, shown installed above, does not require any shelves or supports to be added to the upper case.

Fig. 16-14. Appearing without chime rods in the above view, the Westminster movement requires a shelf and chime rod support.

advantage of this material is its ease of removal when necessary to replace or clean the glass. Force it all the way down into the groove with your fingertips.

The movement used will determine if special shelf and support are required. If the Bim-Bam movement is used, no supports are required as the movement is boxed and simply screwed to the rear of the dial board. If the Westminster movement is used, a shelf and chime rod support will be needed. These are shown in the drawing. However, be sure to have the movement on hand before making these supports as the sizes may vary depending on the make of movement.

The wood is finished by using a paste wood filler followed by two coats of sanding sealer and two coats of semigloss lacquer. The filler used was Golden Oak which contains the stain mixed in with the filler. After applying the filler, allow to dry overnight before applying sealer and lacquer.

The filler, flexible molding, hardware, clock movement and dial are available from Armor Products (see Introduction). Other sources of clock movements and components are listed in the Materials List. Write them for catalogs.

Corner Bookcase/ Desk

CORNERS usually present a problem when decorating a room. Here's an ideal piece of furniture that will fit neatly into that wasted corner and serves as a combination desk andbookcase. The desktop provides ample writing space and storage for stationery,bills, pens, clips, etc. The two bottom shelves hold a stack of your favorite books within easy reach.

The desk is very easy to make as it utilizes ready-made turnings which are available at lumber dealers and home improvement centers throughout the nation. It is made of common pine and only a few basic tools are needed. A drill and saber saw are essential. A router is needed only if you want to shape the edges of the desktop and drawer front. These could be rounded off with a hand plane instead.

The desk measures 30¼ inches high × 40 inches wide × 25 inches deep. The top provides a writing area of more than 3 square feet.

Unless you use plywood, the top and shelves must be glued up to obtain the proper width. The top involves straight or parallel gluing. The shelves, however, must be mitered. This looks tricky but it can be done easily by using cleats and clamps as shown. Select flat boards and arrange them so that knots will not fall on the cutting lines. Lay out the shelves and draw the 45-degree lines for the miter cuts. The cuts can be made in several ways. The table saw, portable saw or saber saw may be used.

Regardless of the saw used, the cut edges must be perfectly square and smooth. After cutting, a router can be used to true up the edge. This is done with a flush trimmer bit. A guide strip of ¾-inch stock is nailed to the bottom of the shelf. Set the strip exactly at 45 degrees using a miter square as a guide. Set the strip so that it is just a trifle in from the edge. About ⅟₃₂ inch will do.

Adjust the cutter so that the bearing will ride on the strip. Take a cut and check the edge. It should be smooth and straight. Incidentally, the edge will be as straight as

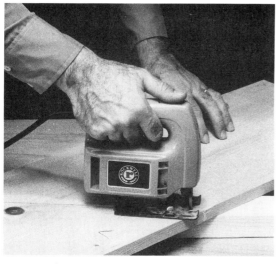

Fig. 17-1. The miter is cut with a saber saw. Be sure to use fine blade, and cut slowly.

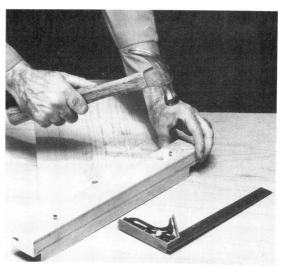

Fig. 17-2. Guide strip's nailed to the underside of shelf. It should be set in from edge.

Fig. 17-3. Insert dowel centers into holes; the sharp point transfers center to mating board.

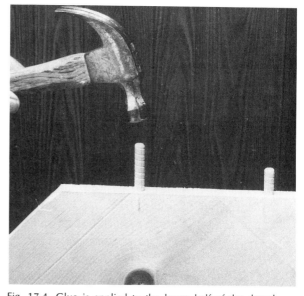

Fig. 17-4. Glue is applied to the lower half of the dowel. Hammer blows drive them home.

the guide strip so be sure to choose a good straight piece for the guide.

Mark the location of the dowels. These should be placed as shown so they will clear the postholes and the curved edge which will be cut later on. A dowel drill-

ing guide is used for the next operation. Several types are available.

The units are self-centering and assure straight accurate holes. Drill ³⁄₈-inch-diameter holes 1¼-inches deep to accept the 2-inch spiral dowels. Dowel centers are used to locate matching holes in the mating pieces.

Insert three dowel centers in the holes drilled into the first piece. Align the two boards then press together. The hole centers will be transferred to the second piece. Drill these holes to the same depth as the first piece.

Because the end grain is porous, it will be necessary to size the edge with a thin

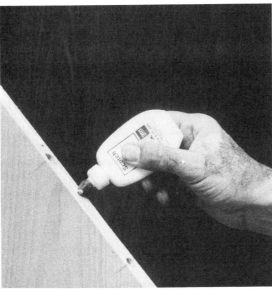

Fig. 17-5. Apply glue to edge grain to size it. Apply second coat before joining the parts.

Fig. 17-6. A yardstick adapted with pivot point is used to draw the radius for the shelf.

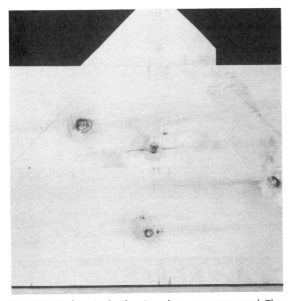

Fig. 17-7. Desktop is glued up in order to conserve wood. The knots should be sound.

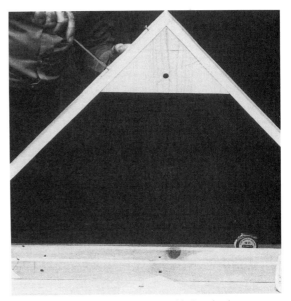

Fig. 17-8. The desk sides are assembled with glue, screws. Predrilled holes are for the legs.

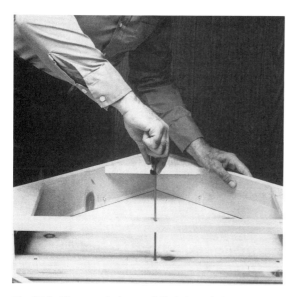

Fig. 17-9. Clearance holes are drilled through the crosspiece to allow screwdriver to enter.

Fig. 17-10. The stock legs are cut apart with back saw. A radial arm saw can also be used.

coat of glue. Apply a bead of glue then spread and allow to dry. Apply some glue to the dowels and insert. Tap with a hammer until the dowels are halfway into the holes. To obtain a good tight joint, attach clamping blocks as shown. Apply more glue to the edges and to the dowels, then join the pieces and clamp tightly. The clamping blocks should be 2- × -3 or 2- × -4 lumber. Draw the pieces together until the glue starts to ooze out of joint. Be sure the boards are flat. Use clamps on both sides.

The top is also glued with dowels. Follow the same procedure to make the holes then clamp using glue strips on the edges. To save lumber for the top piece, you can step the sections as shown.

Set the shelves and top aside, allowing the glue to set thoroughly. In the meantime, you can cut the pieces for the apron and front frame. The rear edges of the side pieces are rabbeted to accept the back panels. Do this with a table saw or use a backsaw and finish off with a chisel.

The bevel cut for the front edge of the sides and the ends of the two strips are cut at a 45-degree angle. After cutting the pieces to size, assemble with screws and glue. After the apron is assembled, invert the top then position the apron as shown. Strips of wood tacked to the front and sides will keep the sections aligned while drilling the screw pilot holes. The holes are drilled diagonally. Use care not to drill through the surface of the top. A guide marked on the drill bit is recommended.

The crosspiece is treated differently. Here the three screws are installed straight. Screwdriver clearance holes are made in the lower piece. The parts are then assembled as indicated. Be sure to use glue at all joints.

The legs are cut from ready-made turnings. (If you have a lathe, you will probably want to turn your own). Choose a suitable turning and cut apart to make up the various lengths as shown. The cutting can be done with a handsaw or on the radial arm saw. Be sure the lengths are uniform and all cuts are square. If done by hand, a miter box should be used. The turnings we used are colonial style 28 inches long. They are manufactured by Michael-Reagan of California and we understand they are available throughout the country.

After cutting the turnings apart, drill the centers to take ½-inch dowels. Make the holes 1½ inches deep and be sure to center them. Drill corresponding holes ½-inch diameter in the two shelves to correspond to the holes previously made in the lower part of the top section. Also shape the edges at this time.

Fig. 17-11. Dowels are driven into the upper section of leg. Be sure to groove dowel.

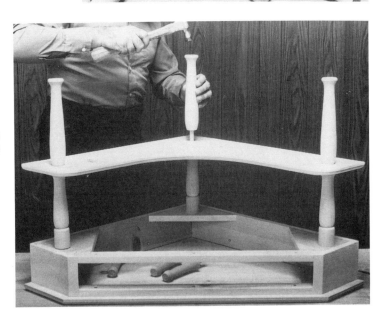

Fig. 17-12. Assembling the desk is simple. Add the shelves and legs to the inverted unit.

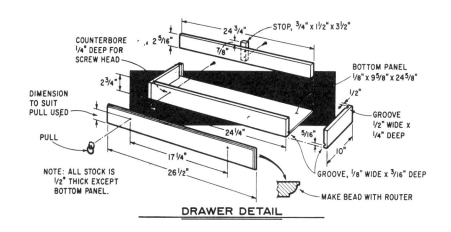

DRAWER DETAIL

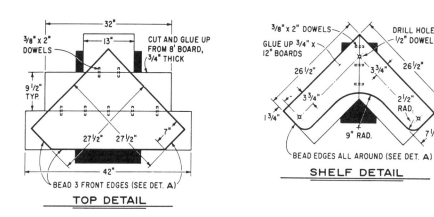

TOP DETAIL

SHELF DETAIL

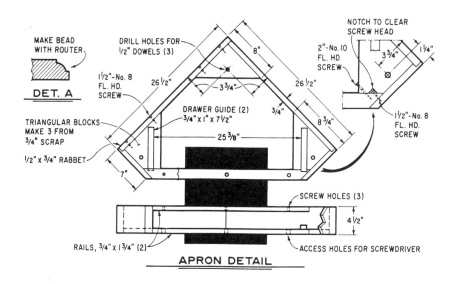

APRON DETAIL

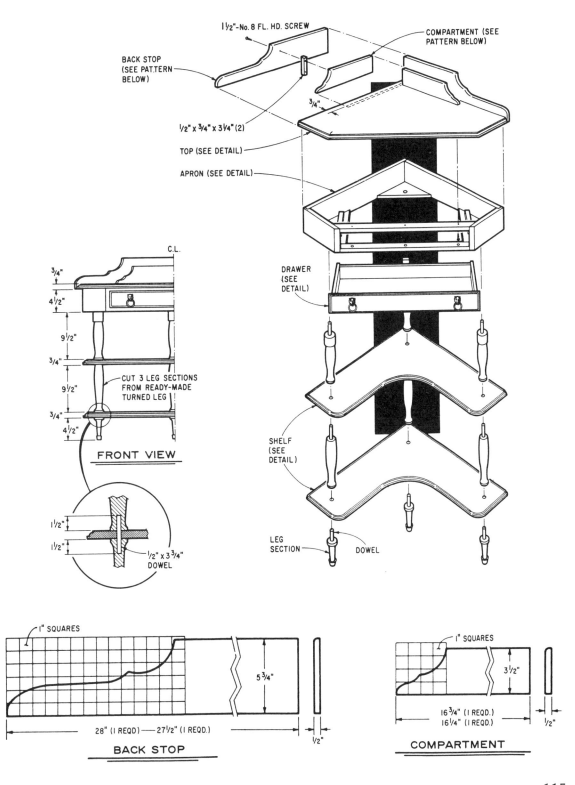

1½"-No. 8 FL. HD. SCREW

COMPARTMENT (SEE PATTERN BELOW)

BACK STOP (SEE PATTERN BELOW)

½" x ¾" x 3¼" (2)

TOP (SEE DETAIL)

APRON (SEE DETAIL)

¾"

DRAWER (SEE DETAIL)

C.L.

¾"

4½"

9½"

¾"

9½"

¾"

4½"

CUT 3 LEG SECTIONS FROM READY-MADE TURNED LEG

FRONT VIEW

SHELF (SEE DETAIL)

LEG SECTION

DOWEL

1½"

1½"

½" x 3¾" DOWEL

1" SQUARES

5¾"

28" (1 REQD) — 27½" (1 REQD.)

½"

BACK STOP

1" SQUARES

3½"

16¾" (1 REQD.)
16¼" (1 REQD.)

½"

COMPARTMENT

115

MATERIALS LIST

Purpose	Size	Description	Quantity
Top	¾″ × 11¼″ × 8″	Pine	1
Back stop	½″ × 5¾″ × 28″	Pine	2
Compartment	½″ × 3½″ × 16¾″	Pine	2
Compartment blocks	½″ × ¾″ × 3″	Pine	2
Rail	¾″ × 1¹¹⁄₁₆″ × 29″	Pine	2
Sides	¾″ × 4½″ × 8″	Pine	2
Corner blocks	¾″ × 7″ × 10″	Pine	3
Shelf (half)	¾″ × 11¼″ × 27″	Pine	4
Turnings	1¾″ dia. × 28″	Pine	3
Kicker	¾″ × 1½″ × 3¼″	Pine	1
Drawer (side)	½″ × 2¾″ × 10″	Pine	2
Drawer (rear)	½″ × 2⁵⁄₁₆″ × 24¾″	Pine	1
Drawer (subfront)	½″ × 2¾″ × 24¼″	Pine	1
Drawer (front)	½″ × 3¼″ × 26½″	Pine	1
Drawer (bottom)	⅛″ × 9⅝″ × 24⅝″	Plywood	1

Note: Top is cut into three lengths and glued as shown.

Screws			
Finishing nails	1½″		
Lion head pulls			2
Spiral dowel	⅜″ × 2″		13
Dowel	½″ × 36″		1

Assemble the parts, starting with the lower shelf first. Cut the dowels to length, then add to the lower turnings (feet). Groove or crimp dowel so that trapped air can be eliminated from the hole. Failure to do so may cause the wood to split.

Add the second shelf in the same manner. Cut the back stops from ½-inch pine and install with screws from the rear. The compartment is also made and added at this time. Screws are driven from the rear where the heads won't show.

The drawer is of simple construction. It is made with an overlapping front. Two pieces of ½-inch lumber are used to make up the front panel. Before assembling the front, shape the edge as desired. A bead cutter used the same shape as the one used for the top, only of smaller size. The side guides are installed with about 1/16-inch clearance between the drawer sides. A small block of wood at the rear of the drawer serves as a kicker and prevents the drawer from tipping when fully extended. It also serves as a stop. It is installed from the bottom opening after the drawer is in place. The pulls are added to complete construction.

Finish the unit with stain and shellac or you may want to try an antique finish. Try a red latex base topped with a dark brown glaze.

Decorative Bookshelf/ Table

SIMPLE IN DESIGN and construction, this unique bookshelf/table in brightly finished walnut is made of prefinished wall panels and molding. This eliminates one of the biggest headaches in furniture finishing. Not only is that tedious operation bypassed, but sanding is eliminated since all exposed edges and surfaces are prefinished.

To most craftsmen, the finishing operation is a necessary evil. And this is especially true when working with open-grained woods which must be filled, sealed, stained, lacquered, rubbed, and waxed. But this is all done before you even start this project, and it's no ordinary finish either. Scientifically applied, the finishes of better panels are similar to those found only in the top grades of furniture. So with half the battle over, you should have no trouble building this attractive contemporary piece.

Costs will vary depending on the panels and molding you use. The table shown was built for very little using a panel of Java walnut with a birch inlay. The panel is grooved, with 16 inches between grooves. The birch strip is only 1 inch wide so little is wasted when ripping the panels. The top is made by joining two sections with a butt joint. If care is used, the joint will be almost invisible. If a one-piece top is desired, a Weldwood flush panel may be substituted. Such panels are higher in price, however. Manufacturers offer a choice of woods.

The prefinished panels are only ¼ inch thick so they must be supported by a heavier wood such as ½-inch fir plywood. This is ideal as the total thickness of ¾ inch is compatible with the stock molding.

To simplify construction, cleats are used throughout the assembly. This eliminates the need for dadoes and rabbets. It also cuts down on the tools needed. A saw, drill, and screwdriver are sufficient.

Start the construction with ripping of the prefinished panel. Cut away the

Fig. 18-1. Using cleats throughout the assembly of the unit not only eliminates the need for rabbets and dadoes, but also cuts down on the number of tools required in the construction.

Fig. 18-2. In this view, the top section is lying upside down and a strip of cove molding has been attached to one of the octagonal sides. The ends of the molding are cut at 45-degree angles.

Fig. 18-3. Because there are so many pieces which look alike, it's a good idea to write an identifying number on the various sections to be joined together, thereby avoiding confusion.

Fig. 18-4. Here the panels are shown in various stages of assembly. The ¼-inch prefinished stock is laminated to the ½-inch plywood backing before the octagonal opening is cut out.

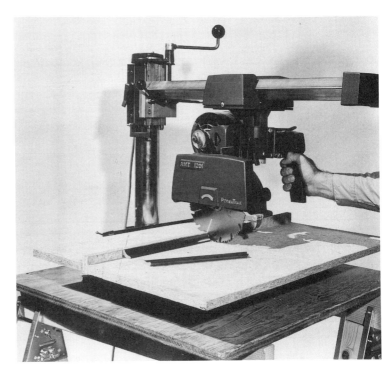

Fig. 18-5. A radial arm saw can greatly simplify the work of trimming and bevel cutting. Use a sharp blade and be sure to check bevels on scrap wood before cutting the prefinished work.

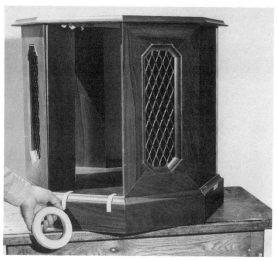

Fig. 18-6. An easy way to hold the moldings in place while the glue sets is to use masking tape, as shown. It's a good idea to first check the fit of all parts before applying the glue.

Fig. 18-7. Partially assembled unit is shown here. Note how diagonals are squared off on the inside. Paint interiors flat black.

MATERIALS LIST

Purpose	Size	Description	Quantity
Outer surfaces	¼″ × 4′ × 8′	Prefinished plywood	1
Inner surfaces	½″ × 4′ × 4′	Fir plywood	1
	¾″ × 30′	Cove molding	
	¾″ × 1″ × 12′	Cleats	
	6″ × 15″	Polished brass grille	4
	1¼″	Round-head screws	as needed
	½″	Round-head screws	as needed

Note: You will also need, white glue and washers.

grooves, then set the panels aside while you cut the ½-inch plywood to the sizes shown for the top and bottom. Note that the top panel is larger than the bottom as it overhangs the sides slightly. The shape of these pieces is octagonal (see detail).

When taking measurements and cutting pieces, bear in mind that the thickness of the material is ¾ inches and not ¼ or ½. This can be confusing to the unwary.

With the top and bottom cut, make the

ALL SHELF CLEATS 1/2" x 1/8" GLUED UNDER

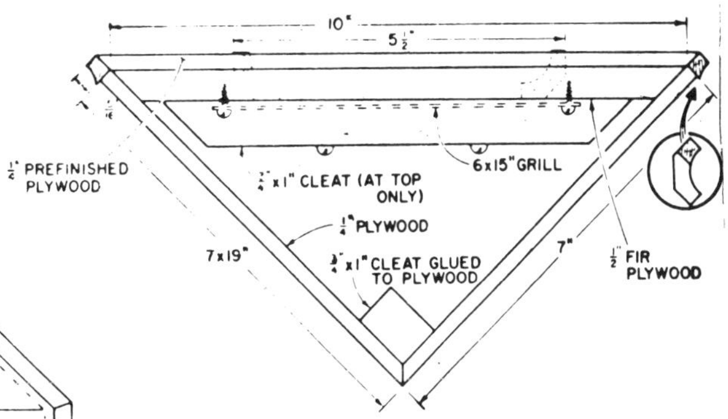
10"
5 1/2"
1/2" PREFINISHED PLYWOOD
3/4" x 1" CLEAT (AT TOP ONLY)
6x15" GRILL
1/4" PLYWOOD
7x19"
3/4" x 1" CLEAT GLUED TO PLYWOOD
7"
1/2" FIR PLYWOOD

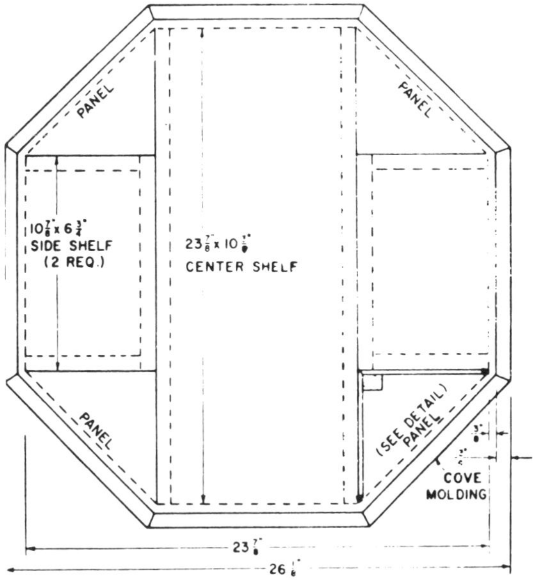
PANEL
PANEL
10 7/8" x 6 3/4"
SIDE SHELF
(2 REQ.)
23 7/8" x 10 1/8"
CENTER SHELF
PANEL
(SEE DETAIL)
PANEL
COVE MOLDING
23 7/8"
26 1/8"

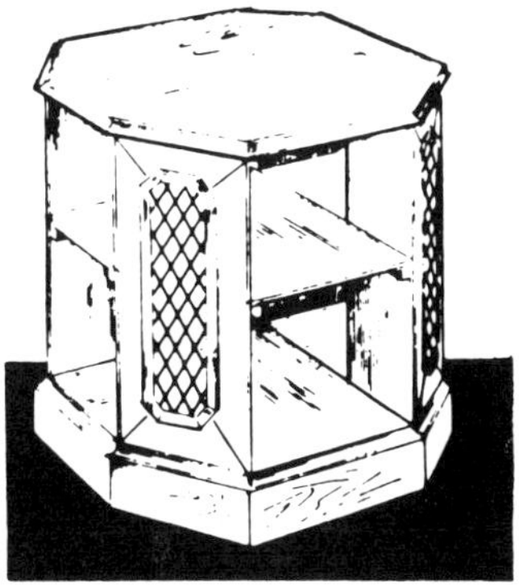

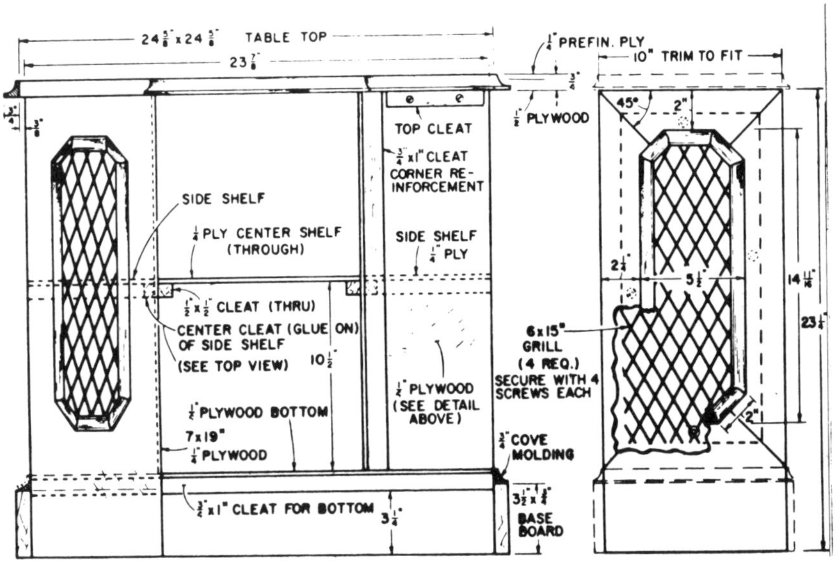
24 5/8" x 24 5/8" TABLE TOP
23 7/8"
1/4" PREFIN. PLY
10" TRIM TO FIT
1/2" PLYWOOD
TOP CLEAT
3/4" x 1" CLEAT CORNER RE-INFORCEMENT
SIDE SHELF
1/4 PLY CENTER SHELF (THROUGH)
SIDE SHELF 1/4" PLY
1/2" x 1/2" CLEAT (THRU)
CENTER CLEAT (GLUE ON) OF SIDE SHELF
(SEE TOP VIEW)
10 1/2"
1/2" PLYWOOD BOTTOM
7x19"
1/4" PLYWOOD
1/2" PLYWOOD (SEE DETAIL ABOVE)
3/4" COVE MOLDING
3/4" x 1" CLEAT FOR BOTTOM
3 1/4"
3 1/2" x 3/4" BASE BOARD
45°
2"
2 1/4"
5 1/2"
14 11/16"
23 1/4"
6x15" GRILL (4 REQ.)
SECURE WITH 4 SCREWS EACH
2"

strips for the base and decorative panels. Cut these sections slightly oversize allowing for trimming after laminating. The best way to treat the panels is to cut the ½-inch part in one piece, adding the ¼-inch facing around the perimeter. The ¼-inch stock is mitered first and then laminated. This procedure makes for a structurally sound panel and saves material on the more expensive ¼-inch panel. Use white glue when laminating and for all assembly work.

The radial arm saw greatly simplifies the work of trimming and bevel cutting. Use a sharp blade and be sure to check bevels on scrap wood before cutting the work. When trimming the molding cut the longest pieces first; this way if you make a mistake, you can recut for the next smaller size. An easy way to hold the moldings in place while the glue sets is to use masking tape, as shown.

It is helpful to install the metal grille before attaching the molding, as it serves as a backstop for the molding and assures perfect line-up. The grille is held with screws and washers. Normally, if the wood needed finishing it would be necessary to remove the grille. Not so here, as no finishing is required.

Before closing off the grilled section, paint the interior flat black. This will contrast nicely with the polished brass of the grille. Use screws and glue in the final assembly.

Maintenance is the same as for any fine piece of furniture. Use a good grade of furniture wax to clean the surface. Avoid abrasive cleaners that might scratch the finish.

Divider Unit With Desk

THE OPEN, INFORMAL DESIGN of the combination desk and storage unit makes it attractive but unobtrusive. You can install it at the end of a room or in a corner, or use it as a divider without overwhelming the rest of the decor.

The unit is not difficult to build and requires few power tools. A power drill, of course would make the work go faster, but accurate holes can be drilled by hand.

One power tool is a must. This is a saw, either a table saw or a portable circular saw, to cut out the parts accurately and to cut the dadoes in the magazine rack (unit A). The latter task could also be done with a router.

If you have no power tools, or don't want to do all the work yourself, have a carpenter build the modules. Then, you can assemble the unit yourself.

Lay out the parts on plywood, as shown in the plans, and cut them out. True the edges with coarse sandpaper and, if necessary, fill any cracks with filler.

Next, cut the 2- × -2s and 1- × -4s to the dimensions shown in the drawing of the framing. If you wish, you can use the dimensions shown or you can extend the uprights to ceiling height.

At the same time, cut the 1- × -4s for the drawer sides and backs and for the table edges. Sand all surfaces smooth and round the edges slightly.

Once the parts are ready, assemble the modules, following the step-by-step instructions in the plans. Do this in your workshop. When they are finished and painted, carry them to the place where you intend to erect the unit. Do the same thing with the framing.

Stain or paint all framing members and allow to dry thoroughly, then move framing into room for assembly.

Predrill and screw together all 2 x 2 and 1 x 4 framing members, attaching members marked 1-4 last.

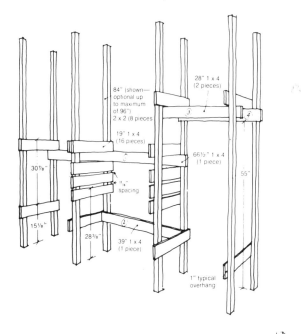

84" (shown—optional up to maximum of 96")
2 x 2 (8 pieces)

28" 1 x 4 (2 pieces)

19" 1 x 4 (16 pieces)

66½" 1 x 4 (1 piece)

30⅞"

⅞" spacing

55"

15⅛"

28⅜"

39" 1 x 4 (1 piece)

1" typical overhang

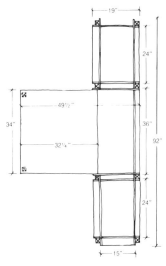

19"

24"

49½"

34"

32¼"

36"

92"

15"

24"

Set up desk as shown. To fold desk down, unlatch screen door hooks on legs, fold legs under and latch with screen door hook. Remove desk assembly from support framing and place assembly into channels directly above the previous channels. Desk top will fold down compactly without touching floor.

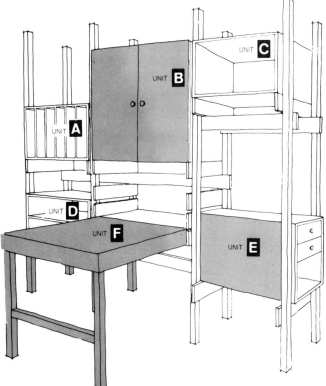

UNIT C

UNIT B

UNIT A

UNIT D

UNIT F

UNIT E

When thoroughly dry, install hinges on doors, and doors on cabinet; apply door pulls and magnetic catches.

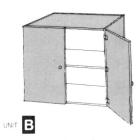

UNIT B

Glue and nail basic cabinet parts together, including the shelf. Countersink nail holes before glue sets, and wipe away excess glue. Fill nail holes, allow to dry, and sand smooth.

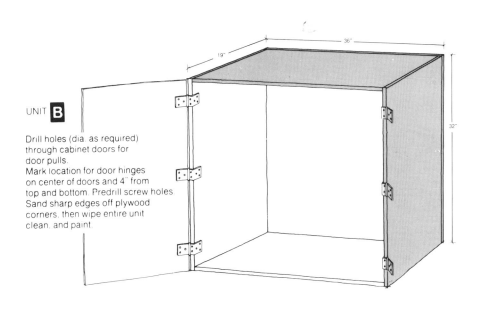

UNIT **B**

Drill holes (dia. as required)
through cabinet doors for
door pulls.
Mark location for door hinges
on center of doors and 4" from
top and bottom. Predrill screw holes.
Sand sharp edges off plywood
corners, then wipe entire unit
clean, and paint.

UNIT **A**

On top and bottom, rout or saw and chisel five
¼" x ¼" channels for dividers, spacing them
as shown. (Note: six additional channels are
shown as optional so dividers can be moved
closer together or farther apart, or to
accommodate up to six additional dividers.

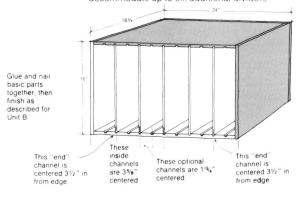

Glue and nail
basic parts
together, then
finish as
described for
Unit B.

This "end"
channel is
centered 3½" in
from edge.

These
inside
channels
are 3⅝"
centered.

These optional
channels are 1¹³⁄₁₆"
centered.

This "end"
channel is
centered 3½" in
from edge.

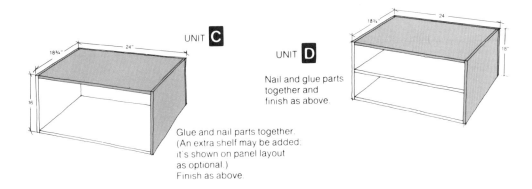

UNIT **C**

UNIT **D**

Nail and glue parts
together and
finish as above.

Glue and nail parts together.
(An extra shelf may be added;
it's shown on panel layout
as optional.)
Finish as above.

125

Cut four strips ¾″ wide by 26½″ long from excess ⅝″ plywood for drawer support runners. Mark their locations on insides of E sides. Glue and nail with brads. Glue and nail box assembly together.

Rout or chisel ¼″ x ¼″ channels inside of drawer fronts to accept drawer bottoms. (Optional: Cut ¾″ wide strips of ⅝″ plywood to length. Nail them inside of drawer fronts for support of bottoms. Reduce length of drawer support runners by ⅝″.)

UNIT **E**

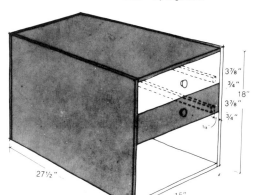

Mark screw hole locations (four per unit) on plywood unit modules where they will attach to 2 x 2 supports. Set unit modules in place, predrill into 2 x 2 supports and fasten securely.

¾″ runner fastened to E side panels.

Drill holes for drawer pulls. Nail and glue drawer assemblies, and finish as described for unit B.

Glue and nail 1x4's to bottom of desk at front, sides and back. Make ¼″ bevel on ends of legs opposite the side on which hinges will be installed. Install butt hinges to both legs. Pre drill and countersink holes in both legs for 2″ flat head screws and attach 2x2″ cross piece. Fill holes, allow to dry, and sand smooth. Then fasten hinged legs to bottom of desk top.

Fasten bottom of desk top section to folding desk top with piano hinge, and finish as above.

UNIT **F**

Center, glue and nail 1x4x34″ support for added stiffness under desk top section.

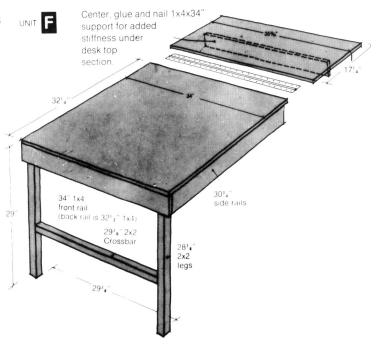

34″ 1x4 front rail (back rail is 32½″ 1x4)

29⅛″ 2x2 Crossbar

28¾″ 2x2 legs

30¾″ side rails

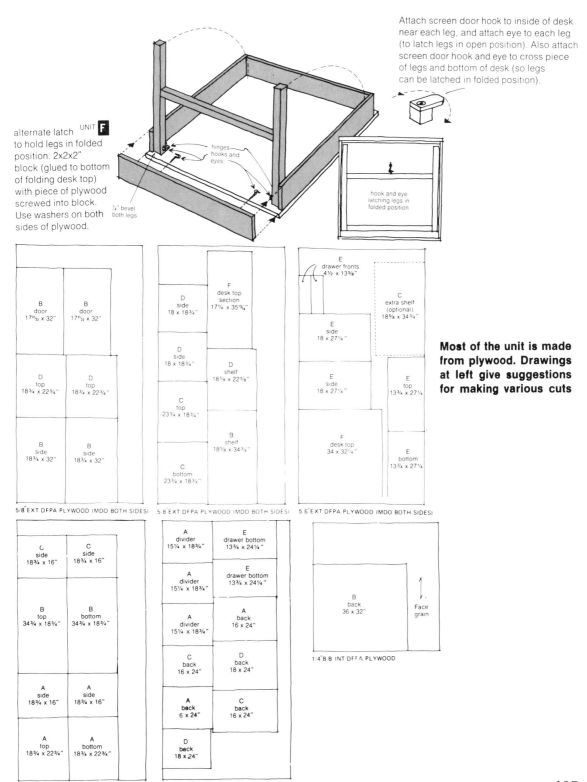

Attach screen door hook to inside of desk near each leg, and attach eye to each leg (to latch legs in open position). Also attach screen door hook and eye to cross piece of legs and bottom of desk (so legs can be latched in folded position).

UNIT **F**

alternate latch to hold legs in folded position. 2x2x2" block (glued to bottom of folding desk top) with piece of plywood screwed into block. Use washers on both sides of plywood.

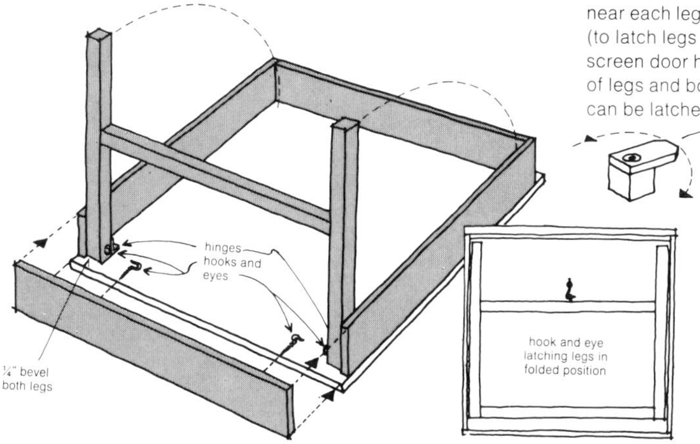

hinges hooks and eyes
¼" bevel both legs
hook and eye latching legs in folded position

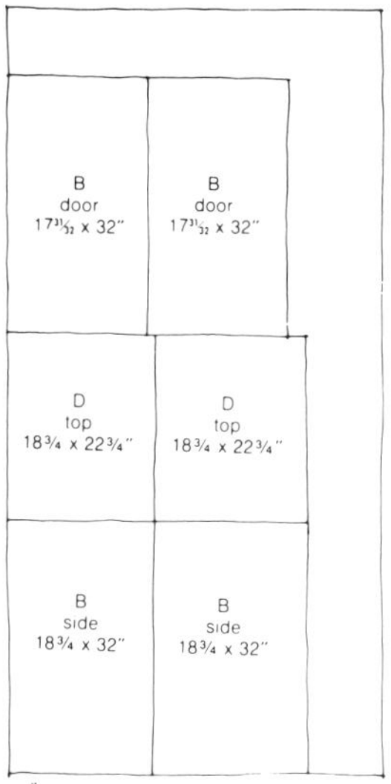

B door 17³¹⁄₃₂ x 32"
B door 17³¹⁄₃₂ x 32"
D top 18¾ x 22¾"
D top 18¾ x 22¾"
B side 18¾ x 32"
B side 18¾ x 32"

5/8" EXT DFPA PLYWOOD (MDO BOTH SIDES)

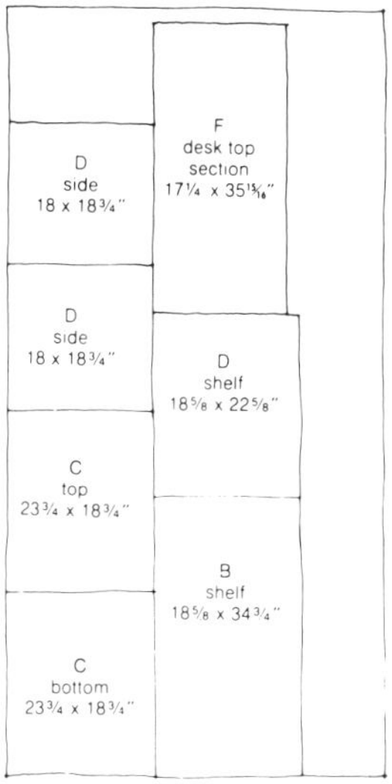

D side 18 x 18¾"
F desk top section 17¼ x 35¹⁵⁄₁₆"
D side 18 x 18¾"
D shelf 18⅝ x 22⅝"
C top 23¾ x 18¾"
B shelf 18⅝ x 34¾"
C bottom 23¾ x 18¾"

5/8" EXT DFPA PLYWOOD (MDO BOTH SIDES)

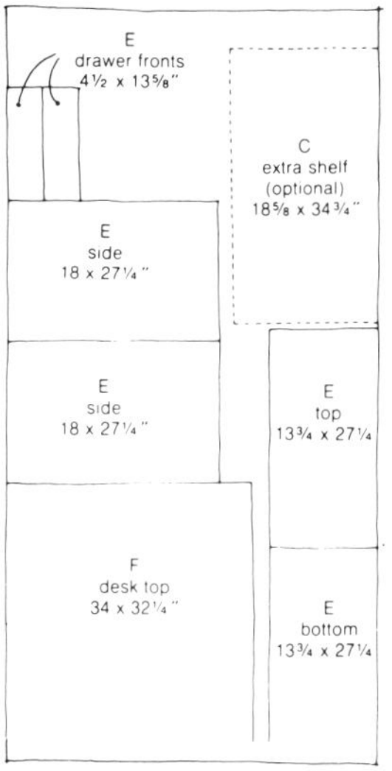

E drawer fronts 4½ x 13⅝"
C extra shelf (optional) 18⅝ x 34¾"
E side 18 x 27¼"
E side 18 x 27¼"
E top 13¾ x 27¼
F desk top 34 x 32¼"
E bottom 13¾ x 27¼

5/8" EXT DFPA PLYWOOD (MDO BOTH SIDES)

Most of the unit is made from plywood. Drawings at left give suggestions for making various cuts

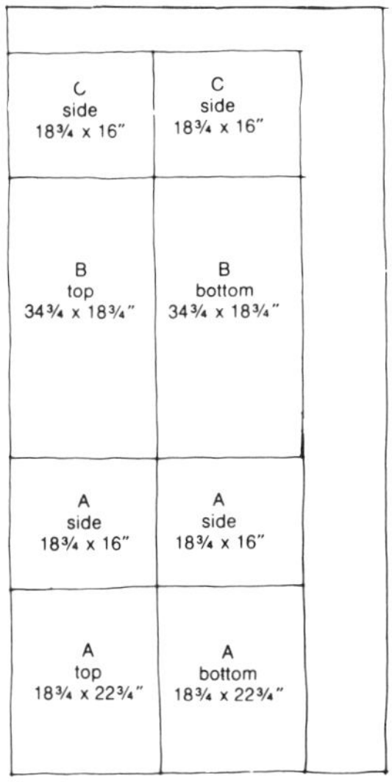

C side 18¾ x 16"
C side 18¾ x 16"
B top 34¾ x 18¾"
B bottom 34¾ x 18¾"
A side 18¾ x 16"
A side 18¾ x 16"
A top 18¾ x 22¾"
A bottom 18¾ x 22¾"

5/8" EXT DFPA PLYWOOD (MDO BOTH SIDES)

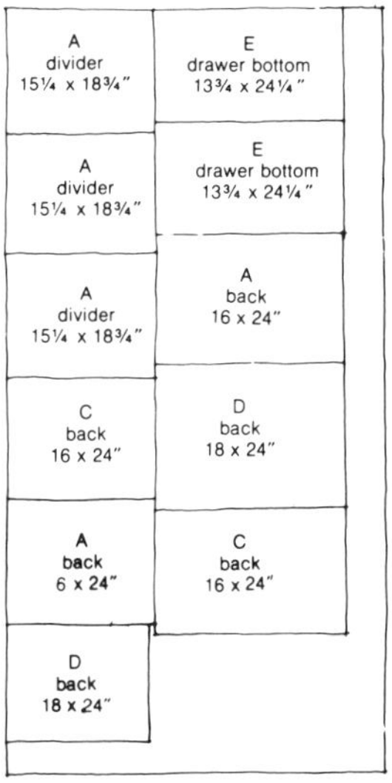

A divider 15¼ x 18¾"
E drawer bottom 13¾ x 24¼"
A divider 15¼ x 18¾"
E drawer bottom 13¾ x 24¼"
A divider 15¼ x 18¾"
A back 16 x 24"
C back 16 x 24"
D back 18 x 24"
A back 6 x 24"
C back 16 x 24"
D back 18 x 24"

1/4" B B INT DFPA PLYWOOD

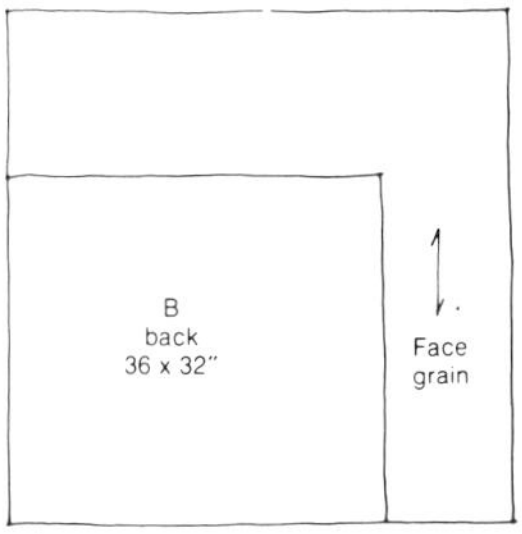

B back 36 x 32"
Face grain

1/4" B B INT DFPA PLYWOOD

MATERIALS LIST

Purpose	Size	Description	Quantity
Cabinets, shelves	⅝″ × 4′ × 8′	EXT-DFPA plywood	4
Dividers, backs, and drawer bottoms	¼″ × 4′ × 8′	B-B INT-DFPA plywood	1½
Frame and desk legs	2″ × 2″ × 72′	Select-grade lumber	1
Frame and desk drawers	1″ × 4″ × 60′	Select-grade lumber	1
	1¼″	No. 8 oval-head screws	as needed
		Finish washers	as needed
	2″	No. 8 flat-head screws	as needed

Note: You will also need cabinet door hinges, door pulls, magnetic door catches, brads, piano hinge, butt hinges, hooks and eyes (small), 6d finishing nails, and finishing materials.

When all the parts and assemblies are on site, erect the unit with screws as shown in the plans. Don't use glue at this stage. You may wish to move the unit some day. If it is merely screwed together, it can be broken down into easily handled parts and reassembled at its new location.

Dough Box End Table

ONE OF THE MOST popular and versatile of Early American creations is the quaint, old-fashioned dough box. It makes an ideal end and lamp table and, since the top is hinged, it provides a roomy storage area for all sorts of miscellaneous items . . . a perfect place for knitting and sewing supplies.

Here is a project that any novice can undertake with success, and it can be completed without an elaborate set of tools. You trace full-size patterns on wood, then saw out and assemble the pieces. You can order the patterns as shown at the end of this article, or enlarge the plans here to full size.

Cut out the two top panels and the bottom piece to the dimensions given on the plans. The two side pieces "B" are each 11½ inches high, 12½ inches long at the top, tapering to 8½ inches at the bottom. The front and back pieces "A" are also 11½ inches high, and are 20 inches long at the top and 16 inches long at the bottom.

Round the top edges of the front, side and back panels.

Glue and nail the end pieces between the front and back panels. Use 3-penny finishing nails and countersink the heads. Fasten the bottom in place as shown, in the same manner.

Round the outside edges of the two top pieces. Abut these together and install the butterfly hinge in the center. Carefully position the entire top so that it overlaps evenly the front, back and side pieces, then nail just one section in place.

The legs and their brackets are available at almost all hardware, lumber and home supply stores. Turn the assembly upside down and screw the brackets in place in each corner so that the legs will project outward from the corners. Then screw the legs into place.

Cover all nail heads with wood putty, and sand smooth. Finish by staining the unit as desired, and follow with at least two coats of a good varnish or similar coating.

129

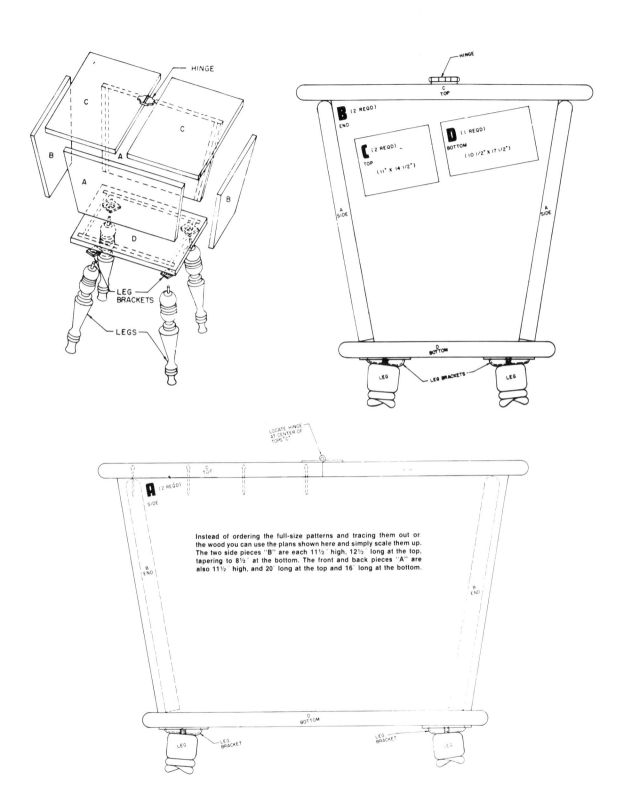

HINGE

C

C

B

A

A

B

D

LEG
BRACKETS

LEGS

HINGE

C
TOP

B (2 REQD)
END

C (2 REQD)
TOP
(11" X 14 1/2")

D (1 REQD)
BOTTOM
(10 1/2" X 17 1/2")

A
SIDE

A
SIDE

D
BOTTOM

LEG   LEG BRACKETS   LEG

LOCATE HINGE
AT CENTER OF
TOPS "C"

C
TOP

A (2 REQD)
SIDE

B
END

B
END

Instead of ordering the full-size patterns and tracing them out on
the wood you can use the plans shown here and simply scale them up.
The two side pieces "B" are each 11½" high, 12½" long at the top,
tapering to 8½" at the bottom. The front and back pieces "A" are
also 11½" high, and 20" long at the top and 16" long at the bottom.

D
BOTTOM

LEG   LEG
BRACKET   BRACKET

LEG   LEG

Purpose	Size	Quantity
Sugar pine, smooth 4 sides	1″ × 12″ × 10″	1
"Gerber" colonial-type legs	12″ long	4
Butterfly-type mounting hinge		1
No. 10 wood screws	⅝″	24
Nails	3-penny	¼ lb.

Sand lightly between coats. A semigloss finish is recommended.

For full-size plans, send $2.50 for Dough Box End Table Pattern No. 280 to Davis Publications, U-Bild Enterprises, P.O. Box 2383, Van Nuys, CA 91409.

Durable Butcher Block Table

THIS STURDY butcher block table will make a fine addition to any kitchen. The end-grain maple top will withstand years of chops and cuts, and its simple lines will fit into any decor. Commercial butcher blocks are usually made 12 inches thick and weigh about 250 lbs.—far too heavy for home use. Ours is made with a dual-thickness top and weighs about 60 lbs. The perimeter blocks are 4 inches thick; the internal blocks are 1½-inch thick. We also added a small drawer to hold knives and other utensils.

The tabletop consists of 82 pieces of end-grain red maple, cut from 8/4 stock. The 8/4 stock (2 inches) has a dressed thickness of 1¾ inch. The technique used calls for some of the blocks to be precut to the fin-ished size before gluing. This greatly simplifies the layout and arrangement of the blocks when alternating the annular rings. However, you may be wondering how as many as 11 pieces can be glued successfully. The trick is to use double-pointed brads. Without the use of these brads, it would be almost impossible for the average home workshopper to accomplish such a job.

Select good flat lumber then set the table saw at 2¹³⁄₁₆ inches and rip enough stock to produce 32 pieces, each 4 inches long. Be sure the fence is set parallel to the blade as any discrepancy now will show up in the finished top later on. These 32 blocks will make up the outer perimeter of the top.

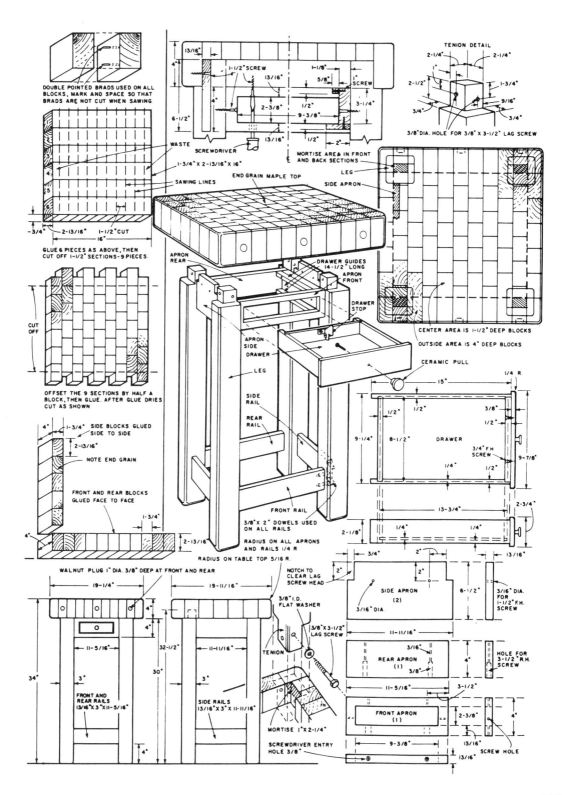

DOUBLE POINTED BRADS USED ON ALL BLOCKS, MARK AND SPACE SO THAT BRADS ARE NOT CUT WHEN SAWING.

WASTE

SCREWDRIVER

1-3/4" X 2-13/16" X 16"

SAWING LINES

2-13/16" — 1-1/2" CUT
16"

GLUE 6 PIECES AS ABOVE, THEN CUT OFF 1-1/2" SECTIONS-9 PIECES.

CUT OFF

OFFSET THE 9 SECTIONS BY HALF A BLOCK, THEN GLUE. AFTER GLUE DRIES CUT AS SHOWN

4" 1-3/4" SIDE BLOCKS GLUED SIDE TO SIDE
2-13/16"
NOTE END GRAIN
FRONT AND REAR BLOCKS GLUED FACE TO FACE
1-3/4"
4" 2-13/16"

WALNUT PLUG 1" DIA. 3/8" DEEP AT FRONT AND REAR

19-1/4"
11-5/16"
3"
34"
FRONT AND REAR RAILS
13/16" X 3" X 11-5/16"

19-11/16"
11-11/16"
3"
32-1/2"
30"
SIDE RAILS
13/16" X 3" X 11-11/16"

13/16"
4"
6-1/2"
1-1/2" SCREW
13/16"
2-3/8" 1/2"
9-3/8"
13/16" 1/2"
1-1/8"
5/8" 1"
SCREW
3-1/4"
2"

MORTISE AREA IN FRONT AND BACK SECTIONS

END GRAIN MAPLE TOP

APRON REAR
DRAWER GUIDES 14-1/2" LONG
APRON FRONT
DRAWER STOP
APRON SIDE
DRAWER
LEG
SIDE RAIL
REAR RAIL
FRONT RAIL
3/8" X 2" DOWELS USED ON ALL RAILS
RADIUS ON ALL APRONS AND RAILS 1/4 R
RADIUS ON TABLE TOP 5/16 R.

TENION DETAIL
2-1/4" 2-1/4"
2-1/2" 1-3/4"
9/16"
3/4"
3/8" DIA. HOLE FOR 3/8" X 3-1/2" LAG SCREW

LEG
SIDE APRON
CENTER AREA IS 1-1/2" DEEP BLOCKS
OUTSIDE AREA IS 4" DEEP BLOCKS

CERAMIC PULL

15" 1/4 R.
9-1/4" 8-1/2" DRAWER 3/8"
1/2" 1/2" 1/2"
3/4" F.H. SCREW
9-7/8"
1/4" 1/2"
13-3/4"
2-1/8" 1/4" 1/4" 2-3/4"
13/16"

NOTCH TO CLEAR LAG SCREW HEAD
3/8" I.D. FLAT WASHER
3/8" X 3-1/2" LAG SCREW
TENION
MORTISE 1" X 2-1/4"
SCREWDRIVER ENTRY HOLE 3/8"

3/4" 2" 2"
SIDE APRON (2)
3/16" DIA
6-1/2"
3/16" DIA. FOR 1-1/2" F.H. SCREW

11-11/16"
3/16"
REAR APRON (1)
3/8"
4"
HOLE FOR 3-1/2" R.H. SCREW

11-5/16" 3-1/2"
FRONT APRON (1)
2-3/8" 4"
9-3/8" 13/16"
13/16" SCREW HOLE

133

Fig. 21-1. Ripped stock is cut to length then arranged, annular rings alternating. Mark off 1½-inch lengths and kerf cuts.

Fig. 21-2. Clamp securely and allow ample time for glue to set. Use cauls under clamp jaws. Then slice into 1½-inch strips.

Arrange the pieces with alternating annular rings, then number each mating piece. Number them 1-1, 2-2, 3-3, etc. Now install the brads.

Normally with soft woods, the brads can be inserted by grasping them endwise with pliers and simply pushing them into the work. However, maple is too hard for this, so you will have to drill the brad holes into one face. Use one of the brads as a drill by chucking it into your drill. A drill press is recommended as the brads must be installed perpendicular to the faces.

Insert two pins about 2 inches apart in one face of the 11 pieces. Keep them in numerical order, working on a flat surface and against a back stop. Clamp the blocks (without glue) to force the pins into the mating pieces. Remove the clamp, separate the pieces, then add glue and reclamp. Use resin glue which is highly water-resistant. Make two sections of 11 pieces (front and rear) and two sections of 5 pieces (sides). The 11 pieces are glued face-to-face. The 5 pieces are glued side-to-side. (See detail drawing).

The blocks for the 1½-inch pieces are made by gluing up 6 pieces of stock 1¾ × 2¹³⁄₁₆ × 16 inches long. Arrange these so the annular rings alternate. Drill two holes in each piece for the double-pointed brads. Make the holes about ¼ inch deep and place them near the ends of each piece. Apply glue then clamp. After the glue has set, slice off 1½-inch wide strips from the block. Use the radial arm saw or table saw for this operation. If the table saw is used, be sure to use a push stick to keep the fingers away from the blade.

The strips are placed on a flat surface and each row is offset alternately by half a block. These are now pinned (one pin at each end), then glued. When the glue has set, trim the protruding ends, preferably using the radial arm saw. Regardless of how much care is taken in preparing and gluing the pieces, the surfaces will have some unevenness. This is objectionable when joining the mating section, such as the front, rear, and sides. These surfaces can be trued up, preferably with a jointer, otherwise with a table saw.

Fig. 21-3. Arrange 1½-inch strips, stagger joints. Double-pointed brads go in each end of face pieces. Trim block with radial saw.

Fig. 21-4. Cut perimeter blocks at saw fence using stop clamp. Arrange for best grain appearance and number. Allow to set.

Fig. 21-5. Mortise for legs is made with one-inch Forstner bit. Lag screw pilot hole made with red hot ¼-inch Phillips screwdriver.

Purpose	Size	Description	Quantity
Block	$1\frac{3}{4}'' \times 2\frac{3}{16}'' \times 4''$	Maple	32
Block	$1\frac{3}{4}'' \times 2\frac{13}{16}'' \times 1\frac{1}{2}''$	Maple	50
Leg	$3'' \times 3'' \times 32\frac{1}{2}''$	Maple	4
Apron side	$\frac{13}{16}'' \times 6\frac{1}{2}'' \times 11\frac{11}{16}''$	Maple	2
Apron front/rear	$\frac{13}{16}'' \times 4'' \times 11\frac{5}{16}''$	Maple	2
Rail, side	$\frac{13}{16}'' \times 3'' \times 11\frac{11}{16}''$	Maple	2
Rail, front/rear	$\frac{13}{16}'' \times 3'' \times 11\frac{5}{16}''$	Maple	2
Drawer guide, side	$1\frac{1}{8}'' \times 3\frac{1}{4}'' \times 14\frac{1}{2}''$	Pine	2
Drawer guide, top	$\frac{1}{2}'' \times \frac{5}{8}'' \times 14\frac{1}{2}''$	Pine	2
Drawer guide, bottom	$\frac{1}{2}'' \times 2'' \times 14\frac{1}{2}''$	Pine	2
Drawer side	$\frac{1}{2}'' \times 2\frac{1}{8}'' \times 15''$	Poplar	2
Drawer subfront	$\frac{1}{2}'' \times 2\frac{1}{8}'' \times 8\frac{1}{2}''$	Poplar	1
Drawer front	$\frac{3}{8}'' \times 2\frac{3}{4}'' \times 9\frac{7}{8}''$	Maple	1
Drawer rear	$\frac{1}{2}'' \times 2\frac{1}{8}'' \times 8\frac{1}{2}''$	Poplar	1
Drawer bottom	$\frac{1}{4}'' \times 8\frac{1}{2}'' \times 13\frac{3}{4}''$	Plywood	1
Plug	$\frac{3}{8}'' \times 1''$	Walnut	6
Drawer pull		(No. 71002)	1
Lag screw	$\frac{3}{8}'' \times 3\frac{1}{2}''$		8
Flat washer	$\frac{3}{8}''$ ID		8
Dowel	$\frac{3}{8}'' \times 2''$	(No. 51017)	16
Double pointed brad		(No. 83007)	80
Screw	$\frac{3}{4}''$	No. 8 FH	2
Screw	$1''$	No. 8 FH	12
Screw	$3\frac{1}{2}'' \times 10''$	RH	2
Brad	$1''$ No. 17		8
Salad bowl finish		(No. 85006)	1 pint
Drawer stop		(No. 78015)	1

Note: If you have difficulty locating the items in parentheses, write to Armor Products, Box 445, E. Northport, NY 11731 and ask for free catalog.

Set the pieces to be trued up onto a flat surface, such as the table saw. Rest the ends onto ¼-inch plywood then clamp two chunky pieces of wood, one at each end, thus forming a bridge as shown in photo. Place the assembly onto the table saw and elevate the blade so it just touches the work. With the work away from the saw blade, turn on the machine then slide the ''bridge'' over the blade and move it from side to side. Advance the work forward a little at a time after each pass. If you find low spots, elevate the blade and repeat. Take only very small bites each time. When done, the surface should be as flat as your saw table.

The walnut plugs for the front and rear blocks are made with a 1-inch plug cutter. The holes for these should be made with a 1-inch Forstner bit. Apply glue to the walls of the hole, then insert the plug.

The final assembly of the top can now

take place. Again, using double-pointed brads glue the sides to the top member. When the glue has set, add the front and rear sections.

The legs are made from solid stock, if available. Otherwise two or more pieces are glued up to make the required thickness. The finished size of the legs are $3 \times 3 \times 32\frac{1}{2}$ inches. Assuming two pieces of $1\frac{3}{4}$-inch stock are glued up, resaw the pieces to obtain the 3-$\times$-3-inch cross section. After sawing, use a jointer to smooth the surface. Otherwise, use a belt sander.

The top end of each leg is tenoned to fit the mortise which will be made at each corner of the top. There are various ways of making the tenon. The easiest way is to use the radial arm saw and make successive cuts on two surfaces. Be sure to clamp a stop to the fence for the first ($2\frac{1}{2}$ inches) cut. After the tenons are cut, drill the holes for the lag screws.

Use the router with a $\frac{5}{16}$-inch rounding bit to round the corners of the legs. After rounding, locate and drill the $\frac{3}{8}$-inch diameter holes for the rail dowels. Make the hole a trifle deeper than 1 inch to ensure that the joint closes fully. Use dowel centers to transfer the holes from the legs to the rails. Using spiral dowels, assemble the leg to the rails and be sure to note that the rails are used in pairs as the lengths vary.

The underside of the top is mortised at each corner to receive the tenoned legs. One simple method of mortising the end-grain makes use of a Forstner bit. This tool is ideal because of its ability to make overlapping cuts without "walking." Lay out the mortise lines, then drill out the waste area. Set the depth to cut $2\frac{1}{2}$-inches deep. Clean out the mortise with a chisel.

Install the legs into the mortises then mark the hole centers for the screws. Remove the legs and drill the $\frac{1}{4}$-inch pilot holes. One hole in each corner can be drilled, but the second hole cannot be drilled because of the space limitations.

We found that heating a 79-cent "bargain" Phillips screwdriver with a torch enabled us to burn the holes required. Fasten the legs with lag screws and flat washers.

The aprons are cut, drilled, and assembled as shown. Note that the side aprons are deeper than those of the front and rear. They are fastened with screws at the sides. The front and rear aprons are fastened with two screws through the edges. The front apron or frame has two additional screws fastened at the ends.

The drawer and guides are cut and assembled as indicated. Use glue and brads to fasten the drawer members. The top is sanded with a belt sander followed by a finishing sander. Start with a coarse belt working down to 120 grit. Dust carefully, then use the finishing sander until the top is glassy-smooth.

The table should be finished with mineral oil or a good salad bowl finish which has been approved for contact with food.

Foldaway
Bed/Storage Unit

DO YOU NEED an extra bed or bookcase? Build this unit and you'll have both—a handsome storage unit and a comfortable bed. This is a modern version of the Murphy bed which was very popular at one time. The Murphy beds folded into a wall when not in use, and you may still see them occasionally on TV reruns of the old Laurel and Hardy films, with one comedian being accidentally slammed into the wall while still asleep.

With living space at a premium today, this unit should find wide acceptance among apartment dwellers and home owners alike. Because of its ease of operation, it takes little effort to convert

from books to bed. Simply roll out the bottom section and tilt. It's a great idea for a small guest room. It occupies little space either open or closed, and it's attractive as well as useful.

The unit shown was made of pine plywood, but solid pine or other woods may be substituted. Construction has been simplified so that even the novice woodworker should have no problem in making the piece. No tricky cuts are involved, and butt joints are used throughout.

The piece consists of three parts: upper shelves, lower bed compartment, and the bed itself. The dummy doors and drawers

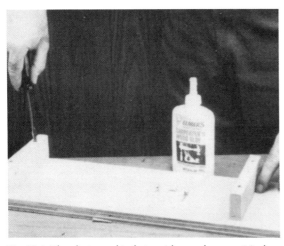

Fig. 22-1. The cleats used to fasten side members are 2 inches wide and receive ³⁄₁₆-inch-diameter holes.

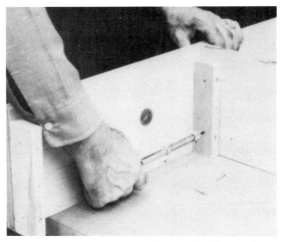

Fig. 22-2. Assembling the side to shelf. Push drill is handy for making the screw pilot holes.

are actually the base of the bed. The bed rides on specially designed non-swivelling casters. These are necessary because they ensure that the bed will roll in and out in a straight line. If conventional casters are used, it becomes very difficult to withdraw and replace the bed without striking the compartment sides.

In order to keep the knobs and pulls clear of the floor when the bed is in use, the edges of the front panel are thickened by the use of appropriate moldings.

The bed consists of a framework supported by four uprights. Crosspieces support a panel which, in turn, supports a camper-type mattress. The camper mattress is ideal since it is only three inches thick and measures 26½ × 70 inches. It remains in place even when the bed is closed or in the upright position. It is held with a pair of straps. A piece of foam of equal thickness may be substituted.

Before starting construction be sure to have the mattress on hand so that you can fit the parts to it. If the mattress you use differs in size, be sure to change the dimensions shown on the drawings

accordingly. Although the area below the bed is open, it can be made with closed sides and bottom to provide additional storage space for blankets, sheets, pillows and the like.

If you choose to use solid boards, the top and side members may have to be glued up, unless you use pine, which is usually available in widths over 12 inches. Since the plywood panels measure 4 × 8 feet, you won't have to do any gluing. Assuming that you are using plywood, lay out and cut the top and side pieces of the compartment either on the table saw or with a portable saw. If you use the portable saw, be sure to use a guide strip to assure a straight cut. The strip should be fastened to the board with clamps, one at each end. The thickness of the strip is governed by the clearance under the saw. Except for some of the smaller trim saws, the guide strip can usually be of ¾-inch stock.

After the three pieces are cut, prepare the two cleats which will be used to fasten the top and side members. Cut the cleats two-inches wide and drill three ³⁄₁₆-inch-diameter holes for the screws in each

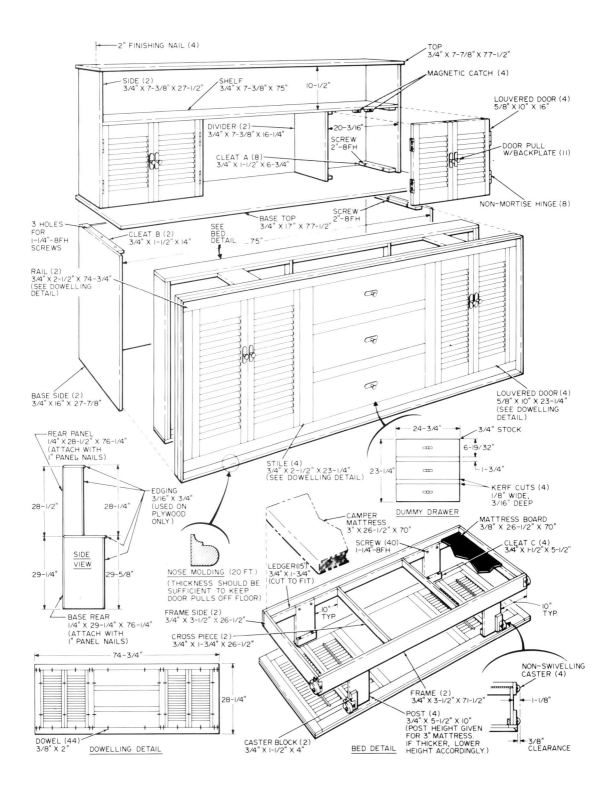

2" FINISHING NAIL (4)

TOP
3/4" X 7-7/8" X 77-1/2"

SIDE (2)
3/4" X 7-3/8" X 27-1/2"

SHELF
3/4" X 7-3/8" X 75"

10-1/2"

MAGNETIC CATCH (4)

LOUVERED DOOR (4)
5/8" X 10" X 16"

DIVIDER (2)
3/4" X 7-3/8" X 16-1/4"

20-3/16"

SCREW
2"-8FH

DOOR PULL
W/BACKPLATE (11)

CLEAT A (8)
3/4" X 1-1/2" X 6-3/4"

NON-MORTISE HINGE (8)

3 HOLES
FOR
1-1/4"-8FH
SCREWS

CLEAT B (2)
3/4" X 1-1/2" X 14"

SEE
BED
DETAIL

BASE TOP
3/4" X 17" X 77-1/2"

SCREW
2"-8FH

75"

RAIL (2)
3/4" X 2-1/2" X 74-3/4"
(SEE DOWELLING
DETAIL)

BASE SIDE (2)
3/4" X 16" X 27-7/8"

LOUVERED DOOR (4)
5/8" X 10" X 23-1/4"
(SEE DOWELLING
DETAIL)

REAR PANEL
1/4" X 28-1/2" X 76-1/4"
(ATTACH WITH
1" PANEL NAILS)

EDGING
3/16" X 3/4"
(USED ON
PLYWOOD
ONLY)

28-1/2"

28-1/4"

SIDE
VIEW

29-1/4"

29-5/8"

STILE (4)
3/4" X 2-1/2" X 23-1/4"
(SEE DOWELLING DETAIL)

24-3/4"

3/4" STOCK

6-19/32"

1-3/4"

23-1/4"

KERF CUTS (4)
1/8" WIDE,
3/16" DEEP

DUMMY DRAWER

CAMPER
MATTRESS
3" X 26-1/2" X 70"

MATTRESS BOARD
3/8" X 26-1/2" X 70"

SCREW (40)
1-1/4"-8FH

CLEAT C (4)
3/4" X 1-1/2" X 5-1/2"

NOSE MOLDING (20 FT.)
(THICKNESS SHOULD BE
SUFFICIENT TO KEEP
DOOR PULLS OFF FLOOR)

LEDGER(15)
3/4" X 1-3/4"
(CUT TO FIT)

FRAME SIDE (2)
3/4" X 3-1/2" X 26-1/2"

10"
TYP.

10"
TYP.

NON-SWIVELLING
CASTER (4)

BASE REAR
1/4" X 29-1/4" X 76-1/4"
(ATTACH WITH
1" PANEL NAILS)

CROSS PIECE (2)
3/4" X 1-3/4" X 26-1/2"

74-3/4"

28-1/4"

FRAME (2)
3/4" X 3-1/2" X 71-1/2"

1-1/8"

POST (4)
3/4" X 5-1/2" X 10"
(POST HEIGHT GIVEN
FOR 3" MATTRESS.
IF THICKER, LOWER
HEIGHT ACCORDINGLY.)

3/8"
CLEARANCE

DOWEL (44)
3/8" X 2"

DOWELLING DETAIL

CASTER BLOCK (2)
3/4" X 1-1/2" X 4"

BED DETAIL

Fig. 22-3. To locate position for dividers, set two doors side by side, make a mark on shelf edge even with door, another mark ³⁄₁₆ inch from first indicates inside edge of divider.

Fig. 22-4. When installing the rear panel, use a temporary spacer to keep the top board from sagging. When nailed in place, the rear panel will prevent the top from sagging.

Fig. 22-5. To accurately position the dividers, use several wood strips, cut to proper length, to provide the correct spacing. Use a clamp to hold wood strip against the top.

Fig. 22-6. Parts of the lower front section are installed with doweled joints. Two dowels are sufficient to hold louvered sections.

Fig. 22-7. Front panel consists of four louvered doors and center panel simulating three drawers. Add stiles, clamp entire assembly.

Fig. 22-8. The top of the bed post must be flush with the ledge strips. A 5½-inch cleat is used to mount the posts to the front panel.

Fig. 22-9. Two of the casters attach to the bed frame. The other two casters attach to the posts by means of 1¼ × 4-inch blocks.

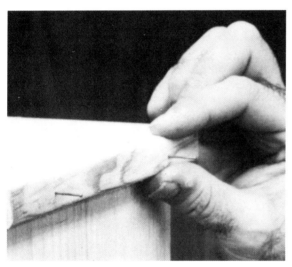

Fig. 22-10. Finishing off the plywood with ³⁄₁₆ × ¾-inch edging. Use glue and brads. For best results, try mitering the corners.

Fig. 22-11. The completed unit is now ready for sanding and finishing. Ours was stained and lacquered, but paint will work just as well.

MATERIALS LIST

Purpose	Size	Description	Quantity
Base side	16″ × 28⅞″		2
Base top	17″ × 77½″		1
Base rear	¼″ × 29¼″ × 76¼″	Plywood	1
Cleat B	¾″ × 1½″ × 14″	Solid pine	8
Door	⅝″ × 10″ × 16″	Louvered	4
Top	7⅞″ × 77½″		1
Shelf	7⅜″ × 75″		1
Side	7⅜″ × 27½″		2
Divider	7⅜″ × 16¼″		2
Cleat A	¾″ × 1½″ × 6¾″	Sold pine	2
Door	⅝″ × 10″ × 24″	Louvered	4
Edging	3⁄16″ × ¾″		40′
Rear panel	1¼″ × 29¼″ × 76¼″	Plywood	1
Stile	2½″ × 23¼″		4
Rail	2½″ × 74¾″		2
Dummy drawer	23¼″ × 24¾″		1
Nose molding	1″		20′
Frame side	3½″ × 26½″		2
Frame	3½″ × 71½″		2
Post	5½″ × 10″		4
Cleat C	1½″ × 5½″	Solid pine	4
Ledger	¾″ × 1¾″	Pine	15′
Crosspiece	¾″ × 1¾″ × 26½″	Pine	2
Caster block	¾″ × 1½″ × 4″		2
Mattress board	⅜″ × 26½″ × 70″		1
Casters			4
Door pull with backplate			11
Magnetic catch			4
Non-mortise hinge			8
Dowel	⅜″ × 2″		40
Screw	2″—8 FH		24
Screw	1¼″—8 FH		40
Panel nails	1″		36
Nails	2″ finishing (for top panel)		4

Note: You will also need white glue, sandpaper, and finishing materials.

face. Install the cleats along the top edge of the side members. Use glue and 2-inch FH screws.

The two side pieces will now have cleats at one end. Put them aside and, while the glue sets, cut the rear panel. This should be ¼-inch plywood. However, since it doesn't show (except when the bed is in use), a less expensive wood, such as fir, can be used. This will help keep costs down. After cutting the panel to size, sand all edges and break the sharp corners. Use a piece of sandpaper wrapped around a block, or a power sander.

Now fasten the sides to the top. Position the sides so the top overhangs equally at both ends. Apply white glue to the joints then assemble with 1¼-inch screws. Before the glue sets, tip the U-shaped assembly forward so the rear edge is upright. Install the rear panel, noting that the lower edge is flush with the lower edge of the sides. The upper edge of the panel should be set back ⅜ inch at the top. The panel is also set back at the sides, but only by ⅛ inch.

Provided that the setbacks are equal at the sides, the assembly will be perfectly square because the rear panel acts like a large square. Fasten the panel with 1-inch panel nails. These are the nails used to install prefinished wall paneling: they are made with annular grooves and have excellent holding power. (Try removing one and you'll see how well they hold.) Use glue at all joints.

This is made as a separate unit which fastens to the base piece. The top, sides, shelf and dividers are of equal width. Set the fence of the table saw to 7⅜ inches and rip the required pieces, then cut them to the lengths shown in the Materials List. Cut the eight cleats to size and, as before, drill the screw clearance holes.

Install the cleats to the side pieces. Position them carefully, especially the upper ones which hold the shelf. The lower ones are fastened flush at the bottom. The cleats for the dividers are mounted flush at top and bottom.

Install the side pieces to the shelf first. Lay the shelf and ends on their backs and be sure to work on a flat surface. Apply glue to the joint, then screw the cleats firmly. To ensure that `the assembly remains square, fasten a diagonal cleat to the back side as shown. Repeat the procedure for the opposite end. The top piece is added next. Center it so the

overhang is equal at both ends and at the front.

To locate the position for the dividers, place two louvered doors side by side without space, as shown in the photo. Place a mark on the shelf edge in line with the door farthest from the side panel. Place another mark ³⁄₁₆ inches from the first. This will indicate the inside edge of the divider. Cut and install the rear panel, then fasten the upper section to the lower.

Install the divider next. To simplify the installation, cut four strips of wood making the length equal to the width of the opening. Place two strips at the top and two at the bottom of the opening between the end panel and the divider. Mark the screw hole locations, apply glue and screw the pieces securely in place.

The doors are hung with non-mortise hinges. These are quickly installed since they do not require a gain to be cut in the door or side panel. The specially designed hinge automatically gives the proper clearance allowance between door and frame. Fasten the hinges to the door, then place into the opening, resting the bottom of the doors on a strip of ⅛-inch wood. Mark the position of the hinges on the frame (side panel and divider), then use an awl to pierce the center marks for the screws. Fasten the rest of the hinges and repeat for the other set of doors.

Drill a ³⁄₁₆-inch-diameter hole in the center stiles of each door for the pulls. Also mount the magnetic catches to the underside of the shelf. Use one catch for each door.

The front panel for the bed is made with louvered doors and a center panel simulating three drawers. Make the center panel first. This should be equal in height to the doors. After cutting the panel to size, cut the double set of grooves representing the rails in between the drawers. Cut the grooves $3/16$ inch deep. Drill the $3/16$-inch holes for the pulls, then set the piece aside temporarily. Trim $3/4$ inch from the door bottoms so they will measure $23\frac{1}{4}$ inches long.

Cut the rails and stiles to size, then lay them on a flat surface with the doors and dummy drawers in place. Be sure that the tops of the doors are oriented (Louvered doors have a top and bottom). With all the pieces aligned, mark a light gauging line on the face of each piece to indicate the dowel locations. Identify each stile with its adjacent part, for example, A-A, B-B, C-C, etc. If you don't, you'll have quite a job trying to match the various parts later on.

Drill $3/8$-inch-diameter holes 1 inch deep for the dowels. A doweling jig is most useful for this operation. It will ensure straight holes perfectly centered and aligned. If you do not use a doweling jig, be sure that the holes are drilled exactly in the center of each piece.

When assembling the front panel install all of the stiles to the doors and drawer panel sides. If you use snug-fitting spiral dowels, you won't need to clamp the assembly. Likewise, you need not clamp the top and bottom rails. The width of the piece was assembled without clamps, because 80-inch clamps are hard to come by. If you have the clamps, use them, but in this instance they are not essential.

The bed is made with a $3\frac{1}{2}$-inch frame formed into a rectangle as shown. Butt joints glued and screwed make up the outer frame. A ledger strip is added to the inner wall of the frame. This, together with the crosspieces, support the mattress board. The four legs are cut to size and installed with the upper edge aligned with the top of the ledger strips. Cleats are used to attach the legs to the front panel. Two spacer blocks are added to the lower legs in order to align the casters.

To keep the pulls clear of the floor when the front panel is tilted downward, a nose molding is applied around the perimeter of the front section. Be sure the molding is deep enough to keep the knobs off the floor.

The cleats should be glued and screwed to the front panel. However, before applying glue, it is advisable to mount the bed without the glue at first as you test the fit between the bed unit and the lower compartment. Make sure that the clearances are okay and that the bed rides in and out freely. If okay, apply glue and secure permanently.

Add the plywood edging, then sand all surfaces and finish as desired. The unit shown was stained and lacquered, but a two-tone painted finish would be another possibility. The unit could also be left natural with several coats of varnish or lacquer.

The hardware and casters should be available locally. If you have difficulty in locating them, write to the Armor Co., Box 290, Deer Park, N.Y. 11729.

Functional Occasional Table

ALTHOUGH classified here as an "occasional" table, you'll find yourself relying more and more on this as an all-around utility table, continually in use rather than occasionally. Because of its solid construction and sturdiness it will withstand daily use and abuse effortlessly. It can be appropriate used as a coffee table, magazine table, lamp table, or whatever. It is ruggedly built of 1¾-inch pine and has three handy storage drawers. The finished table measures 20 × 44 inches and stands 16½-inches high.

The construction is simple and this project is recommended for all classes of woodworkers, from beginners to advanced.

Start with the construction of the top which is made of 1¾-inch stock. Chances are that you won't be able to get a 20-inch board, so you'll probably have to glue up two or more narrower pieces. True up the edges to be glued and if necessary, resaw to eliminate any bumps or dents at the edges. If you have a jointer or power plane, these will do fine.

Next, drill a series of holes to accept the dowels—six holes should do the trick. Use a dowel drilling jig to accurately center the holes. Use dowel centers to transfer the holes to the mating edge. Drill the holes 1⁄₁₆ inches deep, then apply glue to spiral dowels and insert into the drilled holes. Apply glue to both mating surfaces as well as the projecting dowels, then bring the boards together and clamp until the glue sets.

Make the legs next. Use 3- × 3-inch stock, or if not available, you can glue-up thinner material to make up the 2½-inch squares needed. If you have a jointer, clean the surfaces of the squares taking just a light cut. Trim the ends to size so each piece measures 14½ inches long.

The apron is cut next from 1¼-inch stock. The end and rear aprons are solid but the front is made up in the form of a web so it can accept the drawers. Cut the pieces to size and before assembling the web, drill diagonal screw holes through the top piece (three holes) and one each through the ends of the lower part of the front framework or web.

Diagonal screw holes are also drilled into the other three apron pieces. You can do this by hand with an electric drill or on the drill press. Use a 7⁄₃₂-inch drill bit to make the clearance holes to take the No. 10 screws. After the frame is glued-up,

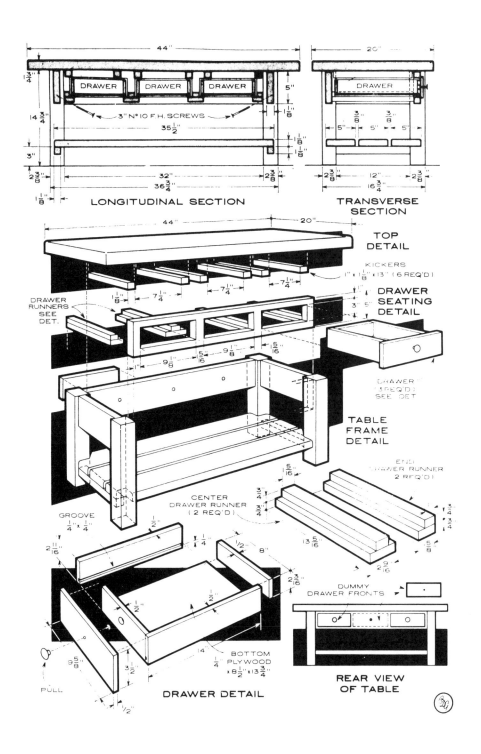

44"

$\frac{3}{4}$"

DRAWER DRAWER DRAWER

5"

$1\frac{1}{8}$"

$14\frac{3}{4}$

3" N° 10 F.H. SCREWS

$35\frac{1}{2}$"

$1\frac{1}{8}$"
$1\frac{1}{8}$"

3"

$2\frac{3}{8}$"

32"

$2\frac{3}{8}$"

$36\frac{3}{4}$"

$1\frac{1}{8}$"

LONGITUDINAL SECTION

20"

DRAWER

$\frac{3}{8}$ $\frac{3}{8}$

5" 5" 5"

$2\frac{3}{8}$" 12" $2\frac{3}{8}$"

$16\frac{3}{4}$"

TRANSVERSE SECTION

44" 20"

TOP DETAIL

KICKERS
1" x $1\frac{1}{8}$" x 13" (6 REQ'D)

$1\frac{1}{8}$" $7\frac{1}{4}$" $7\frac{1}{4}$" $7\frac{1}{4}$"

DRAWER SEATING DETAIL

DRAWER RUNNERS SEE DET.

3 5"

$9\frac{1}{8}$ $5\frac{5}{16}$ $9\frac{1}{8}$ $5\frac{5}{16}$

DRAWER 3 REQ'D SEE DET

TABLE FRAME DETAIL

$5\frac{5}{16}$

END DRAWER RUNNER 2 REQ'D

CENTER DRAWER RUNNER (2 REQ'D)

$\frac{3}{4}$ $\frac{3}{4}$ $\frac{3}{4}$ $\frac{3}{4}$

GROOVE $\frac{1}{4}$" x $\frac{1}{4}$

$1\frac{1}{2}$"

$13\frac{5}{16}$

$\frac{5}{8}$

$2\frac{9}{16}$

$2\frac{11}{16}$" $\frac{1}{4}$ $\frac{1}{2}$ 8"

$2\frac{3}{16}$

$\frac{1}{2}$ $\frac{1}{2}$

$\frac{1}{4}$

DUMMY DRAWER FRONTS

$9\frac{5}{8}$ $3\frac{1}{2}$

BOTTOM PLYWOOD x $8\frac{1}{2}$ x $13\frac{3}{4}$

PULL

$\frac{1}{2}$"

DRAWER DETAIL

REAR VIEW OF TABLE

147

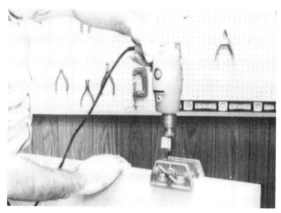

Fig. 23-1. The top is made by joining two or more boards to obtain the necessary width. A dowel jig can help assure accuracy.

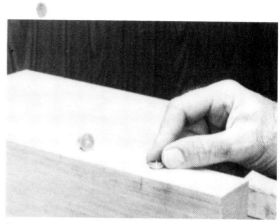

Fig. 23-2. Dowel centers help transfer hole locations. Insert them into drilled holes, then align boards. Centers mark the holes.

Fig. 23-3. Use spiral dowels for best results. Apply glue to both surfaces; join sections.

Fig. 23-4. Scrape glued board to make surface become smooth and even.

Fig. 23-5. Surface rough leg stock on a jointer. A jack plane can be used instead if a jointer is not readily available for your use.

Fig. 23-6. Sections are joined with aid of screws and glue. Be sure to work on a flat surface during the assembly.

Fig. 23-7. In this step the shelf cleat is screwed to the leg as shown. Note the solid, snug fit of the notched corners.

Fig. 23-8. The drawers are of simple butt-joint construction. The bottom panel fits into groove on three sides, is nailed at rear.

Fig. 23-9. The drawers set in place with the corresponding kickers in top panel.

sand the surface flat and it would be a good idea to also sand the surface of the end and rear apron before assembly to tabletop and legs. Break the sharp corners of the legs and bottom of the apron pieces. Use a file, sandpaper or router fitted with a rounding-off cutter.

When assembling the frame, use nails and glue and if possible clamp the work until the glue sets. Note that when you drive the nails at the bottom ends of the frame, you will have to clear the diagonal screw. (See photo.)

The tabletop glue joint should be dry at this point. Trim the top to size and sand the edges. Break all sharp corners with a router.

Next, assemble the apron and legs, working on a flat surface. Apply glue to the ends of the side aprons, then attach to the legs. A clamp should be used to hold the pieces while driving screws. Repeat this procedure until the entire base is assembled.

The drawer guides are made of ¾-inch pine. Note that the two center guides are made differently than the end pieces. Use glue and nails to join the sections, then assemble to the apron using glue and screws driven diagonally. Be sure to space the guides accurately. They must be parallel from side to side to assure that drawers will slide freely.

Drawers are made of ½-inch pine, with butt joints. The fronts are doubled up to eliminate the need for fancy joinery. Cut the sections to size. Then, using the table saw, make the grooves at the lower portion of the side and subfront pieces. The groove is cut to accommodate the drawer bottoms which are of ¼-inch plywood. You can use either a dado blade or you can make several passes with a regular blade.

Check the width of the groove with a piece of the plywood to be sure of the fit. The plywood should slide freely in the groove, but it must not be a sloppy fit. Before assembly, drill the ½-inch screw head-clearance hole in the subfront panels. Assemble the drawers with the 1½-inch finishing nails and glue. Drill a ³⁄₁₆-inch hole in the center of the three drawer fronts before assembling them to the drawers. Use glue and ¾-inch brads, driving the brads from the inside.

Kickers are added to the underside of the tabletop. These are strips of wood used to prevent the drawers from tipping when opened. Space these so they are in alignment with the drawer sides.

The bottom shelf is made next using three pieces of 1⅛-inch stock, 36 inches long. Round the edges and ends of the wood, then join the three with cleats at both ends. The cleats are cut to fit between the legs. Use screws only without glue at this time.

Place the shelf on a flat surface, then place the table in position on top of it. Center the table carefully, then with a sharp pencil, outline the area to be notched so the shelf will clear the legs at the corners. Disassemble the three pieces, cut the notches, then reassemble with glue and screws.

Before gluing, it might be a good idea to reassemble again without glue just to check the fit. If okay, apply glue and assemble. The shelf is held to the legs by driving screws diagonally from the underside of the cleats.

Give the entire table a good sanding, then finish as desired. Finish used on the unit shown was avocado green antique by Arvon Products. It consists of two base coats of latex, followed by a urethane glaze.

Note: All lumber is Northern pine.

Purpose	Size	Quantity
Top	1¾″ × 20″ × 44″	1
Leg	2⅜″ × 2⅜″ × 14¾″	4
Apron end	1⅛″ × 5″ × 12″	2
Apron rear	1⅛″ × 5″ × 32″	1
Shelf	1⅛″ × 5″ × 36″	3
Cleat	1⅛″ × 1⅜″ × 12″	2
Frame vertical (end)	1″ × 1⅛″ × 3″	2
Frame vertical (center)	1⅛″ × 1⅜″ × 3″	3
Frame horizontal	1″ × 1⅛″ × 32″	2
End drawer guide (vertical)	¾″ × 1″ × 13⁵⁄₁₆″	2
End drawer guide (horizontal)	¾″ × 1⅜″ × 13⁵⁄₁₆″	2
Center drawer guide (vertical)	¾″ × 1½″ × 13⁵⁄₁₆″	2
Center drawer guide (horizontal)	¾″ × 2½″ × 13⁵⁄₁₆″	2
Kicker	1″ × 1⅛″ × 13″	6
Drawer front	½″ × 3½″ × 9⅝″	6
Drawer side	½″ × 2¹¹⁄₁₆″ × 14″	6
Drawer subfront	½″ × 2¹¹⁄₁₆″ × 8″	3
Drawer rear	½″ × 2¼″ × 8″	3
Drawer bottom	¼″ × 8⁵⁄₁₆″ × 13⅝″	3
Knobs		6
Screws	3″—No. 10 FH	16
Screws	2″—No. 10 FH	28
Glue		
Nails		

The glaze is applied after the base has dried, using either a brush or cheesecloth, making wiped or streaked patterns as you go. Add pulls to drawers and the table is ready to serve you. Pulls can be bought, also full-size plan No. 00260 for Functional Occasional Table, which is $4 plus 50¢ postage (NY residents add Sales Tax) from Armor Products, P.O. Box 445, East Northport, NY 11731.

Handsome Wardrobe

THIS BEAUTIFULLY DESIGNED and well-proportioned dresser will be welcomed and proudly displayed in any home. Six of the drawers are the pull-out (tote) type, and the other six are conventional drawers. In addition, there are two adjustable shelves for convenient storage.

Construction is simplified greatly by the use of oak plywood. Narrow boards need not be glued-up to make the wide boards for the ends and top—something you would have to do if you were working with solid oak.

Another nice feature is the use of moldings to give the appearance of raised panels. Further simplification in construction is achieved by the use of butts joints.

Although it is a professional-looking furniture piece, it has been designed so that even a novice woodworker can make it without difficulty.

The main part of the case consists of four uprights fastened at the top with a plywood frame. The lower ends are fastened to the floorboard, which extends at the ends and front. Construction is simplified by the use of butt joints, but some woodworkers may prefer to use rabbets and dadoes for joining these parts. If so, the measurements will have to be altered accordingly.

Since plywood is used in the construction, the exposed edges will have to be covered with matching wood tape. The measurements do not include the thickness of the tape as it is nominal. Simply apply the tape to the plywood edges after the parts have been cut to size.

Cut the top frame using fir plywood

Fig. 24-1. The end panel is trimmed to size on a table saw. For a smooth, clean cut, use a plywood blade. Sand before assembly.

Fig. 24-2. Once the frame pieces have been cut, apply glue, insert the splines and clamp. Check to see if all right angles are true.

Fig. 24-3. Fasten the top frame to the end panel with glue and wood screws. Exposed plywood edges are banded with wood tape.

Fig. 24-4. Base piece is best mitered on a radial arm saw; try test cuts on scrap first. A special blade is called for here.

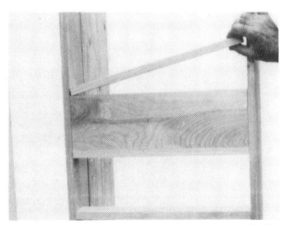

Fig. 24-5. Use a spacer to locate the proper position for the drawer frames within the larger frame; accuracy is very important.

Fig. 24-6. The ends of the rails are grooved in order to accommodate 1/8-inch plywood splines. Keep your fingers away from the blade!

153

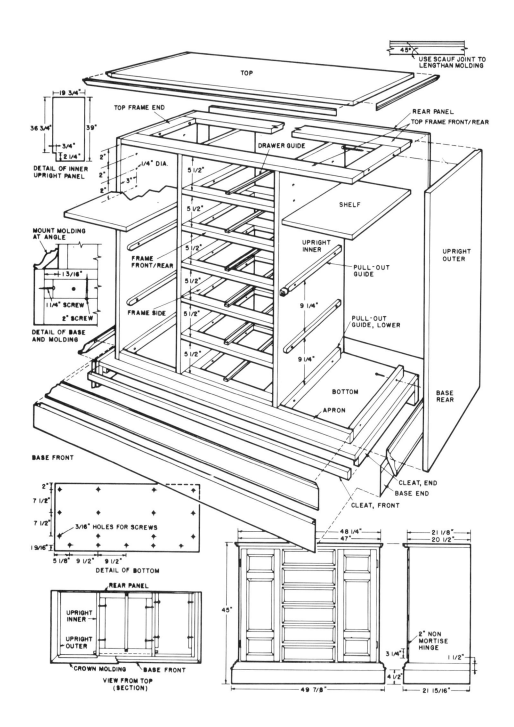

45° USE SCAUF JOINT TO LENGTHAN MOLDING

TOP

19 3/4"

36 3/4"   39"

3/4"

2 1/4"

DETAIL OF INNER UPRIGHT PANEL

TOP FRAME END

DRAWER GUIDE

REAR PANEL

TOP FRAME FRONT/REAR

2"

1/4" DIA.

2"

3"

5 1/2"

2"

SHELF

5 1/2"

UPRIGHT OUTER

MOUNT MOLDING AT ANGLE

FRAME FRONT/REAR

5 1/2"

UPRIGHT INNER

PULL-OUT GUIDE

1 3/16"

1 1/4" SCREW

2" SCREW

FRAME SIDE

5 1/2"

9 1/4"

PULL-OUT GUIDE, LOWER

DETAIL OF BASE AND MOLDING

5 1/2"

9 1/4"

5 1/2"

BOTTOM

BASE REAR

APRON

BASE FRONT

CLEAT, END

BASE END

CLEAT, FRONT

2"

7 1/2"

7 1/2"

3/16" HOLES FOR SCREWS

1 9/16"

5 1/8"   9 1/2"   9 1/2"

DETAIL OF BOTTOM

48 1/4"

47"

21 1/8"

20 1/2"

REAR PANEL

UPRIGHT INNER

UPRIGHT OUTER

45"

2" NON MORTISE HINGE

3 1/4"

1 1/2"

CROWN MOLDING

BASE FRONT

VIEW FROM TOP (SECTION)

4 1/2"

49 7/8"

21 15/16"

154

Fig. 24-7. Here, the rail members for the door frames have been fitted with splines and are ready to be glued on to the stiles.

Fig. 24-8. A clamp tool is great for frame work. Its plastic jaws will not gouge surfaces, and squeeze-out is kept to a minimum.

Fig. 24-9. After you've finished assembling the door frames, break the sharp corners with a router fitted with a bevel-trimmer bit.

Fig. 24-10. The raised panel effect on the doors is achieved with mitered nose & cove molding. Install with glue only—no brads.

Fig. 24-11. Attach the plywood back to the door frame and rabbet the edges of the frame on a table saw. Watch those fingers!

Fig. 24-12. All drawer members are made of birch plywood. The above side member with dado and groove is ready for assembly.

ripped to 3-inch widths. Use splines at the joints. We used ⅛-inch-thick plywood splines because we had the ⅛-inch plywood on hand and the kerf width of our saw blade is exactly ⅛ inch, a perfect match. You can substitute ¼-inch splines if necessary.

After the frame parts are cut, apply glue, insert the splines, then clamp, making sure the frame is square.

Cut the floor board from a piece of ¾-inch fir plywood, then drill the screw clearance holes as in the layout.

The uprights consist of two outer members which measure 20 × 39¾ inches. The inner uprights are cut 19¾ × 39 inches and the lower front edges are notched to fit over the lower rail. Before assembly, cut the ¼- × -⅜-inch rabbets along the rear edges of the two outer panels. Assemble the parts using 2-inch screws except at the top outside, where 3½-inch screws are needed. Fit the rail into place, applying a little glue at the notches. Use glue at the other joints also.

The drawer compartment frames are prepared next. These are cut from ¾-inch plywood. Before cutting the five pieces for the front of the frames, apply the matching wood tape to an 8-foot length of the ripped (2-inch) stock, then cut apart into the individual pieces. These frames are fastened with splines. Before assembling, drill the holes for the screws into the frame sides. Assemble with 2½-inch round-head (RH) screws.

The top is cut to size and edged at the ends and front with ⅝- × -¾-inch nose-and-cove oak molding. Fasten the molding with glue and wire brads. Miter the molding at the ends. If your molding is too short to make the length, use a scarf joint to join the two pieces as shown. Hold the molding

at the mounting angle when cutting the scarf joint and miters. This is especially important when mitering the crown molding at the base.

The top is fastened by driving screws through the top frame. Use 1¼-inch flat-head (FH) screws.

The base consists of the two ends and front, which are mitered and splined. These are then fastened to the bottom board with cleats. The rear base piece is mounted separately without a cleat.

A clamp nail was used for the mitered joints because they pull the joint tight and are far superior to using wood splines. To make the joint, cut the 45-degree miters in the usual manner using the radial arm saw or table saw. Now replace the regular blade with a 22-gauge blade which is made especially for clamp nails. Make the cuts 5/16 inch deep, then join as shown. Be sure to insert the wide or flared end of the clamp nail into the kerf cuts, then drive the nail home with a few hammer blows. Also be sure to apply glue to the mitered surfaces before nailing. Assemble the base with cleats as indicated.

The crown molding is cut to fit, then fastened with glue. Use glue only at the bottom surface as shown. Note that crown moldings are designed with a clearance angle at the back and bottom. If you place a square against the back and bottom, you will note that the angle formed is not 90 degrees, but closer to 112 degrees. This is intentional.

The runners for the pull-out drawers are cut to size and shape as per the drawing. The outer corners are then rounded using a router. Install using round-head screws.

The pull-out drawers are made of ½-inch birch plywood. Cut the members to

Fig. 24-13(A). These optional spring-loaded drawer stops will effectively prevent the drawers from being pulled out too far accidentally.

Fig. 24-13(B). A view of the assembled wardrobe with some of the drawers removed. Leave the back panel off until interior is finished.

size, then rabbet the front and rear panels to take the sides. Cut the ¼-inch groove ⅝ inch from the bottom. Then, before assembling, use the router with a ³⁄₁₆-inch rounding bit to round all top edges. Stop the routing just short of the ends at the insides of the side panels. See detail. Cut the bottom panels to size and insert into place as you assemble the sides, front and rear. Apply glue to the joints and fasten with brads. Do not glue the bottom panel.

The center drawers are also made with ½-inch birch, but they have an additional front made of oak plywood to match the rest of the cabinet.

The grooves and rabbets are similar to the pull-out drawers, but at the rear, the side panels are dadoed since the rear panel is set back ½ inch. The other difference

is that the bottom panel is installed after assembly, and nailed to the bottom of the rear panel.

The subfront is drilled for the two clearance holes and the four mounting holes. The clearance holes are necessary so the drawer pulls can be mounted from inside the drawer. The mounting holes are for the 1-inch screws which fasten the front to the subfront.

The raised panel effect is achieved by the application of molding at the edges of the front panel. Miter these at the corners and fasten with glue only—no brads. Apply the glue with a small brush to the backs of the molding as well as the mitered ends.

The drawer slide is made of hardwood. The ¹³⁄₁₆-inch groove is cut ¼ inch deep using a dado blade. The ¹³⁄₁₆-inch width allows ¹⁄₁₆-inch overall clearance over the ¾-inch wide drawer guide. Center the slide at the bottom of the drawer and fasten with glue.

Each door frame consists of two stiles and four rails. These are fastened with splined joints, and a ¼-inch oak plywood backing is then fastened to the frame. Finally, nose-and-cove molding is mitered and glued into each of the openings for the raised panel effect.

The ¼-inch panel is fastened to the frame with glue and brads. Keep the brads away from the edges which will be rabbeted. The rabbeting can be done with a router or on the table saw using a dado blade or by making two passes using a regular cutting blade.

The doors are hung with non-mortise offset hinges, two per door. A ⁵⁄₁₆-inch hole for the pendant pull is drilled on the inside stiles.

An adjustable magnetic catch is used to hold the door closed. Place the catch in

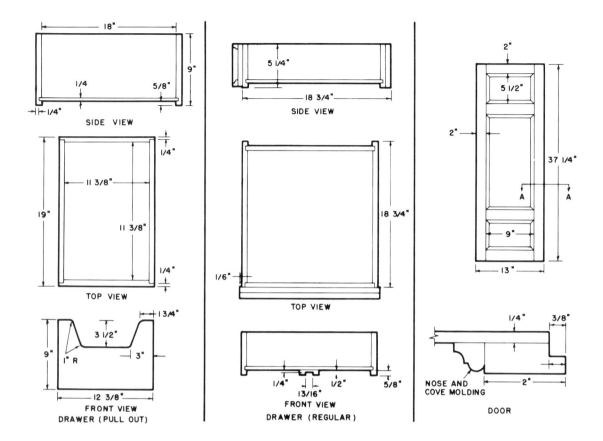

SIDE VIEW

TOP VIEW

FRONT VIEW
DRAWER (PULL OUT)

SIDE VIEW

TOP VIEW

FRONT VIEW
DRAWER (REGULAR)

NOSE AND
COVE MOLDING

DOOR

line with the upper pull-out drawer guide so it will not interfere with the operation of the drawers.

The ¼-inch rear panel is installed using ⅝-inch round-head screws. Do not install the panel until the staining and topcoating operations are completed. With the back panel off, you will be able to finish inside the cabinet from front and rear.

The finishing operation consists of an application of paste wood filler, followed by two coats of sanding sealer and three coats of semigloss lacquer. After a one-week drying time, a final application of rubbing compound is made.

The filler is thinned to a consistency of heavy cream (*not* whipped cream). It should be brushed on with the grain. In a matter of minutes it will start to flatten and appear dull. When this happens, start to remove the surplus filler by wiping across the grain of the wood, using coarse rags—preferably burlap. Finish wiping with clean soft rags, stroking with the grain direction. Allow to dry, then apply the sealer. When the sealer has dried, apply the topcoats of gloss or semigloss lacquer.

MATERIALS LIST

Purpose	Size	Description	Quantity
Cabinet			
Upright, outer	¾″ × 20″ × 39¾″	Oak plywood	2
Upright, inner	¾″ × 19¾″ × 39″	Fir plywood	2
Top	¾″ × 20½″ × 47″	Oak plywood	1
Top frame end	¾″ × 3″ × 14″	Fir plywood	2
Top frame front/rear	¾″ × 3″ × 44½″	Fir plywood	2
Bottom	¾″ × 21³⁄₁₆″ × 48⅜″	Fir plywood	1
Base front	¾″ × 4½″ × 49⅞″	Oak plywood	1
Base end	¾″ × 4½″ × 21¹⁵⁄₁₆″	Oak plywood	2
Base rear	¾″ × 3¾″ × 48⅜″	Fir plywood	1
Rear panel	¼″ × 39¹¹⁄₁₆″ × 45³⁄₁₆″	Fir plywood	1
Cleat, front	¾″ × 1½″ × 48″	Pine	1
Cleat, end	¾″ × 1½″ × 19″	Pine	2
Frame front/rear	¾″ × 2″ × 18″	Fir plywood	12
Frame, side	¾″ × 2″ × 15¾″	Fir plywood	12
Drawer guide	⁷⁄₁₆″ × ¾″ × 18¾″	Solid oak	6
Pull-out guide	¾″ × ¾″ × 18″	Solid oak	8
Pull-out guide, lower	¾″ × 2⁵⁄₁₆″ × 19″	Solid oak	2
Apron	¾″ × 2¼″ × 44½″	Oak plywood	1
Shelf	¾″ × 12⅜″ × 18½″	Oak plywood	2
Door			
Stile	¾″ × 2″ × 37¼″	Oak plywood	4
Rail	¾″ × 2″ × 9″	Oak plywood	8
Door panel	¼″ × 13″ × 37¼″	Oak plywood	2
Drawer (pull out)			
Side	½″ × 9″ × 19″	Birch plywood	12
Front/rear	½″ × 9″ × 12⅜″	Birch plywood	12
Bottom	¼″ × 11¹³⁄₁₆″ × 18⁷⁄₁₆″	Fir plywood	6
Drawer (regular)			
Side	½″ × 5¼″ × 18¾″	Birch plywood	12
Subfront	½″ × 5¼″ × 17¼″	Birch plywood	6
Rear	½″ × 4⅜″ × 17¼″	Birch plywood	6
Front	¾″ × 5⅜″ × 17⅞″	Oak plywood	6
Bottom	¼″ × 17³⁄₁₆″ × 17¾″	Fir plywood	6
Slide	½″ × 2¼″ × 18″	Solid oak	6
Miscellaneous			
Molding, nose and cove	⅝″ × ¾″	Oak	48 ft.
Molding, crown	2½″	Oak	11 ft.
Screw	⅝″—5 RH		16
Screw	3½″—10 RH		20
Screw	1″—8 FH		8
Screw	2″—10 RH		38
Screw	2½″—10 RH		20
Screw	1¼″—8 RH		8

Brad	1″	No. 18	36
Nail	1½″		144
Pull, Chippendale		(No. 70002)	6
Pull, Pendant		(No. 70008)	2
Glue			8 oz.
Wood Tape		Oak type	16 ft.
Hinges, Non-Mortise		(No. 78006)	4
Magnetic Catch		(No. 75002)	2
Shelf Bracket		(No. 77504)	8
Spline	⅛″ × ½″ × 2″	Gum plywood	36
Clamp nail	4″		2

Note: Items enclosed in parentheses are available from Armor Products, P.O. Box 445, East Northport, NY 11731.

Home Office

THIS HIDEAWAY HOME OFFICE is an unobtrusive piece of furniture when closed, but open the two doors and—presto!—you have a large size writing desk, filing space and ample storage. Everything is within easy reach so you can handle the complexities of bills, taxes, credit accounts, and other chores common to all householders.

The size of the cabinet when closed is $20 \times 30 \times 50\frac{1}{2}$ inches. When open, it measures $30 \times 60 \times 50\frac{1}{2}$ inches. The desk surface is 21×56 inches. A unique method is used to support the flaps of the desk: a pin located on the door shelf engages a matching hole in the desk flap. This rigidly supports the flap and locks the door in the open position. Flip-top hinges enable the flaps to fold onto the main desk section: all

can then fold up compactly. Two retractable supports add to the sturdiness of this piece.

Lumber used for this project was $\frac{1}{4}$-, $\frac{1}{2}$-, and $\frac{3}{4}$-inch plywood. Some solid lumber is also utilized. The most difficult part of this project is the mitering of the panels to form the cabinet and doors. All other construction is rather basic and easy to do.

Oak plywood was used in construction but other species may be substituted. Rip the panels to size as shown in the Materials List, then proceed to miter the ends. The mitered joint may be made in several ways, either on the table saw using saw and router, or with the shaper. Choose the method best suited to your equipment and skill. We used the offset miter, which

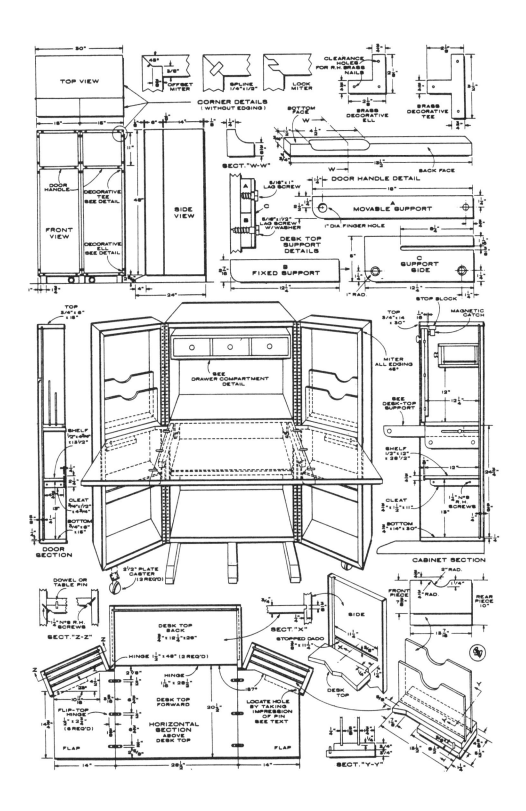

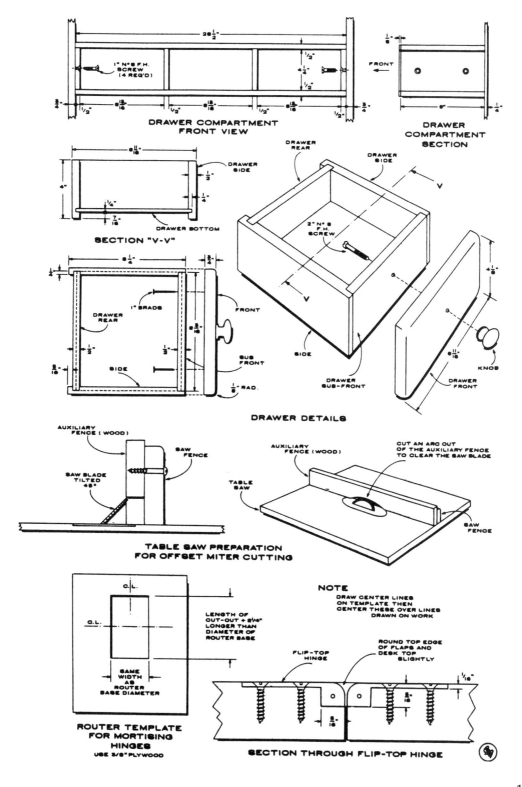

DRAWER COMPARTMENT
FRONT VIEW

DRAWER
COMPARTMENT
SECTION

SECTION "V-V"

DRAWER DETAILS

TABLE SAW PREPARATION
FOR OFFSET MITER CUTTING

ROUTER TEMPLATE
FOR MORTISING
HINGES
USE 3/8" PLYWOOD

NOTE
DRAW CENTER LINES
ON TEMPLATE THEN
CENTER THESE OVER LINES
DRAWN ON WORK

SECTION THROUGH FLIP-TOP HINGE

163

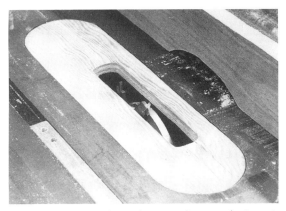

Fig. 25-1. Wide-slot plywood insert replaces regular insert in table saw. Wobble head is used to rabbet panels. Alternative cutting methods are shown in detail drawing.

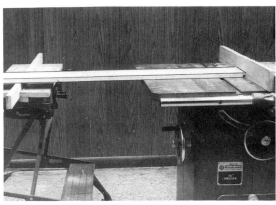

Fig. 25-2. Support is needed for long sides when you are rabbeting them on table saw. Workmate is used here. Wax on the saw table allows the work to slide easily.

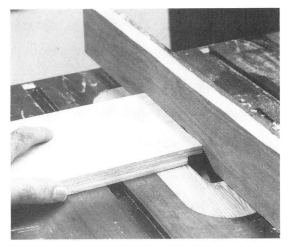

Fig. 25-3. Auxiliary wood fence and the regular saw blade are used to rabbet vertical members (cabinet and door sides). Note arc cut in fence so that it clears saw blade.

Fig. 25-4. Saw blade at 45 degrees is used to make the angle cuts; broken lines indicate the miters here. This joint offers good gluing surface, and keeps corners square.

consists of a miter with a rabbet, but two other methods are shown in the detail: the lock miter and the spline joint. The lock miter should be done with a shaper or router using a matched set of cutters. The spline can be done on the table saw.

To make the offset miter, cut a ⅜- × -¾ -inch rabbet across the ends of the top and bottom panels and the four top and bottom door panels (two tops, two bottoms), using a dado head. Use a Rockwell wobble head for a very accurate cut.

When the tops and bottoms are rabbeted, reset the blade or fence, then proceed to make a ⅜- × -⅜-inch rabbet at the ends of the six vertical members (two cabinet sides and four door sides). Now remove the dado blade and replace it with the regular saw blade, set to an angle of 45 degrees. For this operation, an auxiliary

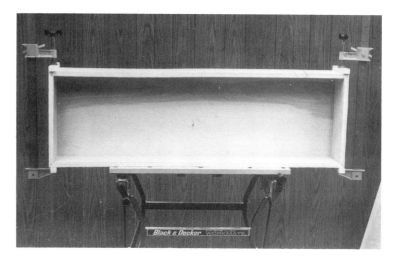

Fig. 25-5. After ¼-inch slot has been cut for rear panel, the panel is installed and cabinet is clamped up on short ends until glue sets. Rear panel floats free in slots.

Fig. 25-6. Closeup of mitered corner; miters should close flush with no space at the joint. In this photo, a wood scrap protects the work from clamp damage while glue sets.

Fig. 25-7. Stopped dado, which will accept the desk top, is cut with a router. Side glides, for accuracy with the router, will be removed later. Study drawings carefully.

wood fence must be fastened to the metal saw fence (most fences are provided with holes for this purpose); simply screw it to the fence as shown in the detail. Before mounting the wood fence, cut an arc out of the piece to clear the saw blade. With the blade set at 45 degrees, adjust the fence to make the angle cuts—and be sure to make them accurately. (See detail.)

The advantage of this joint is that it provides plenty of gluing surface and it helps keep the corners square.

After all miters have been made, cut the stopped dado for the desk piece and the ¼- × -¼-inch groove at the rear of the cabinet members and at the front of the door members. The groove is placed ⅝-inch from the edges. The ¼-inch plywood panels are placed in the grooves and the ends, top and bottom are assembled dry to check the fit: miters should close flush with no space at the joints. If the fit's okay, install the desk piece and other members, apply glue to the miters and clamp

Fig. 25-8. With router guides removed, fit of rabbeted desk top to stopped dado is tested by designer in this photograph. For professional job, fit should be precise.

Fig. 25-9. Though veneer tape can be used to correct exposed plywood edges, solid strips are recommended. Here they are ripped from solid stock. Each strip is ⅛ inch by ¾ inch.

Fig. 25-10. Ends of the strips are mitered and each piece is carefully fitted. Apply glue to the plywood edge and strip and fasten with brads. See text regarding edging brads.

Fig. 25-11. Make pilot holes for hinges slightly under screw size with portable drill; then attach hinge temporarily with end screws for check before proceeding with balance.

Fig. 25-12. Cutting squares for the handles (refer to drawings). Note push stick in photo.

Fig. 25-13. Base pieces are cut from thick stock and then rounded with the router. Round ends where base meets the cabinet, as indicated by pencil in this photograph.

Fig. 25-14. With base pieces attached, casters can be installed with adequate clearance from center base piece. If necessary, you can use shims under caster plates.

securely. *Note:* do not glue in the ¼-inch panel. This should be made to float in the frame or cabinet. The same procedure is followed in making the doors.

Remember when applying clamps to protect the work by using cauls (strips of wood) under the clamps. With the ¼-inch panels in place, the glued-up assembly should be square, but be sure to check for squareness with a large square before the glue sets. Adjust as necessary.

All exposed plywood edges must be concealed. This can be done with veneer tape or with a solid band. The solid band will stand up better and is therefore recommended. Rip the strips from solid stock, making each strip ⅛ × ¾ inches. Let the ends slightly extend the piece to be edged, then measure the pieces carefully and miter the ends. Fit each piece individually, apply glue to the plywood edge and to the back of the band, then fasten with brads.

You can use ordinary brads but "Beauty Brads," especially made for applying molding and edging, are recommended. These very thin brads are made of hardened steel, have no heads, and do not require setting as an ordinary brad does. In use, they are driven into the work

167

Fig. 25-15. Jig made from ⅜-inch plywood is used to mortise desk top for hinges. Flap and desk top must be butted for this operation. Use a ½-inch straight cutter in router.

Fig. 25-16. In its retracted position, the desk support clears flap support permitting the door to close. In use, the finger hole is employed to pull out the support for solidity.

Fig. 25-17. Partially completed drawer. When assembling, insert bottom panel, then glue and brad sides to the subfront and rear. Fronts are fastened in the same way.

Fig. 25-18. Drawer compartment is constructed of ½-inch plywood with butt joints, as indicated in drawing. Oak edging, ½ inch wide, mitered at ends, is applied to plywood.

leaving about ¼ inch exposed, then are snapped across the grain with a hammer blow to the side. The brad will snap slightly below the surface, thus eliminating the need for setting. Also, the hole left is so small that the finishing materials will usually fill it.

The desktop and flaps are cut as indicated, then the three are placed on a flat surface and the hinge locations are laid out. The hinges used are the flip-top type which permits the flaps to flop 180 degrees. The hinges are ½ inch wide and 2¾ inch-

es long and must be mortised so the tops are flush with the desk top. Use a router fitted with a ½-inch straight cutter.

To ensure accuracy and uniformity, you should use a jig (the one shown is made of ⅜-inch plywood). Make the width of the opening equal to the diameter of the router base and the length of the cutout 2¼ inches longer than the diameter of the router base. Note that the hinge is deeper at the center, thus you will have to mortise this part deeper for clearance.

The flaps and desktop must be aligned

at the front edge when cutting the mortise. The rear edges of the flaps must match the shelf when the doors are swung open 157 degrees. Because of possible discrepancies, you may have to rework the rear flap edges to obtain a good fit. You can check this after the side doors are hung.

The piano hinges for the doors measure $1\frac{1}{2} \times 48$ inches and the desk hinge measures $1\frac{1}{16} \times 28\frac{1}{2}$ inches. Install the end and center screws on all hinges and check the fit. If the fit's okay, install the rest of the screws. The plate casters are used under the doors to help take some stress off the door hinges. The casters are installed after the cabinet is mounted onto the base pieces. The base piece height should be the same as the caster height measured from the bottom of the wheel to the top of the plate.

To support the desk flaps, a projection on the door shelves is provided. A locating pin on the shelf prevents the door from swinging away from the flap, which would leave the flap unsupported and place a great strain on the flip-top hinges. Therefore, it is important that whenever the desktop flaps are extended, they must rest on the shelf support provided.

The pins are installed on the shelves as shown. To locate the holes on the underside of the flaps, lower the flaps into place and let the pin point mark the location. A piece of carbon paper placed carbon-side-up on the pin will leave a distinct mark.

The rails near the top of the door fronts serve to break up the monotony of the plain doors and also serve as door pulls. Finger clearance is provided in each piece toward the center. Installed after the staining and finishing operations are completed, they are held firmly by the decorative Tees. No other support is necessary. The finger clearance can be made with a router or shaper. If the proper cutter is not available, you can use a chisel to cut the clearance.

The drawer compartment and drawers are first cut as indicated. The compartment is made of $\frac{1}{2}$-inch plywood with butt joints and oak edging ripped to $\frac{1}{2}$-inch widths is used to conceal the plywood edge. When assembling the drawers, insert the bottom panel, then glue and brad the sides to the subfront and rear. The drawer fronts are fastened to the subfronts with glue and brads. Install the door shelves and large shelf with screws driven through the cleats.

This completes construction. Stain and finish as desired. Try Golden Oak paste wood filler followed by sanding sealer, then clear lacquer. The paste filler stains and fills the open pores of the oak in one operation. In use, the filler is thinned with benzine to the consistency of heavy cream, then is brushed on with the grain. When it starts to set (about 10 minutes) it is rubbed off across the grain using burlap or excelsior. This will work the filler into the pores leaving a smooth surface. Do not do too large an area at one time, for once the filler has set it will be difficult to remove.

Allow the work to dry overnight before applying the sealer coat. Before the sealer is applied, very lightly sand the filled wood then dust with a tac cloth. An informative booklet called Professional Wood Finishing is available for $2.00 postpaid from Armor Products, P.O. Box 290, Deer Park, NY 11729.

When finishing is completed, add the decorative corners and Tees, magnetic catches and brass pulls. The desk supports are also fastened using $1\frac{1}{2}$-inch lag screws.

MATERIALS LIST

Except as noted, lumber used is ¾" oak plywood. Oak, when specified after the measurement signifies solid oak.

Purpose	Size	Description	Quantity
Side	¾" × 14" × 48"		2
Top	¾" × 14" × 30"		1
Bottom	¾" × 14" × 30"		1
Rear	¼" × 29" × 47"	Oak plywood	1
Desktop rear	¾" × 12¼" × 29"		1
Shelf	½" × 12" × 28½"	Oak plywood	1
Shelf edge	⅛" × ¾" × 28½"	Oak	1
Shelf cleat	¾" × 1½" × 11"	Oak	2
Stop	¼" × ¾" × 3½"	Oak	1
Base	1¾" × 2⅝" × 24"		3
Desktop forward	¾" × 20½" × 28¼"		1
Flap	¾" × 14" × 19¼"		2
Support, movable	¾" × 2½" × 18"	Oak	2
Support, fixed	¾" × 2⁷⁄₁₆" × 12¼"	Oak	2
Support, side	¼" × 5" × 12¼"	Plywood	2
Drawer box top	½" × 9" × 28½"	Oak plywood	1
Drawer box bottom	½" × 9" × 28½"	Oak plywood	1
Drawer box side	½" × 4¼" × 9"	Oak plywood	4
Drawer rear	½" × 4" × 8³⁄₁₆"	Oak plywood	3
Drawer subfront	½" × 4" × 8³⁄₁₆"	Oak plywood	3
Drawer front	¾" × 4⅛" × 8¹¹⁄₁₆"	Oak plywood	3
Drawer side	½" × 4" × 8¼"	Oak plywood	6
Drawer bottom	¼" × 7⁷⁄₁₆" × 8³⁄₁₆"	Oak plywood	3
Door side	¾" × 6" × 48"		4
Door top	¾" × 6" × 15"		2
Door bottom	¾" × 6" × 15"		2
Door front	¼" × 14" × 47"		2
Door handle	¾" × ¾" × 13½"		2
Door shelf	¾" × 5¼" × 13½"		2
Separator front	¼" × 7⅜" × 13⁷⁄₁₆"	Oak plywood	2
Separator rear	¼" × 10" × 13⁷⁄₁₆"	Oak plywood	2
Flap support	¾" × 5½" × 8½"		2
Pin	⁵⁄₁₆" × 1"	Dowel	2
Shelf lower	½" × 4¾" × 13½"		2
Shelf edge	¼" × 2¼" × 13½"	Oak plywood	2
Shelf cleat	¾" × 1½" × 4¾"		4
Plywood edging	⅛" × ¾"	Oak	65′
Hinge door	1½" × 48"		2
Hinge desk	1¹⁄₁₆" × 28½"		1
Hinge, flip-top	½" × 2¾" (FTT)		6
Corner	(AC)		8
Tee	(AT)		4
Knob	(Knob)		5
Magnetic catch	(PM)		2
Caster, plate	2½"		2
Screw	1½" × 8 RH		20
Screw	1" × 8 FH		8
Lag screw	⁵⁄₁₆" × 1"		2
Lag screw	⁵⁄₁₆" × 1½"		4
Beauty Brads	(BBDS)		1 pk.
Brads	1"		12

Note: Items in parentheses are available from Armor Products, Box 290, Deer Park, NY 11729.

Lightweight Desk

BUILDING THIS handsome desk is a project that any good craftsman can undertake with confidence. The design could be modified, if so desired, by substituting drawers for a cabinet on the pier.

Start construction by edge-gluing 1-inch stock birch from the top. Clamp and let dry, then plane all the joints and sand to a smooth finish. Cut the shape of the top with a band saw or saber saw, then sand all edges smooth. Next glue-up the stock for the pier section, and sand and plane it. Cut to size, then cut rabbet on bottom edge of sides and back and on back edges of sides. Cut a bottom piece to fit in the rabbet.

Bore upper cleats for No. 10 1½-inch flat-head wood screws, then glue and screw cleats in place, setting them in 1/16 inch from the edges so that when pieces are assembled they will draw up tight at the joints. Assemble the pier section with glue and screws, squaring assembly and then fastening bottom in place with screws.

Install a shelf in the pier section, and hang the door on butt cabinet hinges, with a magnetic catch and brass knob. Cut the pier base pieces to size, mitering corner joints. Bore for No. 11 1½-inch flat-head screws, apply glue, and assemble with corner blocks, making sure it is square. Now fasten base to pier.

Cut the stock for the leg assembly and stretchers. Bore holes for 7/16-inch dowels 2 inches long. Assemble with glue, clamping until glue has set. Remove clamps and plane and sand all joints flush,

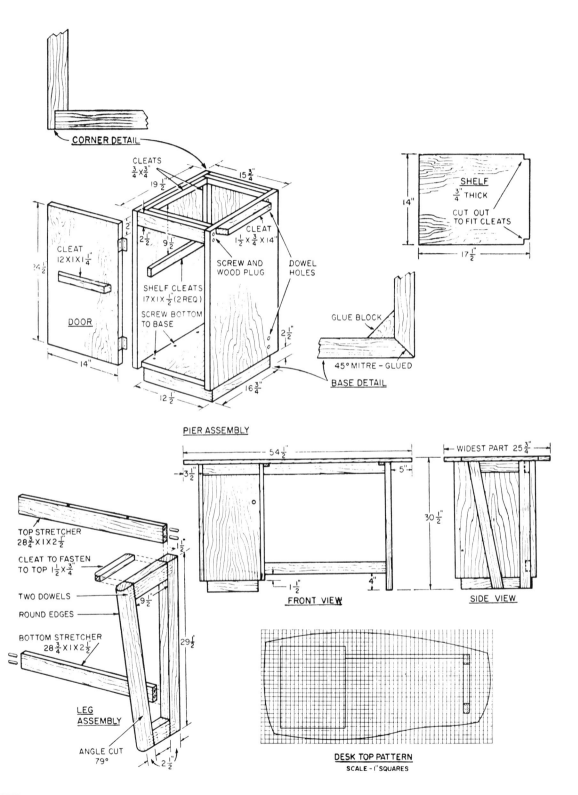

CORNER DETAIL

CLEATS $\frac{3}{4} \times \frac{3}{4}$

19$\frac{1}{2}$

15$\frac{3}{4}$"

2"

2$\frac{1}{2}$"

9$\frac{1}{2}$"

CLEAT $1\frac{1}{2} \times \frac{3}{4} \times 14$"

SCREW AND WOOD PLUG

DOWEL HOLES

SHELF $\frac{3}{4}$" THICK

CUT OUT TO FIT CLEATS

14"

17$\frac{1}{2}$"

CLEAT 12 X I X I$\frac{1}{4}$

26$\frac{1}{2}$

DOOR

SHELF CLEATS 17 X I X $\frac{1}{2}$ (2 REQ)

SCREW BOTTOM TO BASE

14"

12$\frac{1}{2}$

16$\frac{3}{4}$"

2$\frac{1}{2}$"

GLUE BLOCK

45° MITRE - GLUED

BASE DETAIL

PIER ASSEMBLY

54$\frac{1}{2}$"

WIDEST PART 25$\frac{3}{4}$"

3$\frac{1}{2}$"

5"

30$\frac{1}{2}$"

1$\frac{1}{2}$"

4"

FRONT VIEW

SIDE VIEW

TOP STRETCHER 28$\frac{3}{4}$ X I X 2$\frac{1}{2}$

CLEAT TO FASTEN TO TOP I$\frac{1}{2}$ X $\frac{3}{4}$"

TWO DOWELS

ROUND EDGES

9$\frac{1}{2}$"

I$\frac{1}{2}$"

BOTTOM STRETCHER 28$\frac{3}{4}$ X I X 2$\frac{1}{2}$

29$\frac{1}{2}$

LEG ASSEMBLY

ANGLE CUT 79°

2$\frac{1}{2}$

DESK TOP PATTERN

SCALE - I" SQUARES

MATERIALS LIST

Purpose	Size	Description	Quantity
Top	1″ × 12″ × 12′	Birch stock	1
Pier and shelf	¾″ × 12″ × 10′	Birch stock	1
Stretchers	1″ × 2½″ × 60′	Birch	1
Support	1½″ × 2½″ × 80″	Birch	1
Dowels	2″ × ⁷⁄₁₆″		16
Wood screws	1¼″	No. 10 FH	as needed
Wood screws	1½″	No. 11 FH	as needed
Wood screws	2½″	No. 10 FH	as needed

then round the front edge of the leg. Fasten a cleat to the top piece of the leg for fastening to the top.

Bore two holes through the top stretcher for No. 10 2½-inch flat-head screws. Plane and sand stretchers. Bore holes for ⁷⁄₁₆-inch dowels in stretchers, pier, and leg, place glue in holes and assemble pier, leg, and stretchers. Clamp square in all directions.

Place the top upside down, then place the leg and pier assembly on the top. Square and fasten all cleats and the upper stretcher to top, then sand again. Stain to the desired shade, apply a coat of sealer, sand lightly, and apply a finish coat of lacquer.

The trim, modern appearance of this desk will make it a welcome piece of furniture as well as a useful accessory in the living room, bedroom, or den.

Magazine Table

YOU DON'T NEED any fancy equipment to build this fine magazine end table. The Italian provincial legs look difficult to build but indeed they are not. A glance at the drawing reveals that they are built up using a technique called post blocking. This eliminates the almost impossible task of accurately cutting the narrow section between posts with conventional home shop equipment. A simple method of fluting the legs is also utilized to further enhance the project.

Lumber used was pine, but any suitable wood will do. For a stained or natural finish, you may want to try mahogany, cherry or maple. Walnut may also be used—if you can get it. This fine cabinet wood is becoming rare.

Start construction with the legs. These are cut from 2-inch stock. Set the table saw fence for a 1⅝-inch cut then rip the stock to produce a block 1⅝ inches square. After cutting, sand the surfaces or, if you have a jointer, run a pass on each surface to eliminate the kerf marks of the saw. If the jointer is to be used, make the saw cut a trifle more than 1⅝ inches to allow for stock removal on the jointer. After ripping and smoothing the surface, cut the legs to size and taper the lower ends.

The best way to taper the legs is to use a jig on the table saw. The jig consists of a piece of plywood notched out to hold a leg. The notch is positioned at an angle so that when the jig with a leg in place is fed through the saw, a thin wedge section is ripped off the end of the leg. Repeat this operation on all four sides to produce the tapered leg. The angle of the notch determines the amount of taper. This setup can be used for other projects where numerous tapered cuts are required.

The next step is the fluting of the legs. Here again a jig is used for both accuracy and simplicity. The router is mounted to a wooden platform which converts it to a mini shaper. The cutter is made to protrude through the top of the platform to which a fence has been attached. The work is simply held against the fence and fed through

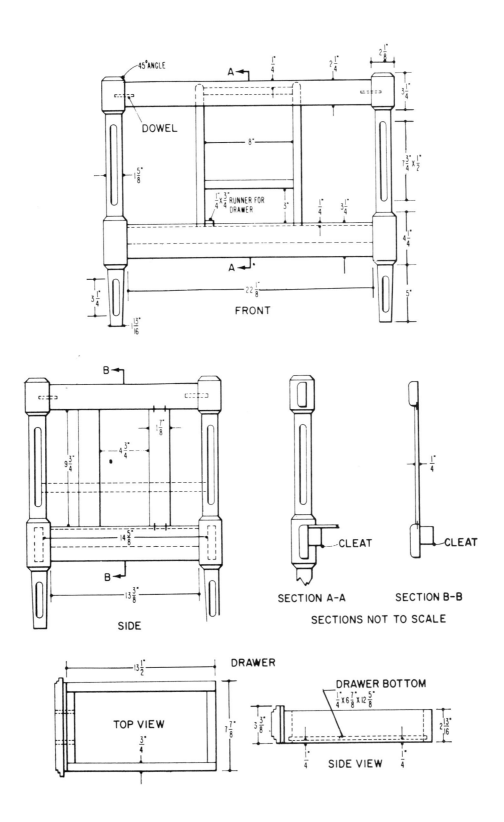

45° ANGLE

DOWEL

A

1/4" 2 1/4" 2 1/8"

3 1/4"

8"

7 3/4" X 1/2"

1 5/8"

1/4" X 3/4" RUNNER FOR DRAWER

3" 1/4" 3 1/4"

4 1/4"

A

22 1/8"

3 1/4"

5"

1 13/16"

FRONT

B

1 7/8"

4 3/4"

9 3/4"

14 5/8"

B

13 3/8"

SIDE

CLEAT

CLEAT

1/4"

SECTION A-A   SECTION B-B

SECTIONS NOT TO SCALE

DRAWER

13 1/2"

TOP VIEW

3/4"

7 7/8"

DRAWER BOTTOM

1/4" X 6 7/8" X 12 5/8"

3 3/8"

2 13/16"

1/4"   SIDE VIEW   1/4"

175

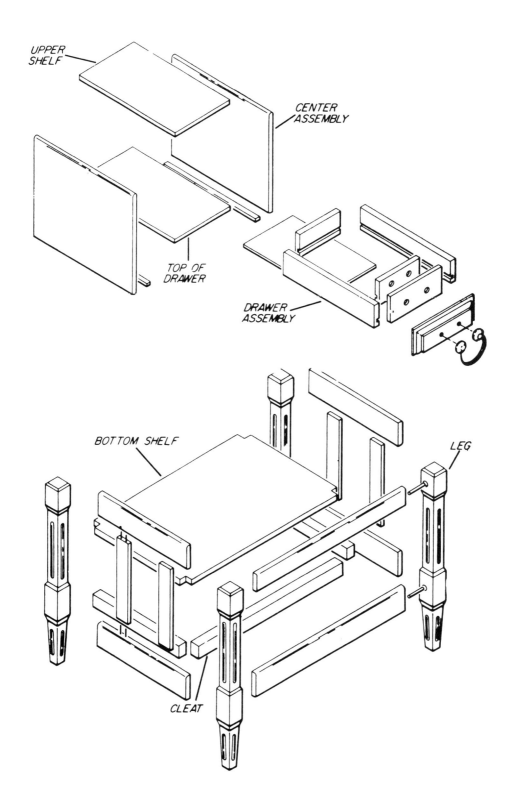

UPPER SHELF

CENTER ASSEMBLY

TOP OF DRAWER

DRAWER ASSEMBLY

BOTTOM SHELF

LEG

CLEAT

176

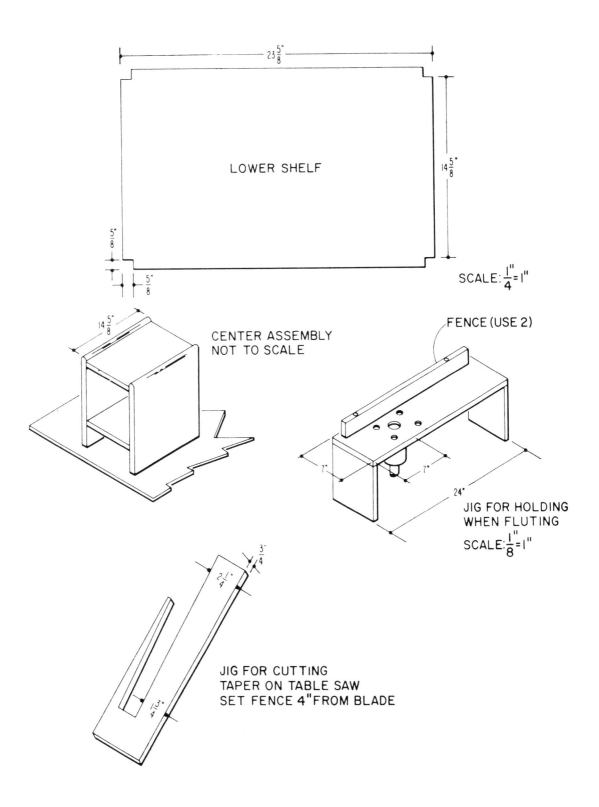

$23\frac{5}{8}"$

LOWER SHELF

$14\frac{5}{8}"$

$\frac{5}{8}"$

$\frac{5}{8}"$

SCALE: $\frac{1"}{4}=1"$

$14\frac{5}{8}"$

CENTER ASSEMBLY
NOT TO SCALE

FENCE (USE 2)

7"

7"

24"

JIG FOR HOLDING
WHEN FLUTING

SCALE: $\frac{1"}{8}=1"$

$\frac{3"}{4}$

$2\frac{1}{4}"$

$4\frac{3}{4}"$

JIG FOR CUTTING
TAPER ON TABLE SAW
SET FENCE 4"FROM BLADE

Fig. 27-1. To taper leg ends, use a table saw jig. Jig is positioned so that the saw blade cuts the leg block at a slight angle.

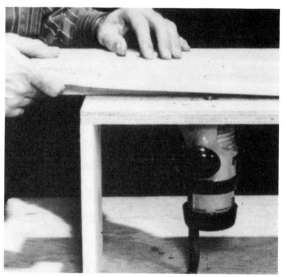

Fig. 27-2. To produce leg fluting, mount router on a frame. Lower work onto cutter, using marks to show where to start and stop.

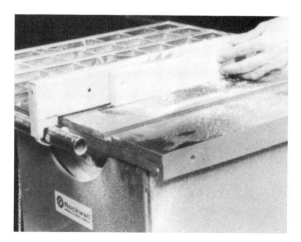

Fig. 27-3. Blocks which will be used to build up legs are ripped from a piece of ¾-inch stick. Cut or sand ends to 45-degree angle.

Fig. 27-4. The legs are built up by attaching the cut and beveled pieces. To attach, use glue, and then clamp for a good bond.

Fig. 27-5. The apron pieces are joined to the legs with dowels. Use dowel locating pins to accurately transfer the hole positions.

Fig. 27-6. The next step is to cut the lower shelf and then install using cleats on underside. Attach it with dowels to legs.

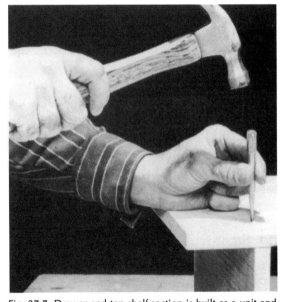

Fig. 27-7. Drawer and top shelf section is built as a unit and installed separately. Assemble with nails, sinking the heads.

the cutter resulting in a flute (or flutes) being cut.

All routers have a removable base plate. The plate is usually held with four screws. Carefully remove these and set aside. Place the plate on a piece of plywood and use a pencil to locate the mounting holes as well as the center opening. Drill the holes for the screws countersinking the heads. The center hole should be large enough to clear the cutter being used. See the drawing for clarification. Make the legs

179

Fig. 27-8. Make drawer with a double front and be sure to make screw clearance holes in subfront so hardware can be installed.

of the platform tall enough so that the bottom of the router will clear the workbench.

Mount the flute cutter in the router, then, using the four screws removed from the router base previously, mount the router in place. Position the fence so that the flute will fall exactly in the center of the leg. Although only one fence is shown for clarity in the photograph, a double fence is recommended to keep the workpiece from swaying.

Some routers are not made with lock-on switches—especially the pistol-grip type. If you have one of these, you will have to have an assistant turn on the power as needed, or you can improvise by taping the switch "on" with masking tape. You can then operate the machine by using the plug as a switch. If you use this method, be sure to remove the tape as soon as the job is done.

Since the flutes are "blind" (they do not run off the edge of the work), you will

have to lower the work onto the cutter and likewise lift it off at the end of the cut. Do this by placing "start" and "stop" marks on the jig. Determine the location of these by making trial cuts in scrap wood the same length as the legs.

Blocking is the next step. Saw ¼-inch-wide strips from suitable stock, then rip two widths. Half the pieces will be ripped 1⅝ inches wide and the rest 2⅛ inches wide. Cut the lengths to size as indicated then bevel the edges on the sander. Set the table for a 45-degree bevel then just touch the work to the disc to produce the bevel. If you do not have a sander, use the table saw to make the bevel.

Glue the strips to the legs as shown. The narrow pieces are installed first. To keep the pieces from shifting, snip the ends of 18 gauge brads so the pointed end is about ¼ inch long. Use a plier to drive the blunt end into the leg leaving just the point protruding. Use two brads per section and hold the pieces with clamps while the glue sets. The wide strips are installed last.

When all the legs have been glued, use a knife or chisel to bevel the square corners of the blocks.

Cut the upper and lower apron pieces to size then round off the edges with the router fitted with a rounding cutter. Note that three edges are rounded on the upper pieces and only two on the lower.

Cut the four slats to size and round off the edges. Again using the blind brad technique, install the slats to the upper and lower apron ends. This time make the brads longer (about ½ inch) and allow them to protrude about ¼ inch. Apply glue and working on a flat surface, bring the parts together. Clamp until the glue sets.

The apron pieces are joined to the legs with dowels. One dowel in each section

MATERIALS LIST

All lumber used is pine (except where noted).

Purpose	Size	Quantity
Lower shelf	¾″ × 14⅝″ × 23⅜″	1
Cleats	¾″ × 1″ × 12″	2
Cleats	¾″ × 1″ × 21″	2
Apron (lower)	¾″ × 3¼″ × 22⅛″	2
End apron (lower)	¾″ × 3¼″ × 13⅜″	2
Apron (upper)	¾″ × 2¼″ × 22⅛″	2
End apron (upper)	¾″ × 2¼″ × 13⅜″	2
Legs	1⅝″ × 1⅝″ × 21½″	4
Blocks	¼″ × 1⅝″ × 3¼″	8
Blocks	¼″ × 2⅛″ × 3¼″	8
Blocks	¼″ × 1⅝″ × 4¼″	8
Blocks	¼″ × 2⅛″ × 4¼″	8
Slats	¼″ × 1⅞″ × 9¾″	4
Compartment slides	¾″ × 12″ × 14⅝″	2
Upper shelf	¾″ × 8″ × 14⅝″	1
Drawer roof	¾″ × 8″ × 14⅝″	1
Drawer sides	¾″ × 2¹³⁄₁₆″ × 13½″	2
Drawer ends	¾″ × 2¹³⁄₁₆″ × 6⅜″	2
Drawer front	¾″ × 3⅜″ × 8¾″	1
Drawer bottom	¼″ × 6⅞″ × 12⅝″	Plywood
Dowels	⅜″ × 2″	16
Pull	3″ centers	

will suffice. Use dowel-locating pins to accurately position the dowels. A dowel drilling jig is first used on the apron ends. Hole positions are then transferred to the legs by means of the pins. (See photo.) Next cut the shelf and install it using cleats on the underside.

The drawer and top shelf compartment is made as a unit and installed separately. Set the lower shelf down about ¼ inch and likewise the upper shelf is set down from the top the same amount.

Make the drawer with a double front as shown and be sure to make screw clearance holes on the subfront so that the hardware can be installed after the finishing operation is completed.

The front edge of the drawer is shaped with a beading cutter.

Sanding and finishing operations complete the project. To facilitate the finishing, the compartment may be lifted out and installed after the finishing is completed.

Mobile Server

THIS MOBILE SERVER is small and compact but when its drop leaves are extended, it measures a full 64 inches. A closed compartment, three drawers and two shelves provide ample storage. And rails on the lower shelf add a decorative touch.

Except for the trim which is solid lumber, the entire cart is made of pine plywood, thus eliminating the need for gluing up boards. Another advantage in using plywood is the fact that it is stable and not subject to expansion and contraction due to weather conditions. Of course, other species of wood may be substituted for pine, such as birch, oak and walnut. To keep construction simple, we have used butt joints throughout. But you can make rabbeted and dadoed joints instead. If you do, be sure to alter measurements accordingly.

Start construction with the cabinet frame. Cut the sides and top choosing the best grain and knot patterns for the outer surfaces. Before cutting any pieces, check your equipment to make sure all cuts will be straight and square. You may find it easier to have the lumber dealer rip the 4- × -8-panel into the necessary working sizes. If you do so, have them cut the pieces slightly oversize so you can trim them to exact size in your shop.

To conserve lumber and cut down on the weight, a web frame is used to support the drawers. In solid lumber construction the long front and rear sections would be splined or doweled to the shorter end pieces. Since we are using plywood, the frame is made by dropping out the center of the panel and using it for one of the doors. Lay out the frame size on the panel, then drill a ¼-inch-diameter hole at each corner and drop the center using a saber saw.

To ensure alignment of the various sections during assembly, temporarily tack blocks of scrap to the sides of the various panels. Locate these pieces carefully, as the accuracy of the entire assembly depends on their placement. In effect, they act as temporary dadoes and rabbets. If you should decide to use dado and rabbet

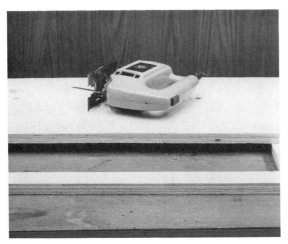

Fig. 28-1. Simplified web frame to support the drawers is made by dropping center panel. You save lumber, eliminate joints.

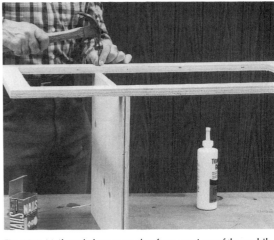

Fig. 28-2. Nails and glue are used to fasten sections of the mobile server. Dropped panel of frame will become cabinet door.

Fig. 28-3. Blocks of scrap wood, temporarily tacked to sides of the panels, assures alignment of sections during assembly.

Fig. 28-4. Shelf is attached to partition before end panel is installed. Glue, nails, and screws are used to fasten sections.

construction, this step would be unnecessary.

Fasten the sections with glue, nails and screws. The nails are used to speed up assembly, but screws are needed for they provide greater holding power than nails. Sink the nail heads and countersink the screw heads only where they will show. The nail heads are filled, but the screws are plugged.

The drawer compartments and guides are made by attaching narrow strips to the underside of the dividers. The strips are cut just long enough to fit within the web frame. The dividers are installed with screws driven from the top. This is necessary especially for the divider placed over the partition. Countersink the screw holes and use 2-inch screws to fasten them to the web frame.

Fig. 28-5. Assembly must be perfectly square. If necessary, use diagonal braces to keep it that way until the glue sets.

The subtop pieces, front and rear are fastened at the ends with screws. Likewise, they are fastened to the tops of the two drawer compartments with screws. Again, nails are used first to align the parts, but screws are needed. Glue all joints.

The top is made in three sections. The end flaps are fastened to the center section with strip (piano) hinges. After cutting the three pieces to size, cut and add the edge strips to both ends of the center piece and to the mating ends of the flaps. Do this before installing the hinges. The edging is ripped from solid stock. Make the strips ⅛ inch thick and install with glue and brads.

Lay the top facedown onto a flat surface, then install the hinges. Also add the cleats near each end of the center section. Position the cleats so their outer edges will align with the cabinet side

Fig. 28-6. Drawer dividers are made to fit web frame. Bottom strip serves as drawer slide. Study preceding drawing carefully.

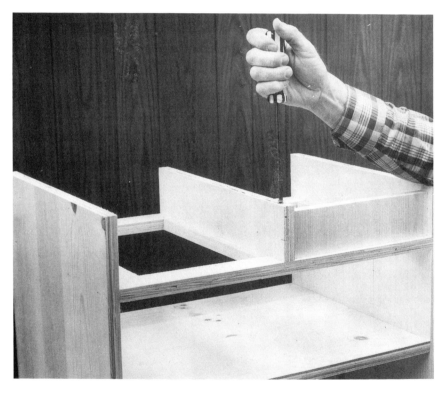

Fig. 28-7. Dividers are fastened with screws at each end as demonstrated in this photo. The temporary spacer assures accuracy.

panels. The nose and cove trim molding may be added now or later when the rest of the trim is added.

The drop leaf brackets we used are the hinged type which fold flat against the side panels when the flaps are down. In order to clear the strip hinge, they are located ¾-inch below the underside of the top. A support block is fastened to the underside of the flap to compensate for the lowered position of the bracket.

The base consists of four corner posts

185

Fig. 28-8. Narrow strips attached to underside of the dividers with nails and screws form drawer compartments and guides.

Fig. 28-9. Underside of top. Hinged-type drop leaf bracket must clear strip hinge. Block compensates for the lower position.

Fig. 28-10. Corner post and decorative apron of server's base. Dowel centers are being used to mark locations on corner post.

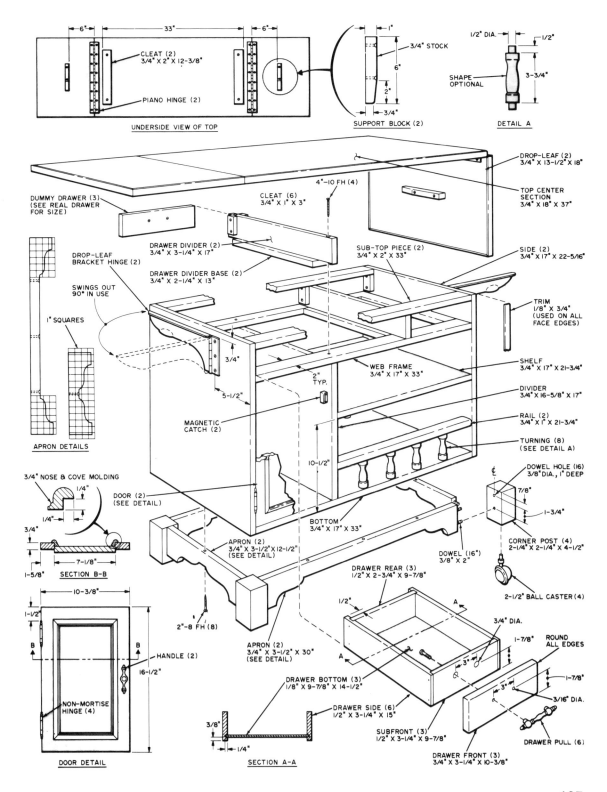

CLEAT (2)
3/4" X 2" X 12-3/8"

PIANO HINGE (2)

UNDERSIDE VIEW OF TOP

3/4" STOCK

SUPPORT BLOCK (2)

1/2" DIA.

SHAPE OPTIONAL

DETAIL A

3-3/4"

DROP-LEAF (2)
3/4" X 13-1/2" X 18"

TOP CENTER SECTION
3/4" X 18" X 37"

DUMMY DRAWER (3)
(SEE REAL DRAWER FOR SIZE)

CLEAT (6)
3/4" X 1" X 3"

4"-10 FH (4)

SIDE (2)
3/4" X 17" X 22-5/16"

DROP-LEAF
BRACKET HINGE (2)

DRAWER DIVIDER (2)
3/4" X 3-1/4" X 17"

DRAWER DIVIDER BASE (2)
3/4" X 2-1/4" X 13"

SUB-TOP PIECE (2)
3/4" X 2" X 33"

SWINGS OUT
90° IN USE

I" SQUARES

TRIM
1/8" X 3/4"
(USED ON ALL FACE EDGES)

SHELF
3/4" X 17" X 21-3/4"

DIVIDER
3/4" X 16-5/8" X 17"

RAIL (2)
3/4" X 1" X 21-3/4"

TURNING (8)
(SEE DETAIL A)

WEB FRAME
3/4" X 17" X 33"

2"
TYP.

5-1/2"

3/4"

MAGNETIC
CATCH (2)

APRON DETAILS

10-1/2"

DOWEL HOLE (16)
3/8" DIA., 1" DEEP

7/8"

1-3/4"

3/4" NOSE & COVE MOLDING

1/4"

1/4"

3/4"

7-1/8"

1-5/8"

SECTION B-B

DOOR (2)
(SEE DETAIL)

BOTTOM
3/4" X 17" X 33"

APRON (2)
3/4" X 3-1/4" X 12-1/2"
(SEE DETAIL)

DOWEL (16)
3/8" X 2"

CORNER POST (4)
2-1/4" X 2-1/4" X 4-1/2"

2-1/2" BALL CASTER (4)

10-3/8"

1-1/2"

B

B

HANDLE (2)

16-1/2"

NON-MORTISE
HINGE (4)

DOOR DETAIL

2"-8 FH (8)

APRON (2)
3/4" X 3-1/2" X 30"
(SEE DETAIL)

DRAWER BOTTOM (3)
1/8" X 9-7/8" X 14-1/2"

DRAWER SIDE (6)
1/2" X 3-1/4" X 15"

3/8"

1/4"

SECTION A-A

DRAWER REAR (3)
1/2" X 2-3/4" X 9-7/8"

1/2"

A

A

3"

SUBFRONT (3)
1/2" X 3-1/4" X 9-7/8"

DRAWER FRONT (3)
3/4" X 3-1/4" X 10-3/8"

3/4" DIA.

1-7/8"

ROUND
ALL EDGES

1-7/8"

3/16" DIA.

DRAWER PULL (6)

3"

187

Fig. 28-11. Dowel (and caster) holes are bored with ⅜-inch bit, 1 inch deep. The long apron has already been glued in photo.

Fig. 28-12. Bar clamps are used for final gluing. Omitted for clarity here, protective scraps should be under clamp jaws.

Fig. 28-13. Before applying glue to trim of the mobile server, check fit carefully. This is good procedure on all shop projects.

Fig. 28-14. Water putty can be used to fill gap caused by rounded edging. Alternatives: wood putty or notching of crosspieces.

and a decorative apron. Dowels are used to fasten the assembly. Cut the corners from solid stock. The scalloped design is cut with a saber saw. The long straight section on the front and rear pieces can be made on the circular saw by blind cutting. Such cutting requires that the cut starts and stops short of the ends.

To make the cut, the workpiece is carefully positioned against the fence with the saw blade lowered below the table surface. While holding the work firmly with one hand, slowly raise the blade with the other. As the blade breaks through the surface, continue raising until the kerf reaches the forward limit of the cut. Now

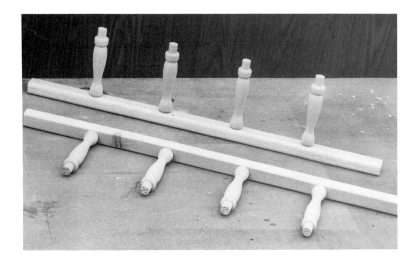

Fig. 28-15. Small turnings for rails have ½-inch tenons at each end. If you make yours, be sure tenons are ½ inch in diameter.

Fig. 28-16. Recessed door for cabinet of the server is made by lowering center panel. The molding has been rabbeted to fit.

Fig. 28-17. Moldings are clamped to the frame while glue sets. Scrap block is used under the clamps to prevent marring.

start feeding the work and stop just a trifle before the scallop starts. Stop the machine and when the blade stops rotating, lift the work away from the blade. Cut the scallops and drop the waste. You will note a slight undercut at each end of the scallop on the rear side of the work. This will not show in the finished piece. If you like, you can cut a sliver of wood to fit the kerf and glue it into place.

When all the pieces have been cut, mark the locations of the dowel and caster holes and bore with a ⅜-inch bit. If you

have a dowel jig, use it to bore the holes in the apron ends. Bore the holes 1 inch deep. Use dowel centers to transfer the hole locations onto the corner posts. Be sure to work on a flat surface to assure accurate alignment.

Gluing should be done in two stages. First, glue the posts to the long apron pieces. When the glue has set, join the long sections to the shorter ones. If all the holes have been drilled straight and square, the assembly should square up when the clamps are applied, but it's a good idea to

Fig. 28-18. Drawers are solid pine with hardwood bottom. Note false front. Rear panel fits dadoes cut into the drawer sides.

check the assembly anyway. If necessary, use temporary braces to hold it square.

The doors are made with recessed panels. This is easily accomplished by the use of molding. Ordinary nose and cove molding is rabbeted on the outer rear edge; it is then mitered and dropped into the frame cut into the door panel. The center panel cut from the door is glued to the back side of the molding. A pair of clamps and a scrap piece of wood across the door will hold it firmly while the glue sets. If you use non-mortise-type hinges, you won't have to mortise out a gain in the door or frame.

The drawers are made with a false front. The lumber used is solid pine. The rear panel fits into dadoes cut into the side panels. Rabbets are cut at the front end of the sides to take the subfront panel. A ⅛-inch groove near the bottom of the side and front panels takes a ⅛-inch hardboard bottom piece. Before assembling the parts, drill the necessary holes for the drawer pulls. Make the holes in the subfront large

enough to clear the screw heads for the pulls. Assemble the drawer with glue and 1¼-inch finishing nails. Do not glue the bottom panel. Simply nail it into the lower edge of the rear panel.

The three extra drawer fronts are installed at the rear of the cabinet and held to small cleats attached to the compartment sides. The rear door is also a dummy and is also fastened with cleats.

Use a piece of ¾-inch stock for the rail. Drill the four ½-inch-diameter holes for the turnings and drill four matching holes in the bottom panel. Round the edges of the rail with a router then sand smooth. The turnings are turned on the lathe.

If you lack a lathe, you can substitute straight dowels or you can purchase the turnings ready-made. If you make your own, be sure the tenons are exactly ½ inch in diameter. It is not necessary to glue the rails to the cabinet sides. Gluing the tenons into the bottom holes will suffice.

The edging and trim are added to complete the project. If you use plywood edging, you will find it has a slight radius on the outer edges. This rounded edge will form a gap where two pieces butt. You can leave the gap and fill with wood putty or you can notch out the crosspieces slightly to eliminate the problem.

If you decide on the filler, color the filler to match the stain you intend to use. Some fillers can be colored with earth colors. Check the instructions of the product you are using.

Sink and fill all nail heads then sand the entire cabinet. Break all sharp edges. Dust, then stain as desired, followed by several clear topcoats of varnish or lacquer.

MATERIALS LIST

All lumber is ¾″ pine plywood except "pine", which is solid pine.

Purpose	Size	Description	Quantity
Top center	18″ × 37″		1
Top end	18″ × 13½″		2
Top cleat	¾″ × 2″ × 12⅜″	Pine	2
Top lid support	¾″ × 1″ × 6″	Pine	2
End	17″ × 22⁵⁄₁₆″		2
Bottom	17″ × 33″		1
Divider	16⅝″ × 17″		1
Shelf	17″ × 21¾″		1
Web frame	17″ × 33″		1
Top support	¾″ × 2″ × 33″		2
Drawer divider	3¼″ × 17″		1
Drawer divider base	2¼″ × 13″		2
Rail	¾″ × 1″ × 21¾″	Pine	2
Spindle	¾″ × 3¾″		8
Base end	3½″ × 12½″		2
Base front	3½″ × 30″		1
Base rear	3½″ × 30″		1
Base corner	2¼″ × 2¼″ × 4½″	Pine	4
Door	10⅜″ × 16½″		2
Drawer front	¾″ × 3¼″ × 10⅜″	Pine	6
Drawer subfront	½″ × 3¼″ × 9⅞″	Pine	3
Drawer side	½″ × 3¼″ × 15″	Pine	6
Drawer rear	½″ × 2¾″ × 9⅞″		3
Drawer bottom	⅛″ × 9⅞″ × 14¾″	Hardboard	3
Dummy drawer front cleat	¾″ × 1″ × 3″		6
Nose and cove molding	⅝″ × ¾″		30
Plywood edging	⅛″ × ¾″		32
Lid support bracket			2
Magnetic catch PM			2
Hinge, non-mortise	2″		4
Dowels	⅜″ × 2″		8
Ball casters			4
Strip hinge	1½″ × 18″		2
Door pulls			2
Drawer pulls			6

Add sockets for the ball casters then insert the stem.

The turnings, hinges and brackets, should be available locally. Should you experience difficulty in locating them, write to Armor Products, Box 290, Deer Park, N.Y. 11729.

Modern Storage Cabinet

THIS MODERN CHINA cabinet/storage unit, elegantly sleek and stylishly simple in appearance, will blend in well with other contemporary furniture pieces. The simplicity of its design and lack of ornamentation makes it fairly easy to build. It features a storage compartment at the bottom and smoked glass doors at the top. The center section is left open. It is made entirely of plywood except for the edging which is cut from solid stock.

The pivot hinges for the glass doors are quite novel. They do not require holes to be drilled into the glass. Instead, they are furnished with nylon studs which securely hold the glass. Another feature of these new hinges is the built-in bullet catch stop.

The two basic tools needed for this project are the table saw and router. Dado joints are used throughout and this is where the router comes in handy.

The lumber used was ¾-inch red birch plywood and solid stock. You will need two 4- × -8-foot panels and one ¼-inch panel for the back. Most lumber yards will rip the plywood free or for a nominal charge. If your lumber dealer will do it, have the boards ripped to 16-inch widths. This will make it easier to carry. You can then recut the boards to the final width in your shop. Lumberyard dealers can rough-cut the stock to size but most will not or cannot maintain the accuracy required in

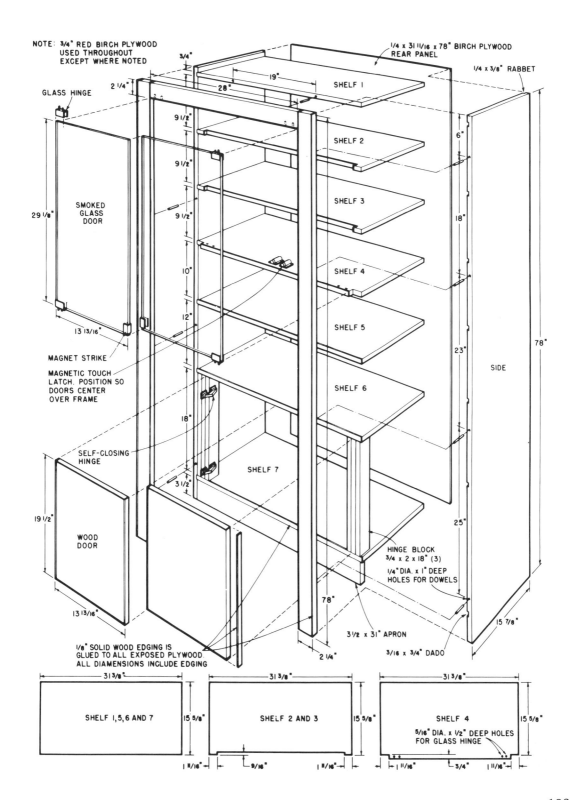

NOTE: 3/4" RED BIRCH PLYWOOD
USED THROUGHOUT
EXCEPT WHERE NOTED

GLASS HINGE

1/4 x 31 11/16 x 78" BIRCH PLYWOOD
REAR PANEL

1/4 x 3/8" RABBET

3/4"

2 1/4"

19"

28"

SHELF 1

6"

9 1/2"

SHELF 2

9 1/2"

SHELF 3

18"

29 1/8"

SMOKED
GLASS
DOOR

9 1/2"

SHELF 4

10"

SHELF 5

23"

13 13/16"

12"

MAGNET STRIKE

SHELF 6

SIDE

78"

MAGNETIC TOUCH
LATCH. POSITION SO
DOORS CENTER
OVER FRAME

18"

SELF-CLOSING
HINGE

SHELF 7

3 1/2"

25"

19 1/2"

WOOD
DOOR

HINGE BLOCK
3/4 x 2 x 18" (3)

1/4" DIA. x 1" DEEP
HOLES FOR DOWELS

13 13/16"

78"

2 1/4"

3 1/2 x 31" APRON

3/16 x 3/4" DADO

15 7/8"

1/8" SOLID WOOD EDGING IS
GLUED TO ALL EXPOSED PLYWOOD.
ALL DIAMENSIONS INCLUDE EDGING

31 3/8"

31 3/8"

31 3/8"

SHELF 1,5,6 AND 7

15 5/8"

SHELF 2 AND 3

15 5/8"

SHELF 4

5/16" DIA. x 1/2" DEEP HOLES
FOR GLASS HINGE

15 5/8"

1 11/16"

9/16"

1 11/16"

1 11/16"

3/4"

1 11/16"

193

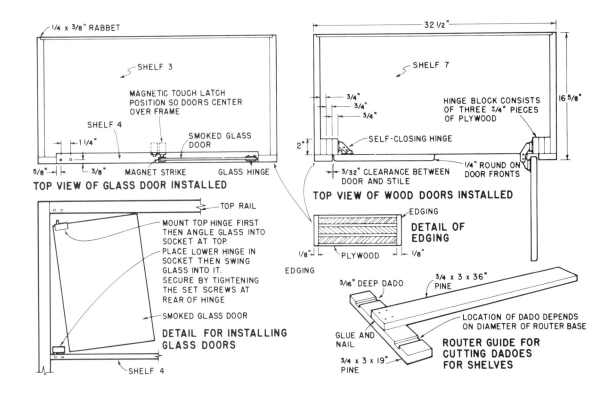

1/4 x 3/8" RABBET

SHELF 3

MAGNETIC TOUCH LATCH
POSITION SO DOORS CENTER
OVER FRAME

SHELF 4

SMOKED GLASS
DOOR

1 1/4"

5/8"   3/8"   MAGNET STRIKE   GLASS HINGE

TOP VIEW OF GLASS DOOR INSTALLED

32 1/2"

SHELF 7

16 5/8"

3/4"
3/4"
3/4"

HINGE BLOCK CONSISTS
OF THREE 3/4" PIECES
OF PLYWOOD

SELF-CLOSING HINGE

2"

1/4" ROUND ON
DOOR FRONTS

3/32" CLEARANCE BETWEEN
DOOR AND STILE

TOP VIEW OF WOOD DOORS INSTALLED

TOP RAIL

MOUNT TOP HINGE FIRST
THEN ANGLE GLASS INTO
SOCKET AT TOP.

PLACE LOWER HINGE IN
SOCKET THEN SWING
GLASS INTO IT.
SECURE BY TIGHTENING
THE SET SCREWS AT
REAR OF HINGE

SMOKED GLASS DOOR

**DETAIL FOR INSTALLING
GLASS DOORS**

SHELF 4

EDGING

**DETAIL OF
EDGING**

1/8"   PLYWOOD   1/8"

EDGING

3/16" DEEP DADO

3/4 x 3 x 36"
PINE

LOCATION OF DADO DEPENDS
ON DIAMETER OF ROUTER BASE

GLUE AND
NAIL

3/4 x 3 x 19"
PINE

**ROUTER GUIDE FOR
CUTTING DADOES
FOR SHELVES**

Fig. 29-1. The use of a homemade
dado guide eases the cutting of dadoes
for the cabinet sides. Use a guide for
straight cuts.

cabinetmaking, such as for this project. Also, they use coarse blades leaving less than smooth edges.

Start construction with the two side members. Trim them to the proper length then rip them to the necessary width. Place them on the work table back-side up and proceed to lay out the double line for the dado. The lines are to be exactly ¾ inch apart. No need to run the lines across the board. Marking them along one edge will suffice.

One of the most effective ways for cutting dadoes requires the use of a router guide. This is a homemade gadget and consists of a T square made of ¾-inch stock. Make the guide as shown and bear in mind that it must be perfectly "square." If it is off, the dadoes will likewise be off.

Fit your router with a ¾-inch straight cutter, preferably carbide tipped. Set the depth of cut to ³⁄₁₆ inch then clamp the guide to a piece of scrap wood, and take two cuts, one on either side of the straightedge. These will serve as locators when cutting the dadoes.

To cut the dadoes, slide the guide along the work until the pencil marks previously drawn at the edge of the board line up with the dado groove in the guide. Clamp the guide at the far end then proceed to cut the dado. When done, slide the guide to the next set of marks and repeat the procedure. To prevent damage to the work, be sure to use a wood pad under the clamp where it contacts the work.

When the dado operation is completed, run a ¼- × -⅜-inch rabbet along the rear inner edges to accept the rear panel. If the router left fuzz at the edges of the rabbet or dadoes, clean with a piece of 220-grit sandpaper.

Fig. 29-2. The dadoes cut in the sides of the cabinet will hold the shelves, so be certain they are equal for level shelves.

The shelves are made next. Cut the seven pieces to length (31⅜ inches), but not to width. The solid wood strip must be added to the front edge of the shelves. You can cut these strips and add them with glue and brads. A better method is to glue a thicker piece to the edge, then trim it later. The advantage here is that the thicker piece assures better contact under clamping pressure and easier handling.

Prepare the edging by ripping ⅞-inch-wide strips of hardwood to match the red birch plywood. The ⅞-inch width will leave a slight overhang which will be trimmed off later.

Edging clamps are ideal for this operation, but are not essential. Regular clamps can be used in the conventional manner. When clamping, be sure to center the ⅞-inch strip over the ¾-inch shelf. Apply glue to both surfaces then clamp and watch out for the strip creeping.

When all the edges have been glued, set the saw table fence so that ⅛ inch of the trim will be left on the edge. Next, reset the saw fence to 15⅝ inches, then recut the shelves trimming off the excess at the rear edge of the shelves.

You will note that four of the shelves are identical rectangles, and the other three are not. Shelves No. 2 and No. 3 are notched along the front edge to allow clearance for the swinging glass doors. Shelf No. 4 is deeper than the others and

Fig. 29-3. The edging is prepared by ripping 7/8-inch wide strips of hardwood to match the plywood. Trim the overhang.

Fig. 29-4. Edging clamps are in place and glue is applied to fasten the edging. When clamping, center the strip over the 3/4-inch shelf.

is notched at the front corners. The added depth is necessary to support the sockets for the glass hinge.

When all shelves are cut, add the solid edging to the fronts. Note that the dimensions shown are for the shelves with the edging included.

The assembly and gluing of the shelves to the sides must be done with great care. A pair of sawhorses is recommended. Straddle them with a pair of 2- × -3's about 7 feet long. These will support the cabinet and also serve as cauls under the clamps. The rear panel should be cut to size at this time.

To ensure a good strong joint, glue size the ends of the shelves. Do this by thinning some glue with water and brush on the ends of all the shelves. Allow to dry about 15 minutes. The glue used was an aliphatic resin type, which is strong and fast-drying. This fast-drying feature may pose a problem unless you work fast and with an assistant. If you are too slow in this operation, the first-glued joints may start to set before you get to the last joint. If you think this will be a problem, it is suggested that you use a glue with a longer standing time. Most hide glues will serve this purpose.

Apply undiluted glue to the dado grooves and to the shelf ends, then install the shelves into the grooves. Add glue to the other ends of the shelves and to the grooves of the other side member. Assemble carefully, then apply the clamps as shown.

To ensure that the assembly is square, insert the rear panel temporarily. If the top or bottom shelf is parallel to the end of the

MATERIALS LIST

All lumber is ¾" red birch plywood except as noted.

Purpose	Size	Quantity
Side	¾" × 15⅞" × 78"	2
Rear	¼" × 31¹¹⁄₁₆" × 78"	1
Shelf	¾" × 15⅝" × 31⅜"	6
Shelf	¾" × 16⅜" × 31⅜"	1
Hinge block	¾" × 2" × 19"	6
Apron	¾" × 3½" × 31"	1
Frame top	¾" × 2¼" × 28"	1
Frame side	¾" × 2¼" × 78"	2
Dowel	¼" × 1⁷⁄₁₆"	10
Door, wood	¾" × 13¹³⁄₁₆" × 19½"	2
Door, glass, smoked	13¹³⁄₁₆" × 29⅛"	2
Edging	⅛" × ¾", solid birch	40'
Glass hinge (GDH)		2 pr.
Hinge, self-closing (IH)		2 pr.
Touch Latch (TL)		2
Strike (MAS)		2

Note: Items in parentheses are available from Armor Products, P.O. Box 290, Deer Park, NY 11729. Write for catalog.

Fig. 29-5. Apply undiluted glue to the shelf ends and dado grooves.

Fig. 29-6. After sliding the shelves into the grooves of both side members, clamp securely. Check for squareness before allowing glue to dry.

Fig. 29-7. The frame members are fastened to the cabinet sides with ¼-inch dowels. Fasten them with glue and clamp securely till dry.

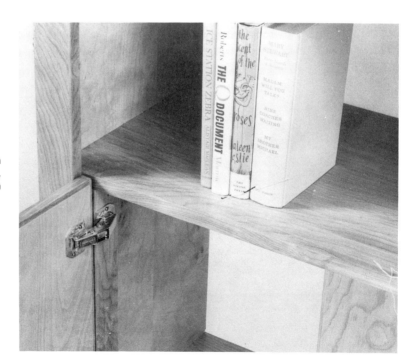

Fig. 29-8. Special hinges are used in this project. They are self-closing, adjustable, surface mounted and open flush with inside.

Fig. 29-9. Detail shows the strike for the glass doors before it has been fully inserted. These strikes keep the doors closed.

Fig. 29-10. The glass is held in place by tightening the nylon screws at the rear edge. Lower hinge is placed into socket first.

rear panel, the assembly will be square. After the panel is removed, you can check for squareness with a builder's square.

The front frame consists of two side stiles and a top rail. Rip these to size then edge and recut so they will be 2¼ inches wide. The frame members are fastened to the cabinet sides with ¼-inch dowels. Locate and drill the holes in the front edges of the side and top shelf. Use dowel centers to transfer the hole locations to the frame members. The holes in the cabinet are drilled one-inch deep and those in the frames ½ inch deep. Fasten the frame members to the cabinet with glue and clamp securely.

The apron and hinge blocks are added next. The blocks are necessary if you use the hinges shown. These are self-closing, adjustable and surface mounted. They open flush with the inside, but they are designed to be used from zero to full overlay.

Cut the doors to size then edge with the side edging running the full length of the docr. (See drawing.) To allow for clearance, the outer corners of the door must be rounded.

The glass doors are purchased cut to size. Ask for smoked glass. These are ¼-inch plate glass and are quite expensive, so be sure the size is correct. To make sure the size shown will fit your cabinet, you may want to make a pair of dummy doors out of ¼-inch plywood. Install them and check them out carefully. The doors should clear the side stiles as well as the No. 2 and No. 3 shelves.

Install the glass doors by fastening the top hinge to the glass. Hold in place by tightening the nylon screws at the rear edge. Now place the lower hinge into the lower socket then swing the glass into place.

Sawhorse Toolbox

THIS IS NOT just a sawhorse, but a workshop which will save you many steps around the house because it can be easily moved from one job to another. Hand tools can be stored in the space beneath the top, while bins located between the legs hold small portable electric tools, such as a drill, sander and saw. A shelf holds a carry-all toolbox for additional storage.

The toolbox also serves as a base into which a rack may be inserted to make a support the same height as the sawhorse. When used in conjunction with the sawhorse, this rack is useful for supporting full sheets of plywood or long lengths of lumber when sawing them to smaller pieces, or for dressing down doors.

To ensure the proper fitting of the parts for the sawhorse, pay particular attention to the compound angles to which these parts are cut. Unlike making right angle ripping or crosscuts on a circular saw, the compound angles used here require settings of either 4 or 15 degrees, or a combination of both.

While the circular saw simplifies the cutting of these compound angles, satisfactory results can be obtained with a crosscut handsaw. The blade of a T-bevel, set to the proper degree with the aid of a protractor, is used as a visual guide for determining the required slant at which the saw is held. The handle of the T-bevel is positioned on the work at a 90-degree angle from the cutting line. The 4- and 15-degree bevels on the edges can also be made with a hand plane.

Retail lumberyards will rip stock to the widths designated in the Materials List. Unless otherwise specified, all ¾-inch stock members for the sawhorse and toolbox are joined with coated 8d common wire nails, and an adhesive applied to the joints.

Cut all of the pieces for the sawhorse from the dimensions given in the drawing and start assembling them by nailing the compartment sides and ends together to form a frame. Add the compartment bottom which is beveled 15 degrees on all four edges. The four legs are sawed alike in size and shape up to the point when the rail notches are made. Make duplicate notches on the legs.

When notching the legs, the cutting angles of the first set of legs are the reverse of those used on the second set. Attach the

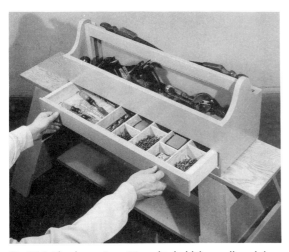

Fig. 30-1. The drawer is partitioned to hold the small workshop necessities such as screwdrivers, chisels, bits, and assorted nails and screws. To protect the cutting edges of the chisels, install some special brackets or clips in the larger compartment.

Fig. 30-2. Convenient bins at each end can hold an assortment of portable electric tools such as a drill, sander and saw. Hand tools can be stored in space below top—their weight prevents the sawhorse from creeping when planing boards held in vise.

Fig. 30-3. When assembling the tool box, mount the tray and the handle to one of the sides, then add the other side.

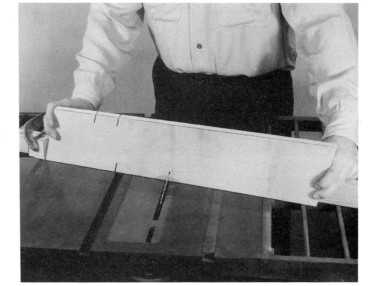

legs to the compartment sides, cutting off or clinching over any nails which protrude on the inside. Add the rails next, then install the shelf.

Fasten the bin bottom fillers to the rails with 6d nails and nail the bin backing to the legs with 4d nails. Before installing the hooks, eyes and chain to the top, give the wood (except for the working surface of the top) an enamel undercoating. When dry, smooth with steel wool and apply two coats of an interior enamel. Give the unpainted portion of the top two coats of boiled linseed oil.

203

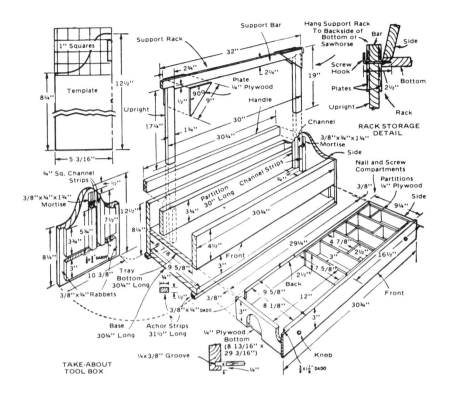

Take-About Tool Box

- 1" Squares
- Template — 12½", 8¼", 5 3/16"
- Support Rack
- Support Bar
- Hang Support Rack To Backside of Bottom of Sawhorse
- Bar, Side, Screw Hook, Bottom, Plates, Upright, Rack — 2½", 19"
- **RACK STORAGE DETAIL**
- 32", 2¾", 2¼"
- Plate ¼" Plywood, 90°, 9°, ½", 9"
- Handle
- Upright — 17¼", 1¼"
- 30", 30¾"
- Channel
- 3/8"x¾"x1¼" Mortise
- Side
- Nail and Screw Compartments
- Partitions ¼" Plywood — 3/8", Side, 9¼"
- ¼" Sq. Channel Strips — ½", 12½", 8¼"
- 3/8"x¾"x1¼" Mortise
- 7½", 5¼", 3¼"
- Channel Strips
- Partition 30" Long
- Channel Strips — ¼"
- 30¾", 3¾", 4½"
- Front — 3"
- 30¾"
- 29¼", 4 7/8", 2½", 16¼"
- 3", 7 5/8", 2½"
- Back — 9 5/8", 12"
- 8 1/8", 3"
- Front
- 8¼", 3", 1"x1" DADOS
- Tray Bottom 30¾" Long
- 9 5/8", 10 3/8", 3"
- 3/8"x¾" Rabbets
- Base 30¾" Long
- Achor Strips 31½" Long
- 3/8"x¾" DADO
- ¼x3/8" Groove
- ¼" Plywood Bottom (8 13/16" x 29 3/16")
- Knob
- ¾"x1¼" DADO
- ¼"

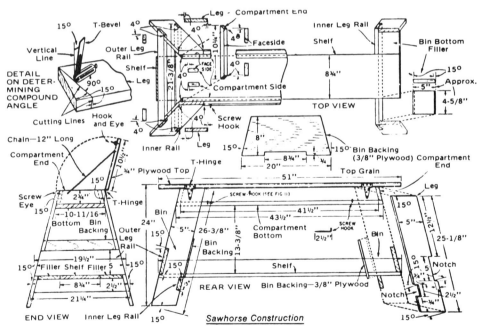

Sawhorse Construction

- 15°, T-Bevel
- Vertical Line
- DETAIL ON DETERMINING COMPOUND ANGLE — 90°, 15°
- Cutting Lines
- Outer Leg Rail, Shelf, Leg
- 4°, 10¾", 21-3/8", FACE SIDE, 4°
- Leg - Compartment End
- Faceside
- Compartment Side
- Inner Leg Rail, Shelf — 8¾"
- Bin Bottom Filler — 15°, Approx., 5", 4-5/8"
- **TOP VIEW**
- Hook and Eye, 4°, Screw Hook, Leg, Inner Rail, 4°
- 8", 15°, 8¾", 20", ¾"
- Bin Backing (3/8" Plywood) Compartment End
- Top Grain
- Chain—12" Long
- Compartment End — 10½", 15°
- ¾" Plywood Top
- T-Hinge
- Screw Eye — 15°, 2¾", T-Hinge, 10-11/16"
- Bottom Bin Backing
- Outer Leg Rail
- 19½", Filler Shelf Filler 5, 15°
- 8¼", 2½", 21¼"
- **END VIEW** — Inner Leg Rail, 15°
- 24", 15°, 5", 26-3/8", 13-3/8"
- Bin, Bin Backing
- 51", 41½", 43½"
- SCREW HOOK (SEE FIG 11)
- Compartment Bottom
- SCREW HOOK — 2½"
- Shelf
- **REAR VIEW** — Bin Backing—3/8" Plywood
- Leg — 15°, 5", 12½", 25-1/8"
- Notch — 5", Notch — 2½", ¾"
- 15°

204

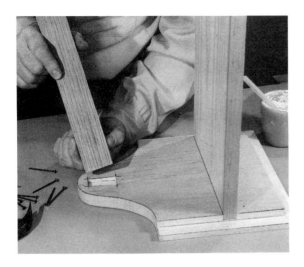

Fig. 30-4. Making the lateral cuts in the legs for the rail notches. Note the stop block clamped to the 2-inch-high fence which in turn, is fastened to the miter gauge extension.

MATERIALS LIST FOR TOOL BOX

Purpose	Size	Description	Quantity
Box sides	¾″ × 10⅜″ × 12½″	Pine	2
Box tray bottom	¾″ × 8⅞″ × 30¾″	Pine	1
Box handle	¾″ × 1¾″ × 30¾″	Hardwood	1
Box base	¾″ × 9⅝″ × 30¾″	Pine	1
Box front	¾″ × 4½″ × 30¾″	Pine	1
Box back	¾″ × 8¼″ × 30¾″	Pine	1
Box channel strips	¾″ × ¾″ × 5¾″	Pine	2
Box channel strips	¾″ × ¾″ × 7½″	Pine	2
Box partition	¾″ × 3¾″ × 30″	Pine	1
Anchor strips	¾″ × ½″ × 31½″	Pine	2
Drawer front	¾″ × 3″ × 30¾″	Pine	1
Drawer sides	¾″ × 3″ × 9¼″	Pine	2
Drawer bottom	¼″ × 8¹³⁄₁₆″ × 29¹⁄₁₆″	Plywood	1
Drawer back	¾″ × 3″ × 29¼″	Pine	1
Nail compartment ends and partitions	¼″ × 2½″ × 7⅝″	Plywood	6
Nail compartment front and back	¼″ × 2½″ × 16½″	Plywood	2
Nail compartment partitions	¼″ × 2½″ × 3″	Plywood	4
Support rack uprights	¾″ × 1¾″ × 17¼″	Pine	2
Rack support bar	¾″ × 2¼″ × 32″	Hardwood	1
Support rack plates	¼″ × 4½″ × 9″	Plywood	4

Note: Also required are knobs, screw hooks and finishing materials.

MATERIALS LIST FOR SAWHORSE

Purpose	Size	Description	Quantity
Compartment sides	¾″ × 3″ × 41½″	Pine	2
Compartment ends	¾″ × 3″ × 10¼″	Pine	2
Compartment bottom	¾″ × 10¹¹⁄₁₆″ × 43½″	Pine	1
Legs	¾″ × 5⅛″ × 26½″	Pine	4
Inner leg stretchers	¾″ × 2¾″ × 21¼″	Pine	2
Outer leg stretchers	¾″ × 5¼″ × 19½″	Pine	2
Shelf	¾″ × 8¾″ × 51¼″	Pine	1
Bottom bin fillers	¾″ × 4¾″ × 5⅛″	Pine	4
Bin backing	⅜″ × 8″ × 20″	Plywood	2
Top	¾″ × 10½″ × 51″	Plywood	1
Link or safety chain	24″		1
Round-head screws	¾″	No. 7	as needed

Note: You will also require T-hinges, hooks and eyes, glue, coated wire nails, finishing nails, lath nails, enamel, enamel undercoater and boiled linseed oil.

Scribe the cutting lines for the contoured portions of the side or ends with the aid of a cardboard half-template, as shown in the drawing. After cutting the dadoes, rabbets and handle mortises, join the sides to the tray bottom and handle. Next add the base, front and back.

When installing the channel strips, check their spacing so that the ¾-inch stock, used for the uprights of the supporting rack, slides freely in the channels thus formed. Shape the upper ends of the longer channel strips to conform to the contoured portion of the sides. The partition, which forms a compartment for handsaws, rests against the channel strips and is anchored with 8d finishing nails driven in through the sides. Anchor strips nailed to the bottom prevent the toolbox from sliding off the shelf.

Cut the end dadoes on the drawer front and sides and then make the ¼- x -⅜- inch grooves in these members (including the back) for the bottom. Join the sides to

the front, slide the bottom in the grooves and add the back. Crossnail with 6d finishing nails. Assemble the parts for the nail and screw compartments with ¾-inch brads and glue before installing in the drawer. Anchor the unit in place with brads and add the knobs to complete the drawer.

The support rack is made of a hardwood bar (preferably oak) and two uprights. Drive 10d finishing nails through the bar and into the uprights. Coat the plywood plates with glue and attach them to the rack with lath nails. When not in use, the rack can be hung on the sawhorse.

Recess the heads of the finishing nails and paint the box, except the sides, back, bottom, and inside of the drawer, with an enamel undercoat. When dry, fill the nail holes with wood putty and smooth the surface with steel wool. Apply two coats of interior enamel of the same shade as you used on the sawhorse. Coat the unpainted surfaces with boiled linseed oil.

Spice Racks

SPICE RACKS ARE OFTEN merely functional shelves built onto the insides of cabinet doors. If you have the available wall space, why not bring the spice rack out into the open where it is more accessible, and where it can add a distinctive decorative touch.

Either of these racks will do even more. Both provide drawers for storage of recipe cards and other small items; one also has a clock for timing cooking to perfection.

The rack components can be assembled using conventional joining methods. However, to save time and labor, consider using a Thermogrip electric glue gun that utilizes stick glue. This type of adhesive sets in less than a minute, and there is no need to use clamps of any kind; simply apply the hot glue with the gun, then hold the sections together by hand until the bonding material sets. The glue guns are available in most hardware stores.

The Early American-style rack is made of pine finished with a warm stain that is in keeping with your colonial kitchen decor. Use a jigsaw, saber saw, or even a hand coping saw to cut the curved front, end and back sections. The front is preferably cut from a single piece of wood, or it can be assembled from separate pieces glued together. Both front and back pieces lap over the ends, not vice versa.

The rack will look better if you round the curved edges. A shaper does this best, but careful handworking can also yield a creditable job. Note that the center drawer—used for filing recipe cards—differs from the other two; the sides are shaped so as to permit tilting for installation, and a tab at the rear acts as a drawer stop.

The Nautical-style rack, with the clock, is even easier to build since it calls for no curved pieces and needs no face panel. It is more appropriate in a contemporary style kitchen. Use a combination of gum wood and dark mahogany—the latter for the drawer fronts and the clock face.

Note that the lipped drawer fronts sim-

207

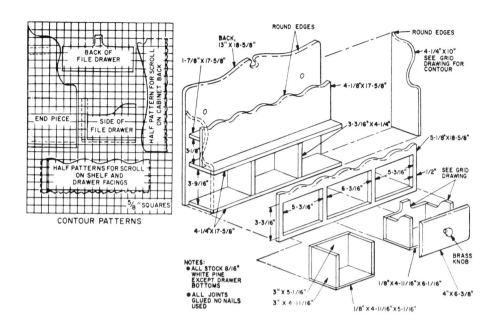

CONTOUR PATTERNS

BACK OF FILE DRAWER

END PIECE

SIDE OF FILE DRAWER

HALF PATTERN FOR SCROLL ON CABINET BACK

HALF PATTERNS FOR SCROLL ON SHELF AND DRAWER FACINGS

5/8" SQUARES

ROUND EDGES

BACK, 13" X 18-5/8"

1-7/8"X17-5/8"

ROUND EDGES

4-1/4"X10" SEE GRID DRAWING FOR CONTOUR

4-1/8"X17-5/8"

3-3/16" X 4-1/4"

3-1/8"

3-9/16"

5-1/8"X18-5/8"

5-3/16"

1/2" SEE GRID DRAWING

6-3/16"

5-3/16"

3-3/16"

4-1/4"X17-5/8"

NOTES:
- ALL STOCK 8/16" WHITE PINE EXCEPT DRAWER BOTTOMS
- ALL JOINTS GLUED NO NAILS USED

3" X 5-1/16"
3" X 6-11/16"

1/8" X 4-11/16" X 6-1/16"

BRASS KNOB

4" X 6-3/8"

1/8" X 4-11/16" X 5-1/16"

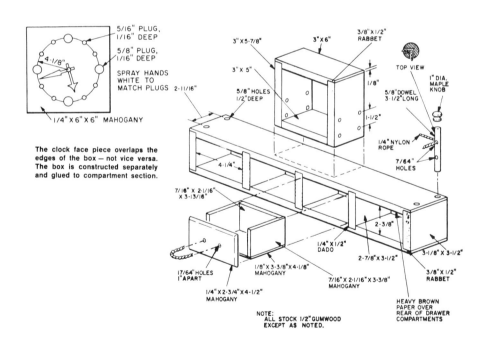

5/16" PLUG, 1/16" DEEP

5/8" PLUG, 1/16" DEEP

4-1/8"

SPRAY HANDS WHITE TO MATCH PLUGS

2-11/16"

1/4" X 6" X 6" MAHOGANY

The clock face piece overlaps the edges of the box — not vice versa. The box is constructed separately and glued to compartment section.

3" X 5-7/8"

3" X 5"

5/8" HOLES 1/2" DEEP

4-1/4"

7/16" X 2-1/16" X 3-13/16"

17/64" HOLES 1" APART

1/4" X 2-3/4" X 4-1/2" MAHOGANY

3" X 6"

3/8" X 1/2" RABBET

TOP VIEW

1/8"

1-1/2"

5/8" DOWEL 3-1/2" LONG

1" DIA. MAPLE KNOB

1/4" NYLON ROPE

7/64" HOLES

1/8" X 3-3/8" X 4-1/8" MAHOGANY

1/4" X 1/2" DADO

7/16" X 2-1/16" X 3-3/8" MAHOGANY

2-7/8" X 3-1/2"

2-3/8"

3-1/8" X 3-1/2"

3/8" X 1/2" RABBET

HEAVY BROWN PAPER OVER REAR OF DRAWER COMPARTMENTS

NOTE: ALL STOCK 1/2" GUMWOOD EXCEPT AS NOTED.

ply butt against the compartment framework. Lengths of nylon rope, glued into holes, serve as handles.

The clock box is made separately, and then glued in place as shown. The dial for the clock is made by gluing short lengths of dowel into holes drilled into a ¼-inch-thick piece of mahogany along a circle that will bring them close to the tips of the clock hands. Use the hands that come with the clock mechanism. Note that the clock face laps over the edges of the box.

The posts at the top of the cabinet are intended to simulate a ship's capstans. The nylon ropes attached to them are anchored in place with bits of melted glue.

Super Workbench

A STURDY, DURABLE workbench is one of the most important items in any workshop, whether it be large or small, amateur or professional. This particular one features a novel hardwood top which is laminated to a plywood base. The combination provides the necessary stiffness and the hard surface will withstand abuse without splintering or denting. Hardwood strip flooring is ideally suited for this purpose because it is end-matched with tongue and groove edges which greatly simplify installation.

Other features of this fine workbench are a pegboard tool rack, roomy drawer, large storage compartment, and a work support for supporting long boards held in the vise. It also features a plug-in strip which is fastened to the underside of the tool rack. This is not visible in the photos as it is placed toward the rear of the shelf as a safety precaution.

Also included are two frame-type pegboard panels which are mounted at the ends of the bench to utilize the otherwise wasted space.

The basic frame consists of 2-×-4 lumber fastened with lag screws which contribute to the sturdiness of this bench. Select straight 2 × 4's and try to choose those with a minimum of knots. Cut the various components to length then notch the legs to accept the stretchers. The method of notching depends on the tools available to you. If you have a band saw notching will be greatly simplified. Otherwise, you can use a handsaw and chisel for this operation.

Carefully locate and layout the notches on the leg members. Note that only the lower rear notches are U-shaped. All others are L-shaped and thus edge cut. If the band saw is to be used, make the layouts on the proper face so the throat of the machine will not interfere. If you use a handsaw be sure to make the cuts straight and square.

After notching the pieces set them aside and prepare the stretcher to take the

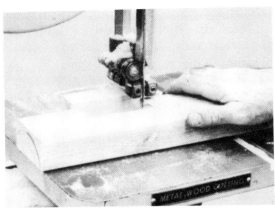

Fig. 32-1. The notches on the leg piece are cut with a band saw. If none is available use a handsaw and chisel as an alternate.

Fig. 32-2. After the hole is drilled in the stretcher piece transfer location of bolt to the leg by placing in the hole and tapping with hammer.

Fig. 32-3. After the holes are drilled, screw in the bolt with a ratchet. Remember to use washer under the bolt head to prevent wood from crushing. Drill hole deep enough for a good bite into the center brace.

Fig. 32-4. Once the framework for the bench is bolted up, glue and clamp the front frame. Make sure to check the frame for squareness before the glue dries. Your workbench is already working for you.

lag screws. Locate the hole centers as indicated, then, using a 1-inch-diameter spade-type bit, bore the lag screw clearance to a depth of ⅜ inch. This will allow room for the head and washer. The screw body hole is bored next. This is 5/16-inch diameter and is bored through the center of each clearance hole.

Next, transfer the mounting holes to the cross members. Do this by aligning the pieces so the edges are flush, then insert the lag screws and tap gently with a hammer. When all the holes have been located, bore the 3/16-inch root diameter for the lag screw, then assemble the frame. Be sure to place a washer under the head of each screw. Tighten securely, using a socket wrench. Be sure to work on a flat surface to ensure that the frame will assemble straight and square. Check for accuracy with a large square.

The front frame is made of pine lumber, but you may substitute hardwood if you like. Rip the parts to size, then trim them to length. The Materials List shows the stiles (the two vertical members of the front frame) as being 1¾ inches wide. It's a good idea to make them 2 inches wide.

This will permit final trimming to size, thus ensuring that the width of the frame will align with the bench ends. Also, making the pieces oversize eliminates the need for cauls under the clamps. The dents left by the clamp jaws are simply trimmed off after assembly.

Two dowels per joint are used to assemble the frame. Locate the holes for the dowels carefully. Use dowel centers, a

Fig. 32-5. After the frame is assembled, squared up and the glue has dried attach it to the bench frame. The front was cut oversize to ensure a perfect fit during sanding of the final assembly.

Fig. 32-6. The notches in the floor panel were cut by using the end of the leg as a template. Apply a bead of glue to the stretchers and crosspieces and finish installation with 1-inch, 16 gauge brads.

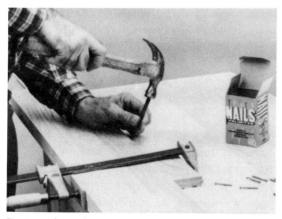

Fig. 32-7. The work area of the bench is topped with hardwood flooring. Rip the groove from the first strip. If possible the first strip should run the entire length of the bench. Fasten the flooring with 1½-inch spiral flooring nails.

Fig. 32-8. The overhang of the strip flooring is trimmed with a panel saw. Leave about ¹⁄₁₆ inch for final trimming with a router. Strips should be staggered at least 8 inches. The last piece of flooring at the rear may have to be trimmed with a plane.

Fig. 32-9. Use a good quality wood filler to fill in all the cracks and spaces between strips. Allow to dry and then sand. You may need to do this several times for a seamless finish.

Fig. 32-10. The end and front edges of the top have been covered with a strip of trim ¼ inch thick × 1½ inches wide. To prevent cupping each sliding door is made up of 4 pieces with the annular rings reversed. These are glued up and installed.

doweling jig or a combination of both. Bore the ⅜-inch-diameter holes, 1¹⁄₁₆ inches deep. Spiral groove dowels are recommended. If you use smooth dowels, groove them with the splined jaws of a plier. This will permit air to escape as the dowel is driven into the hole. Failure to do this could result in the wood splitting.

Prepare the parts for assembly by applying a thin coat of glue to the three horizontal members of the frame. This is called sizing and its purpose is to prevent excessive absorption of glue, which would result in a dry or weakened joint. Allow the glue to set about 15 minutes, then recoat and join the parts. If the pieces were cut properly, the assembled frame should square up. However, be sure to check for squareness after applying the clamps. If necessary, adjust and square up before the glue sets.

The end panels and bench floor are made from ¼-inch plywood. Cut these to size as indicated. The end pieces should line up with the front and rear edges of the 2- × -4 legs. Apply a bead of glue to the sides of the legs and crosspieces then

install and assemble the ends, using 1-inch, 16-gauge brads.

The front frame is installed now. Use glue and 2-inch finishing nails. Be sure to let the overhang at each end be equal. Allow the glue to set, then trim the overhang using a plane or router.

The top consists of a ¾-inch plywood base topped with hardwood flooring. Cut the plywood to size then fasten it to the plywood frame. If the top is to be fastened permanently, you can drive screws from above through the plywood into the 2 × 4's. If you prefer to make the top removable, fasten it from the underside by boring holes through the 2- × -4 frame then fasten with 3-inch lag screws.

The flooring is available in maple or oak and is sold at all lumber yards. It is sold by the bundle in random lengths. Size of the bundles varies so be sure to order enough to cover the 10 square feet of the workbench top.

The front or leading edge strip should be ripped to remove the groove as indicated. Do this on the table saw or use a plane. If possible, the first strip should

213

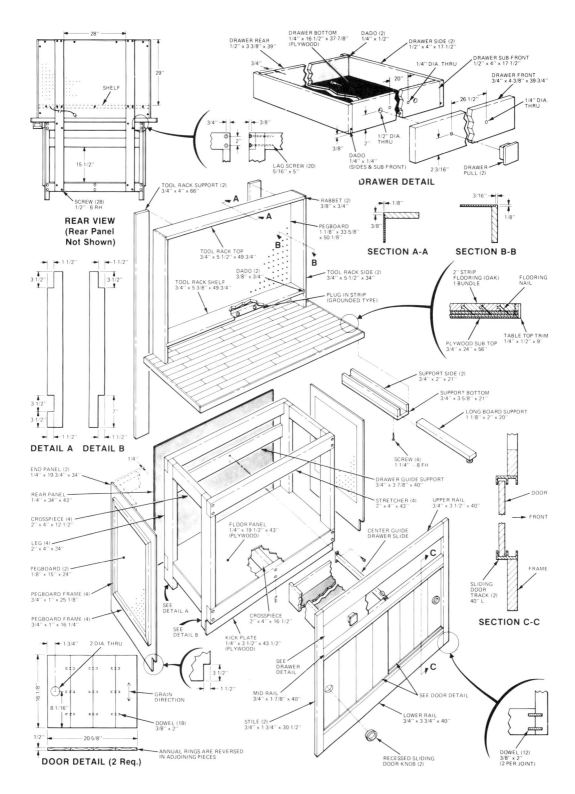

REAR VIEW
(Rear Panel
Not Shown)

SHELF

28"

29"

15 1/2"

SCREW (28)
1/2" 6 RH

3/4"   3/8"

2"

LAG SCREW (20)
5/16" x 5"

DRAWER REAR
1/2" x 3 3/8" x 39"

DRAWER BOTTOM
1/4" x 16 1/2" x 37 7/8"
(PLYWOOD)

DADO (2)
1/4" x 1/2"

DRAWER SIDE (2)
1/2" x 4" x 17 1/2"

1/4" DIA. THRU

3/4"

20"

DRAWER SUB-FRONT
1/2" x 4" x 17 1/2"

DRAWER FRONT
3/4" x 4 3/8" x 39 3/4"

1/4" DIA.
THRU

26 1/2"

1/2" DIA.
THRU

2"

3/8"

DADO
1/4" x 1/4"
(SIDES & SUB-FRONT)

2 3/16"

DRAWER
PULL (2)

DRAWER DETAIL

TOOL RACK SUPPORT (2)
3/4" x 4" x 66"

RABBET (2)
3/8" x 3/4"

PEGBOARD
1 1/8" x 33 5/8" x 50 1/8"

TOOL RACK TOP
3/4" x 5 1/2" x 49 3/4"

TOOL RACK SHELF
3/4" x 5 3/8" x 49 3/4"

DADO (2)
3/8" x 3/4"

TOOL RACK SIDE (2)
3/4" x 5 1/2" x 34"

PLUG IN STRIP
(GROUNDED TYPE)

A   A

B

B

1/8"

3/8"

3/16"

1/8"

SECTION A-A   **SECTION B-B**

2" STRIP
FLOORING (OAK)
1 BUNDLE

FLOORING
NAIL

PLYWOOD SUB-TOP
3/4" x 24" x 56"

TABLE TOP TRIM
1/4" x 1/2" x 9'

1 1/2"   1 1/2"

3 1/2"   3 1/2"

3 1/2"   7"

3 1/2"

1 1/2"   1 1/2"

DETAIL A   DETAIL B

SUPPORT SIDE (2)
3/4" x 2" x 21"

SUPPORT BOTTOM
3/4" x 3 5/8" x 21"

LONG BOARD SUPPORT
1 1/8" x 2" x 20"

SCREW (4)
1 1/4" – 8 FH

END PANEL (2)
1/4" x 19 3/4" x 34"

1/4"

REAR PANEL
1/4" x 34" x 43"

CROSSPIECE (4)
2" x 4" x 12 1/2"

LEG (4)
2" x 4" x 34"

PEGBOARD (2)
1/8" x 15" x 24"

PEGBOARD FRAME (4)
3/4" x 1" x 25 1/8"

PEGBOARD FRAME (4)
3/4" x 1" x 16 1/4"

FLOOR PANEL
1/4" x 19 1/2" x 43"
(PLYWOOD)

SEE
DETAIL A

SEE
DETAIL B

CROSSPIECE
2" x 4" x 16 1/2"

KICK PLATE
1/4" x 3 1/2" x 43 1/2"
(PLYWOOD)

DRAWER GUIDE SUPPORT
3/4" x 3 7/8" x 40"

STRETCHER (4)
2" x 4" x 43"

CENTER GUIDE
DRAWER SLIDE

UPPER RAIL
3/4" x 3 1/2" x 40"

DOOR

FRONT

FRAME

SLIDING
DOOR
TRACK (2)
40" L

SECTION C-C

C

C

SEE
DRAWER
DETAIL

MID RAIL
3/4" x 1 7/8" x 40"

SEE DOOR DETAIL

1 3/4"

2 DIA. THRU

16 1/8"

8 1/16"

DOWEL (18)
3/8" x 2"

1/2"

20 5/8"

GRAIN
DIRECTION

3 1/2"

1 1/2"

ANNUAL RINGS ARE REVERSED
IN ADJOINING PIECES

DOOR DETAIL (2 Req.)

STILE (2)
3/4" x 1 3/4" x 30 1/2"

LOWER RAIL
3/4" x 3 3/4" x 40"

RECESSED SLIDING
DOOR KNOB (2)

DOWEL (12)
3/8" x 2"
(2 PER JOINT)

extend the length of the top in one piece. Let the ends overhang and fasten the strip with 1½-inch spiral flooring nails. These are driven diagonally through the tongue of the strip.

Before installing the first strip, bore six ³⁄₃₂-inch-diameter holes, ¼ inch in from the leading edge. Counterbore these holes with a ⁵⁄₃₂-inch-diameter bit and make this hole ⅛ inch deep. Align the edge of the strip with the edge of the plywood and drive nails into each of the holes. Now proceed with the diagonal nailing. Drive the nails at a 45-degree angle and to a point where the nailheads are still slightly above the wood surface, then complete nailing with a nail set. This will prevent damage to the strip edges.

The strips for the second course are installed with the groove fitted tightly against the tongue of the preceding course. Use a scrap of flooring to tap the strips tightly into place before nailing.

When nailing near the strip ends, it may be necessary to drill pilot holes for the nails to prevent splitting. The end joints in each course must be staggered at least 8 inches apart. Each course must be installed so the ends overhang slightly. When the last row is installed, use the same procedure as used in the first course. Bore holes near the rear edge and drive the nails straight down. If necessary, trim the rear strip.

The overhang is now trimmed with a saber saw or circular saw. Trim close to the plywood but leave about ¹⁄₁₆-inch overhang. This is then retrimmed using a router fitted with a panel trimming bit. Set the cutter so the guide of the bit rides against the end of the plywood edge. The result will be a cleanly trimmed edge with both the plywood and the hardwood perfectly flush. Be wary of voids in the plywood edge as this could cause the router bit to dip and cut an indent in the hardwood edge.

The end and front edges of the top are covered with a piece of trim ¼ inch thick by 1½ inches wide. Install the ends first, then follow with the front. Hold with brads.

The sliding doors are made of ½-inch pine. To prevent cupping, each door should be made of at least four pieces of wood, glued up to form the panel. Cut each door from a length of stock and reverse the annular rings as indicated on the drawing. This will ensure that the doors will remain flat. Use dowels or if you have a shaper, you may want to use a glue joint instead. Make the doors slightly oversize in height, then trim to the necessary size. Note sliding door track varies among manufacturers so be sure to have the track installed before cutting the doors to height.

The drawer is made of ½-inch stock except for the front which is ¾ inch thick. Cut and assemble the pieces as indicated. The front and subfront are installed temporarily with two screws installed in oversize holes bored through the subfront. This will allow adjustment of the front panel over the drawer opening.

Because of the width of the drawer, two drawer runners are used as indicated.

The frame for the pegboard is assembled from ¾-inch stock. Rabbet the rear edges of the sides and top member to take the pegboard. Install the pegboard with flat-head screws.

The tool rack may be wall or table mounted. If wall-mounted, install it so it just clears the bench top. If mounted to the

MATERIALS LIST

Purpose	Size	Description	Quantity
Leg	2″ × 4″ × 34″		4
Stretcher	2″ × 4″ × 43″		4
Crosspiece	2″ × 4″ × 12½″		4
Crosspiece	2″ × 4″ × 16½″		1
Floor panel	¼″ × 19½″ × 43″	Plywood	1
End panel	¼″ × 19¾″ × 34″	Plywood	2
Kick plate	¼″ × 3½″ × 43½″	Plywood	1
Rear panel	¼″ × 34″ × 43″	Plywood	1
Stile	¾″ × 1¾″ × 30½″	Pine	2
Upper rail	¾″ × 3½″ × 40″	Pine	1
Mid rail	¾″ × 1⅞″ × 40″	Pine	1
Lower rail	¾″ × 3¾″ × 40″	Pine	1
Drawer guide support	¾″ × 3⅞″ × 40″	Pine	1
Subtop	¾″ × 24″ × 56″	Plywood	1
Top	2″ strip flooring	Bundle oak	1
Door	½″ × 16⅛″ × 20⅝″	Pine	2
Drawer front	¾″ × 4⅜″ × 39¾″	Pine	1
Drawer subfront	½″ × 4″ × 38⅝″	Pine	1
Drawer side	½″ × 4″ × 17½″	Pine	2
Drawer rear	½″ × 3⅜″ × 39″	Pine	1
Drawer bottom	¼″ × 16½″ × 38⅞″	Plywood	1
Tool rack side	¾″ × 5½″ × 34″	Pine	2
Tool rack top	¾″ × 5½″ × 49¾″	Pine	1
Tool rack shelf	¾″ × 5⅜″ × 49¾″	Pine	1
Pegboard	⅛″ × 33⅝″ × 50⅛″		1
Pegboard	⅛″ × 15″ × 24″		2
Pegboard frame	¾″ × 1″ × 16¼″	Pine	4
Pegboard frame	¾″ × 1″ × 25⅛″	Pine	4
Long board support	1⅛″ × 2″ × 20″	Pine	1
Support side	¾″ × 2″ × 21″	Pine	2
Support bottom	¾″ × 3⅝″ × 21″	Pine	1
Table top trim	¼″ × 1½″ × 9′	Pine	
Tool rack support	¾″ × 4″ × 66″	Pine	2
Center slide hardware			
Drawer pull			
Sliding door track			
Recessed sliding door knob			
Plug-in strip (grounded type)			
Finishing nails	2″		
Finishing nails	1½″		
Lag screws	⅝″ × 5″		20
Screws	1¼″	No. 8 FH	16
Screws	½″	No. 6 RH	28

bench, let it rest on the bench and support it at the rear with two boards which span the frame.

The long work support is placed at the end of the table opposite the end where the vise is installed. The support is fitted with a knob on the underside and pulls out as required when working on long boards held by the vise. Installation details are shown on the drawing.

The small frames are made with mitered joints. The backs are rabbeted similar to the tool rack.

Add the rear panel to the bench to complete construction. Add the plug-in strip after the bench has been finished. The bench shown was finished with three coats of white shellac. The pegboard was given a couple of coats of semigloss latex paint.

3-In-1 Patio Unit

THIS VERSATILE PIECE of patio furniture is actually three pieces in one. With the top down it serves as an informal table for deck or poolside parties. Need a bench? Just raise the rear section and presto, you have a neat bench with an 18-inch backrest. To convert to a chaise lounge merely fold the hinged back down again, then tilt one end up to any of three positions. The compartment underneath can be used to store cushions.

The piece is made of redwood and measures 6 feet long, 3 feet wide, and 16 inches high. We used clear redwood for the flat boards and construction grade 2 × 4's for the framework. Lag screws were utilized where structurally required. Hot-dipped galvanized finishing nails were used to fasten the flat boards. The galvanized nails have tremendous holding power; the surface is rough so they really hold, and being galvanized they won't rust.

The double-jointed top is assembled with 8 butt hinges. The ones we used were exactly ¼-inch thick, the same as the spacing used between the boards. The hinge thickness is not critical however. The closed width is more important; it should be ¾ inch or close to it.

The lumber used is 2 × 4's and 1 × 6's, nominal size. Actual measurements are 1½ × 3 inches and ¾ × 5½ inches. Choose knot-free pieces for the six legs then cut them to 16-inch lengths. You can do this on the radial arm saw or table saw, but be sure that all lengths are exact.

The tops of each legs must be notched to fit around the 2 × 4 crosspieces. This

Fig. 33-1. Legs are notched on table saw. Stop clamped to the fence limits length of cut. Band saw is used to complete cut.

Fig. 33-2. Screws should pass over each other without interference. Flat washers should be installed under screw heads.

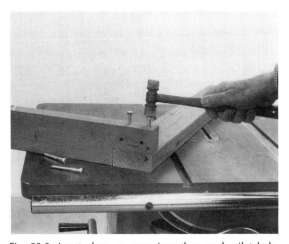

Fig. 33-3. Locate legs on crosspiece then mark pilot hole locations using lag screws to indent centers and to fasten with.

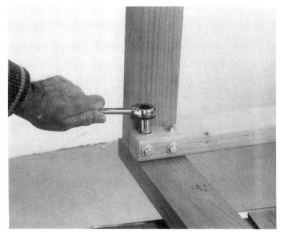

Fig. 33-4. The rail is added to complete the frame assembly. Do not overtighten screws. Notched rails are supported by blocks.

can be done entirely with the band saw, but we found it more practical to use the table saw for greater accuracy.

The crosscut is made first. Elevate the table saw blade to a height of 1¾ inch then, with a small piece of ¾-inch stock against the fence, place the work against the ¾-inch wood and set the fence to cut into the leg exactly 3½ inches from the end of the

piece. Use the miter gauge to hold the work on edge then remove the ¾-inch scrap, turn on the power and make the blind cut. The scrap piece is used to keep the end of the stock clear of the fence while the cut is being made to avoid kickback.

The rip cut is made next. Elevate the blade as high as it will go then set the rip fence 1¾ inches to the outside of the blade.

Make a test cut on a piece of scrap 2 × 4. The remaining stock should be exactly 1¾ inches wide.

Clamp a stop block to the fence to limit the length of the cut. The bottom of the saw blade should cut into the leg 3½ inches. The waste will not cut off completely because of the curvature of the blade. Complete the cut with a handsaw or band saw.

Drill the ⅜-inch-diameter holes for the lag screws, noting that the holes are offset slightly so the screws will pass over each other where they cross. The rails and crosspieces are cut to size then joined at the corners by means of the lag screws. The center crosspiece is notched at two places as shown. Do this by making two vertical saw cuts then clean out the notch with a chisel.

Make the notches ¾ inch deep. Install the legs centered on the rail. This will place the middle crosspiece slightly off center. Cut, drill and mount the 10-inch support blocks. The two blocks mounted on the center crosspiece should be offset about one inch to allow the lag screws to clear each other.

Make the two support members next. These are built from 2- × -4 stock which has been ripped in half. The unit for the bench support is made to hinge because of space limitations. A strap hinge provides sufficient strength and is narrow enough to fit the 1¾-inch-wide stock. The sliding bolt keeps the support from accidentally folding when in use. The unit pivots on a 3-inch lag screw. The end of this piece and the other support (for the chaise) are shaped to conform to the mating part.

The lower rail is made by ripping a 64-inch-length of 2 × 4. Drill the screw holes then mount as shown.

The lower compartment panels are cut to length then installed with a ¼-inch space between the boards. Before installing, round all corners with a router fitted with a ⁵⁄₁₆-inch rounding bit. The two center boards and the two end boards must be notched to fit around the legs. Notch the two center boards then install the rest of the boards working from center out. Notch the end boards as required to clear the legs. Install the boards with 1½-inch H.D. finishing nails.

The top boards are cut to 18-inch

Fig. 33-5. Panels are spaced using a stick with ¼″ dowels at each end to ensure alignment. Check squareness of panels.

Fig. 33-6. Bench back is held with two-piece support. Notched end fits corner of seat support. Sliding bolt holds support.

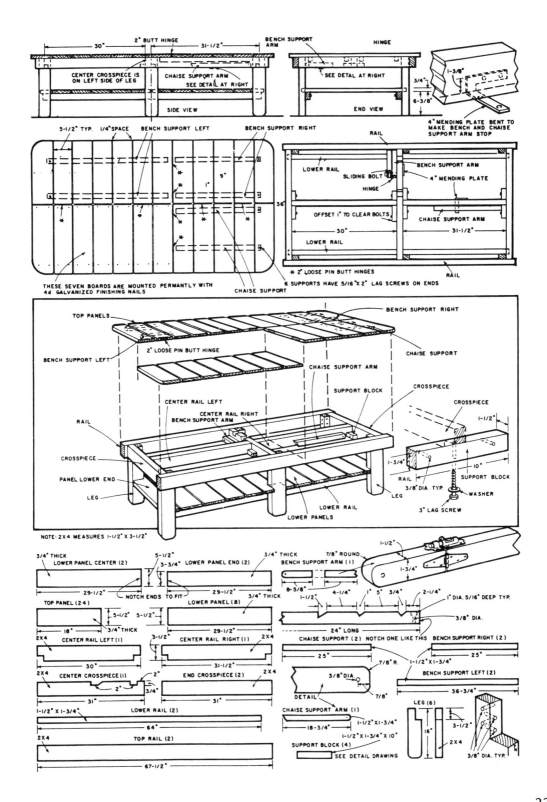

CENTER CROSSPIECE IS ON LEFT SIDE OF LEG

2" BUTT HINGE
30"
31-1/2"
BENCH SUPPORT ARM
CHAISE SUPPORT ARM
SEE DETAIL AT RIGHT
SIDE VIEW

HINGE
SEE DETAIL AT RIGHT
END VIEW

1-3/8"
3/4"
6-3/8"
4" MENDING PLATE BENT TO MAKE BENCH AND CHAISE SUPPORT ARM STOP

5-1/2" TYP. 1/4" SPACE
BENCH SUPPORT LEFT
BENCH SUPPORT RIGHT

1"
9"

THESE SEVEN BOARDS ARE MOUNTED PERMANENTLY WITH 4d GALVANIZED FINISHING NAILS

CHAISE SUPPORT

RAIL
LOWER RAIL
SLIDING BOLT
HINGE
BENCH SUPPORT ARM
4" MENDING PLATE
OFFSET 1" TO CLEAR BOLTS
CHAISE SUPPORT ARM
30"
31-1/2"
LOWER RAIL
36
RAIL

* 2" LOOSE PIN BUTT HINGES
6 SUPPORTS HAVE 5/16" X 2" LAG SCREWS ON ENDS

TOP PANELS
BENCH SUPPORT RIGHT
2" LOOSE PIN BUTT HINGE
BENCH SUPPORT LEFT
CHAISE SUPPORT
CHAISE SUPPORT ARM
SUPPORT BLOCK
CENTER RAIL LEFT
CROSSPIECE
CENTER RAIL RIGHT
BENCH SUPPORT ARM
CROSSPIECE
RAIL
1-1/2"
CROSSPIECE
PANEL LOWER END
LEG
1-3/4"
RAIL
SUPPORT BLOCK
10"
3/8" DIA. TYP.
LEG
WASHER
LOWER RAIL
LOWER PANELS
3" LAG SCREW

NOTE: 2X4 MEASURES 1-1/2" X 3-1/2"

3/4" THICK
LOWER PANEL CENTER (2)
29-1/2"

5-1/2"
3-3/4" LOWER PANEL END (2)
29-1/2"
NOTCH ENDS TO FIT
3/4" THICK

7/8" ROUND
BENCH SUPPORT ARM (1)
1-1/2"
1-3/4"
8-5/8"
4-1/4"
1" 5" 3/4"
2-1/4"
1" DIA. 5/16" DEEP TYP.
1-1/2"
3/8" DIA.

TOP PANEL (24)
5-1/2" 5-1/2"
18"
3/4" THICK

LOWER PANEL (8)
29-1/2"
3/4" THICK

24" LONG
CHAISE SUPPORT (2) NOTCH ONE LIKE THIS

2X4 CENTER RAIL LEFT (1)
30"
3-1/2"
2X4 CENTER RAIL RIGHT (1)
31-1/2"

25"
7/8" R.
1-1/2" X 1-3/4"
BENCH SUPPORT RIGHT (2)
25"

2X4 CENTER CROSSPIECE (1)
2"
2"
3/4"
END CROSSPIECE (2)
31"
2X4
31"

3/8" DIA.
7/8" R.
DETAIL
7/8"
BENCH SUPPORT LEFT (2)
36-3/4"

1-1/2" X 1-3/4"
LOWER RAIL (2)
64"

CHAISE SUPPORT ARM (1)
18-3/4"
1-1/2" X 1-3/4"
1-1/2" X 1-3/4" X 10"

LEG (6)
3-1/2"
16"
2X4
3/8" DIA. TYP.

2X4
TOP RAIL (2)
67-1/2"

SUPPORT BLOCK (4)
SEE DETAIL DRAWING

MATERIALS LIST

All lumber is redwood. All measurements are in inches.

Purpose	Size	Quantity
Rail	1½″ × 3½″ × 67½″	2
Crosspiece	1½″ × 3½″ × 31″	3
Leg	1½″ × 3½″ × 16″	6
Lower rail	1½″ × 1¾″ × 64″	2
Panel top	¾″ × 5½″ × 18″	24
Panel, lower	¾″ × 5½″ × 29½″	10
Panel, lower end	¾″ × 3¾″ × 29½″	2
Support block	1½″ × 1¾″ × 10″	4
Center rail, left	1½″ × 1¾″ × 30″	1
Center rail, right	1½″ × 1¾″ × 31½″	1
Bench support, left	1½″ × 1¾″ × 36¾″	2
Bench support, right	1½″ × 1¾″ × 25″	2
Chaise support	1½″ × 1¾″ × 25″	2
Bench support arm	1½″ × 1¾″ × 8⅝″	2
Chaise support arm	1½″ × 1¾″ × 18″	1
Lag screw	5⁄16″ × 3″	44
Lag screw	5⁄16″ × 2″	6
Flat washer	5⁄16″ ID	46
Finishing nails	4d galvanized	1 lb.
Butt hinge	2″ loose pin	8
Hinge, strap	3″	1
Sliding bolt	3″	1
Mending plate	4″	2

lengths and the four outer pieces are rounded with a ¾-inch radius. All of the boards are rounded with the router and 5⁄16-inch rounding bit. Seven boards are mounted permanently to the lower left section of the frame.

Start the first board 39½ inches from the left end of the rail and let it overhang one inch. Fasten the boards with the coated nails. Because of the smaller bearing surface at the ends due to the overhang, the end pieces are reinforced with 2-inch lag screws.

The board supports for the back and end are ripped from 2 × 4's. They are then drilled and notched as indicated. Mount the boards to these with the ¼-inch-spacing and be sure that the ends are aligned perfectly. The three sections are hinged to each other and to the fixed boards as shown. The use of loose pin hinges simplifies installation. Mount the hinges so they are flush with the top of the boards.

The entire top should be sanded smooth then finished. We used a semi-transparent redwood stain.

3-In-1 Sports Gear Cabinet

WHETHER YOU ENJOY hunting, fishing, camping, tennis, golf, or skiing you can adapt this basic cabinet design to hold your gear—or you can build a row of them, each with a different interior arrangement to suit your own needs.

To build the hunting cabinet, first lay out the parts on three sheets of plywood as shown on the plans. True the edges with 1/0 sandpaper on a block and rabbet one end of each side panel for the top.

Assemble the cabinet on its back on the floor with resin glue and finishing nails. Use your square frequently to ensure accurate work.

While the glue is setting, glue and nail the door framing strips and the door panel together, following clearance all around as indicated.

When the glue of the cabinet has set, build the interior shelves and drawers as shown on the plans. Use glue and finishing nails to join the parts to each other and to the cabinet.

Cutouts for the gun stock and barrel racks are made as shown in the plans. The surest way to establish the correct height for each (so the weapons will fit in the case) is by trial and error. With your guns in the cabinet, try them at various heights. When the correct height is reached, hold the rack in place and mark the position. When the position of each rack is marked, remove the guns and glue and nail the racks in place. Install a hinged bar and a lock on front of the upper rack.

Next, build the shelves and facings in the door. The facing should be flush with the framing strips. Note how quarter-round molding is used to strengthen the inside corners of the facing.

Smooth all joints and slightly round the corners with 3/0 sandpaper. Fill any nail holes and exposed plywood edge grain with wood filler, smooth the entire cabinet with 3/0 sandpaper.

Place the cabinet on its back and attach the door to the cabinet with four pin-

SKI, GOLF AND TENNIS CABINET

NOTE: Bill of Materials is on following page

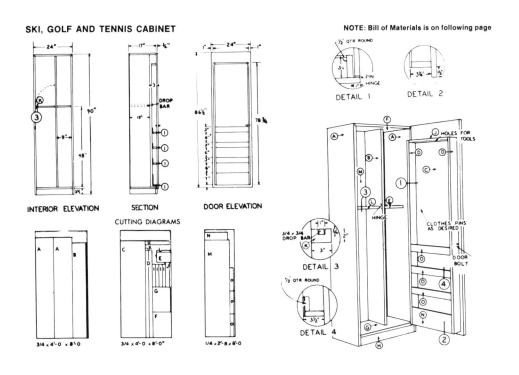

INTERIOR ELEVATION   SECTION   DOOR ELEVATION

DETAIL I   DETAIL 2

CUTTING DIAGRAMS

3/4 x 4'-0 x 8'-0   3/4 x 4'-0 x 8'-0"   1/4 x 2'-8 x 8'-0

DETAIL 3

DETAIL 4

HUNTING-FISHING CABINET

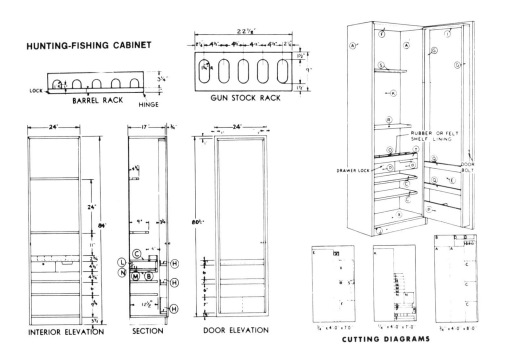

BARREL RACK   GUN STOCK RACK

INTERIOR ELEVATION   SECTION   DOOR ELEVATION

CUTTING DIAGRAMS

3/4 x 4'-0 x 7'-0   1/4 x 4'-0 x 7'-0   3/4 x 4'-0 x 8'-0

MATERIALS LIST

Purpose	Size	Description	Quantity
Sides	¾″ × 17″ × 84″	A-D interior plywood	2
Drawer shelf	¾″ × 12″ × 22½″	A-D interior plywood	1
Shelves	¾″ × 12½″ × 22½″	A-D interior plywood	3
Drawer fronts	¾″ × 4½″ × 11¼″	A-D interior plywood	2
Door	¾″ × 24″ × 80½″	A-D interior plywood	1
Top	¾″ × 17″ × 23¼″	A-D interior plywood	1
Door frame	¾″ × 3¼″ × 77¼″	A-D interior plywood	2
Door shelves	¾″ × 3″ × 20½″	A-D interior plywood	3
Base	¾″ × 3½″ × 22½″	A-D interior plywood	1
Door top shelf	¾″ × 3¼″ × 22″	A-D interior plywood	1
Gun stock rack	¾″ × 9″ × 22½″	A-D interior plywood	1
Barrel rack	¾″ × 4¼″ × 22½″	A-D interior plywood	1
Bottom shelf	¾″ × 16¾″ × 22½″	A-D interior plywood	1
Back	¼″ × 23¼″ × 80⅛″	A-D interior plywood	1
Drawer backs	¼″ × 3″ × 11″	A-D interior plywood	2
Drawer sides	¼″ × 3¾″ × 12⅛″	A-D interior plywood	4
Drawer bottoms	¼″ × 10¾″ × 12⅛″	A-D interior plywood	2
Dividers	¼″ × 2″ × 3½″	A-D interior plywood	4
Door shelf fascia	¼″ × 7″ × 20½″	A-D interior plywood	1
Door shelf divider	¼″ × 3″ × 6¼″	A-D interior plywood	1
Door shelf fascia	¼″ × 2″ × 20½″	A-D interior plywood	2
Gun shelf face	¼″ × 2¾″ × 22½″	A-D interior plywood	1
Gun shelf face	¼″ × 2⅜″ × 22½″	A-D interior plywood	1
Backing	¼″ × 20½″ × 56″	Cork	1
Lining	9″ × 22½″	Rubber or felt	

Note: You will also need rack hinge and lock, drawer lock, door bolt, pin hinges, 4d and 6d finishing nails, glue, clips and finishing materials.

hinges. The door may be hinged at either side. Install a suitable catch or lock.

Give the whole cabinet a coat of primer and then finish it with two coats of semigloss enamel. Install any lining material you feel is appropriate and any fixtures or hardware needed to accommodate your gear.

The camping cabinet and the ski, golf, and tennis cabinet are made in the same way as the hunting and fishing cabinet with different arrangements for the interior shelving as shown on the plans.

In addition, using the basic design for the cabinet shell and door, you can easily improvise your own interior design to accommodate almost anything.

For indoor uses, such as in these cabinets, plywood can be joined with resin glue (white glue) and nails. Use 6d finishing nails for ¾ and ⅝-inch plywood, 3d or 4d nails for ⅜-inch, and 1-inch brads for ¼-inch plywood.

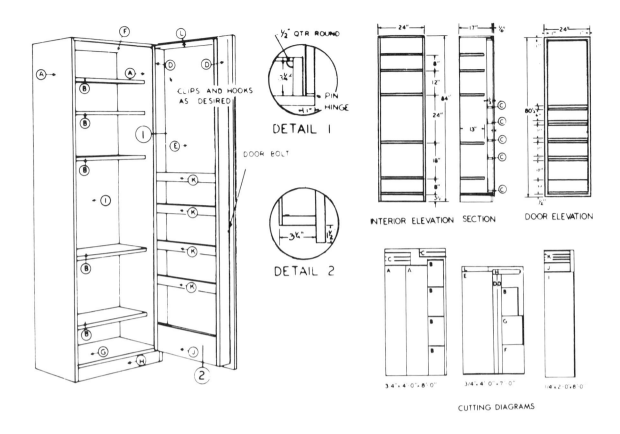

CLIPS AND HOOKS AS DESIRED

DETAIL 1

DOOR BOLT

DETAIL 2

INTERIOR ELEVATION   SECTION   DOOR ELEVATION

CUTTING DIAGRAMS

MATERIALS LIST

Purpose	Size	Description	Quantity
Sides	¾″ × 17″ × 84″	A-D interior plywood	2
Shelves	¾″ × 13″ × 22½″	A-D interior plywood	5
Door shelves	¾″ × 3″ × 20½″	A-D interior plywood	5
Door side frame	¾″ × 3¼″ × 78″	A-D interior plywood	2
Door top frame	¾″ × 3¼″ × 20½″	A-D interior plywood	1
Door	¾″ × 24″ × 80½″	A-D interior plywood	1
Top	¾″ × 17″ × 23¼″	A-D interior plywood	1
Bottom shelf	¾″ × 17″ × 22½″	A-D interior plywood	1
Base	¾″ × 3½″ × 22½″	A-D interior plywood	1
Back	¼″ × 23¼″ × 80⅛″	A-D interior plywood	1
Door shelf fascia	¼″ × 7″ × 20½″	A-D interior plywood	1
Door shelf fascia	¼″ × 2″ × 20½″	A-D interior plywood	4
	¼″ × ¼″ × 30″	Quarter round molding	1

Note: You will also need pin hinges, door bolt, 4d and 6d finishing nails, glue, clips, hooks and finishing materials.

MATERIALS LIST

Purpose	Size	Description	Quantity
Sides	¾″ × 9″ × 13″	A-D interior plywood	2
Standard	¾″ × 17″ × 23¼″	A-D interior plywood	1
Door	¾″ × 16¾″ × 22½″	A-D interior plywood	1
Door side frame	¾″ × 3½″ × 22½″	A-D interior plywood	2
Shelf	¾″ × 3″ × 20½″	A-D interior plywood	1
Top	¾″ × 3¼″ × 20½″	A-D interior plywood	1
Bottom shelf	¾″ × 2″ × 3″	A-D interior plywood	1
Base	¾″ × ¾″ × 12¾″	A-D interior plywood	1
Door shelves	¼″ × 23¼″ × 86⅛″	A-D interior plywood	4
Top door tool shelf	¼″ × 7″ × 20½″	A-D interior plywood	1
Drop bar catch	¼″ × 3″ × 20½″	A-D interior plywood	1
Drop bar	½″ × ½″ × 30″	Quarter round molding	1
Back	¾″ × 17″ × 90″	A-D interior plywood	1
Door shelf fascia	¾″ × 13″ × 85″	A-D interior plywood	1
Door shelf fascia	¾″ × 24″ × 86½″	A-D interior plywood	3
	¾″ × 3¼″ × 78¾″	A-D interior plywood	1

Note: You will also need hinge for drop bar, door bolt, pin hinges, 4d and 6d finishing nails, glue and finishing materials.

Tile-Top Table with Built-In Planter

IF YOU'RE SEARCHING for a coffee table that is beautiful, distinctive and unique, you won't be able to resist this one. This table features a lovely ceramic tiled top (your own selection) and a planter insert which can hold real live plants for the green thumbed or artificial plants for the nongardener. The planter is made with acrylic plastic and is easily removable so you can plant, replant, or transplant plants away from the table without fear of messing it up with soil or water.

The table is made of butternut wood which has a lovely grain pattern. This wood must be handled carefully however, as it tends to split easily. The ceramic tiles are 8 inches square and ⅜ inch thick. Ceramic tiles for a tabletop make a lot of sense. They are durable, not affected by

alcohol or heat, easily cleaned, require no upkeep, and pattern choices and colors are almost limitless. We used ⅛-inch Plexiglas for the plants, which is readily available at most glass shops.

Simplified construction methods have been devised so even the novice can make this table without much difficulty. A router is used to form the flutes on the lower part of the apron. It is also utilized for the cove cut at the upper part of the legs and for the add-on strip at the bottom edge of the apron.

The legs are constructed first. Glue-up two pieces of 1-inch stock. Note that 1 inch refers to the nominal size of the lumber. The dressed size is the actual size of the stock and it is ¾ inch for softwoods and ¹³⁄₁₆ inch for hardwoods. Although the

228

Fig. 35-1. A leg is set up for cutting flutes with the router. Note jig clamped to base of router to position and limit the cut.

Fig. 35-2. The legs are then clamped together in pairs to bore the half rounds. This is best done, as here, on a drill press.

Fig. 35-3. To smooth out the half round sandpaper is wrapped round a dowel which is fixed in the drill as a sanding drum.

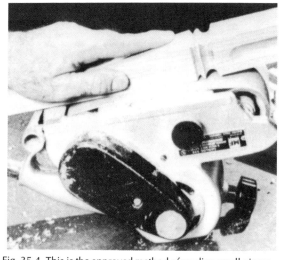

Fig. 35-4. This is the approved method of sanding small pieces with a belt sander. If tool is lightweight, clamp it to table.

difference between the two is not very great, it can cause problems. If you use hardwood, follow the measurements shown; otherwise make the slight adjustment needed for softwoods.

After the glue has set, the leg squares must be cut to size. Next lay out the shape of the leg on one face of each piece. Mark the center line for the ½-inch concave cut on each piece, then square over the line around each piece using a try square. Clamp two legs as shown, and drill a ½-inch-diameter hole through each pair.

After each hole is drilled, rotate each

leg 90 degrees, clamp, and repeat the drilling operation. When done, each leg will have a clean semicircular cut as shown. The angular cuts just below the curved section are made with a saber saw or band saw.

The narrow kerf cuts near the bottom of each leg must be made while the legs are still square. Square a pencil line around the

leg 1½ inch from the bottom end. Use a hack saw to make the kerf cuts. Make them ⅜ inch deep and be sure they are in perfect alignment around the leg.

The tapers are cut with the saber saw or band saw. An alternative is to use the table saw for taper ripping with a tapering jig. This method works very well, but because of the small size of the legs, the

Fig. 35-5. Here the tapers are being cut on a band saw. Note that the pencil lines for the second side will have to be redrawn.

Fig. 35-6. Pieces of scrap wood should be used to raise it to the proper height when the dowel holes are being transferred.

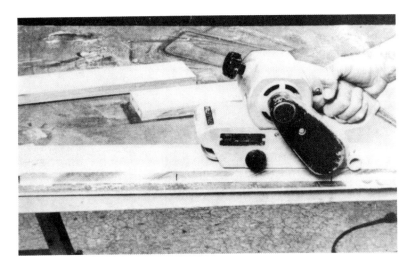

Fig. 35-7. The apron pieces which make up the sides of the coffee table planter must be sanded before the basic unit is finally put together. The final sanding, shown here, should be done with an oscillating belt-type sander loaded with fine grit paper.

230

Fig. 35-8. A special procedure must be used in assembling the top frame. Parts must be installed in pairs, one long and one short per section. Then the sections are drawn together in this jig, made from scrap wood and assembled with drawn bars shown.

Fig. 35-9. The apron is fastened to the top with screws. Note that the holes are counterbored. The pieces of pine which are used as supports for the tiles are cut and screwed to the crosspieces in position. The other end will be held with a cleat.

hands are rather close to the blade and this could be dangerous. The drawing shows how the jig is made and used. A push stick is recommended for this operation.

The legs are fluted using a core box cutter and a jig which is clamped to the router base. The router is used upside down and in this manner it works like a shaper. The jig is cut in the shape of an L. A scrap piece of ⅜-inch or ½-inch plywood works fine. The long side of the L serves as a fence against which the work is pushed. The short part of the L acts as a stop, limiting the length of the flute.

In the example, one wide flute was made, but you might prefer to substitute a narrower cutter and make two or even three flutes. You will have to move the jig for each cut however. Regardless of the number of flutes you make, test the cut on scrap wood the same width as the legs before cutting the actual pieces.

After the legs are cut and shaped, they must be sanded. The curved part is best done with a piece of sandpaper wrapped around a ½-inch dowel. Use it by hand or mount the dowel in a drill for a faster and smoother operation. The tapered part can

Fig. 35-10. The planter support is being installed here. It will be held in place with screws driven diagonally through ends.

Fig. 35-11. This view shows how the tiles rest on the tile base. And this, in its turn rests on the tile-bases supports.

be done on a belt sander. If you use a portable belt sander, mount it upside down and move the work back and forth until flat and smooth.

The aprons are ripped to size, then cut to the proper length. Note that we have made a series of 9/16-inch-deep kerf cuts on the back side of the long pieces. This was done because the wood was badly bowed. If your lumber is flat, disregard this operation.

The double flute near the lower edge of the apron is made with the router. This can be done in the conventional manner by clamping a guide strip on the work, or by clamping one to the router base. If you have a router guide, set it for the proper depth and cut the flutes first, one on all the pieces, then reset to cut the second flute.

The strip at the bottom of the apron is ripped to size then rounded at the outer edge. After shaping, sand it smooth and likewise sand the face of the apron, then add the strip to the lower edge of the apron.

Use glue and brads.

Drill and counterbore the apron mounting holes. The depth of the counterbore must be fairly accurate or you may find the mounting screws penetrating the top frame. If you use the drill press, set the depth gauge. If you use a portable drill, wrap a piece of tape on the drill bit to indicate the proper depth.

Drill the dowel holes at each end of the apron. Make these holes 1¼ inch deep, then drill the mating holes in each of the legs ¾ inch deep. (Note: If you are to use a doweling jig to drill the holes into the apron ends, do this before adding the strip at the bottom as it will interfere with the jig.)

The legs are glued to the long aprons first. After the glue has set, the two assemblies are glued to the short aprons. To attempt to glue and clamp the four aprons and four legs at one time would be tricky. You will need long bar clamps when gluing the legs to the long aprons.

232

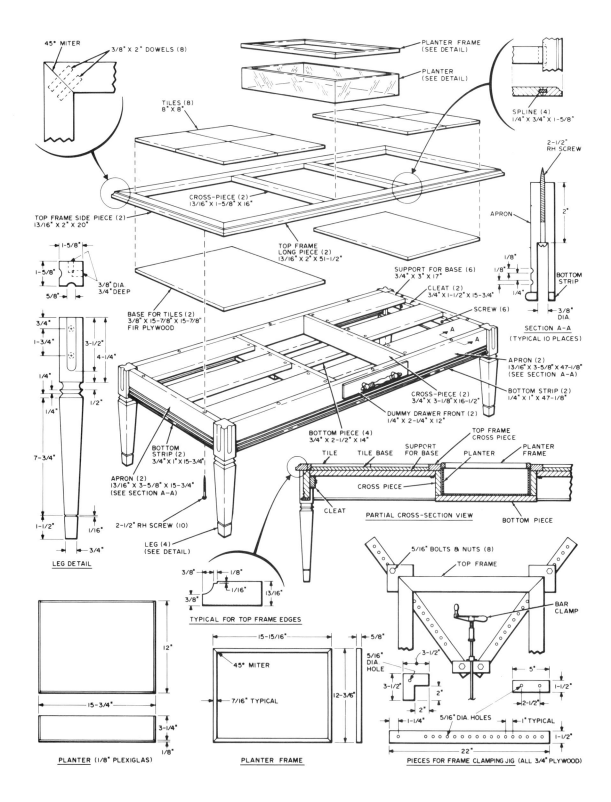

MATERIALS LIST

Except where noted, all lumber is $^{13}/_{16}$" butternut.

Purpose	Size	Description	Quantity
Apron, short	$3^5/_8$" × $15^3/_4$"		2
Apron, long	$3^5/_8$" × $47^1/_8$"		2
Apron trim short	$^1/_4$" × 1" × $15^3/_4$"		2
Apron trim long	$^1/_4$" × 1" × $47^1/_8$"		2
Leg	$1^5/_8$" × $1^5/_8$" × $14^1/_2$"		4
Crosspiece	$1^5/_8$" × 16"		2
Spline	$^1/_4$" × $1^5/_8$" × $^3/_4$"		2
Top, short	$2^1/_8$" × $20^1/_4$"		2
Top, long	$2^1/_8$" × $51^1/_4$"		2
Planter frame, long	$^7/_{16}$" × $^5/_8$" × 16"		2
Planter frame, short	$^7/_{16}$" × $^5/_8$" × $12^1/_4$"		2
Dummy drawer front	$^1/_4$" × $2^1/_4$" × 12"		2
Planter compartment side	$3^1/_8$" × $16^1/_2$"		2
Planter compartment bottom	$^3/_4$" × $2^1/_2$" × $13^3/_4$"	Pine	4
Tile base support	$^3/_4$" × 3" × 17"	Pine	6
Tile base support cleat	$^3/_4$" × $1^1/_2$" × $15^3/_4$"		2
Tile base	$^3/_6$" × $15^7/_8$" × $15^7/_8$"	Fir plywood	2
Planter	$^1/_8$"	Plexiglas	
Side	$3^1/_4$" × $15^1/_2$"		2
End	$3^1/_4$" × 12"		2
Bottom	12" × $15^3/_4$"		1

As a substitute, you can use a wedge-type clamp, utilizing your workbench top or other flat surface for this purpose. Screw or clamp a stop at one end of the table.

At the other end fasten a wedge-shaped piece the same way with clamp or screws. Position the wedge so another wedge can fit between it and the workpiece. Carefully strike the loose wedge with a hammer so it tightens up the assembly. Leave it until the glue sets.

The top frame is made with mitered corners. Cut the stock to the proper width and make each slightly oversize. Mark the lengths accurately then miter. Be sure the corners are perfect 45-degree cuts.

The grooves for the crosspieces are made with the router. Keep the router setting the same and cut the grooves in the ends of the two crosspieces. The best way to groove the crosspieces is to make the groove in a wide board which has been cut to exact length. After grooving, rip into the narrow strips required. Cut plywood splines and insert them into the ends of the crosspieces. Use glue. Drill the dowel holes into the mitered frame ends.

A special procedure must be used in assembling the top frame. If three sides of the frame were doweled and assembled, it would be impossible to install the last section. The parts must be installed in pairs, one short and one long per section. Bear in mind that the assembly cannot be delayed too long as the glue will start to set and of course hits can ruin the job.

Take four dowels and sand them so they fit the holes easily without force. Set them aside. Prepare a miter frame clamp. This is easily made with scrap wood. Drill a series of holes, spaced 1 inch apart, then assemble with corners and draw bars as shown. Use 5/16-inch bolts in assembling the parts. The jig is self-adjusting and can be used for all miter frame gluing.

Apply dowels and glue to two diagonal corners and to one end only of the crosspieces. Insert the loose-fitting dowels into the other diagonal corners. Do not use glue here. Install the jig and draw the parts together by tightening the clamp. Align the crosspieces making sure they are in proper position.

After the glue has set, separate the two sections, replace the dowels with proper fitting ones, apply glue to the miters and dry end of the splines and repeat the clamping operation. Note that if you prefer to glue and clamp the entire frame at one time, a slow-setting glue should be used.

The supports for the tiles and planter are made of pine. Cut the pieces to size and fasten with screws. If you use 7/16-inch-thick tiles, the tile base should be 3/8-inch plywood. When this is placed onto the base supports, the tiles will fit into the recess with the top surface flush with the frame. We did not use a grout between the tiles. If you use grout, select one that matches the tiles.

The planter is made of 1/8-inch Plexiglas. Cut the pieces to size then assemble using thickened solvent cement. Simply apply a bead to the joint edge and gently join the pieces. Clamp or hold firmly until set. The resulting high-strength joint will not be affected by moisture. A wood frame is made to loosely fit into the opening and rest on the planter.

The table should be given a good sanding, followed by stain and suitable topcoat. If the wood used has open grain, paste wood filler should be used to fill the pores. The filler can be mixed with the stain. Follow the manufacturer's directions for the proper procedure.

The tiles used are Bizantino Orange No. 67 and are made by United Ceramic Tile Co. Your local tile dealer should be able to get these for you. If you have difficulty, write the company directly at 923 Motor Parkway, Hauppauge, New York, 11787.

To use the planter for living plants, place a layer of gravel at the bottom. Over this place a layer of charcoal, followed by potting soil.

Trestle Desk

THIS FINE DESK can be easily built with ordinary tools. It features three full-depth drawers which provide ample storage for stationery, books, and so on. The dividers at the rear are useful for keeping bills, letters, and important papers in order. The large writing area allows you to write easily without feeling cramped.

The material used for the main part of the desk is ⁵⁄₄-inch pine (which is 1⅛ inch dressed). However, ½-inch pine and plywood are also utilized. In addition, 1¾-inch stock is used for the pedestal base. The ½-inch pine is used to keep costs down. The desktop and shelf are both made of ½-inch material with the edges built up to give the appearance of heavier lumber. The side pieces are 11 inches wide, and while it is available in one piece, ⁵⁄₄ × 12 inches, the cost is much higher than narrower boards, and so we decided to glue-up to make the necessary width. Also, wider boards have a tendency to warp and cup. Gluing-up narrower pieces eliminates this problem. The plywood is used for the bottom of the desk compartment.

Construction starts with the side pieces. Assuming that you will use two or more pieces to make the necessary width, rip enough stock for both side pieces. Allow a little extra stock for trimming after gluing. The glued joint should be doweled. In order to place the dowels properly, make a kraft paper pattern of the side section using the squares provided.

Lay out the pattern carefully, then cut with a scissor or razor blade. Use the pattern as a guide to determine where to place the glue line. Bear in mind that the dowels will penetrate each section by 1 inch. The pieces to be glued must be square and true. After ripping, the edges should be trued up with a jointer or jack plane. Take light cuts; only remove enough stock to clean the glue line edges.

The dowels used are ⅜ × 2 inches. The dowel holes must be accurately located and aligned. Perhaps the best way to drill these holes is with a doweling jig which will ensure perfect alignment of the mating pieces automatically. Drill the holes about 1⅛ inch deep.

Insert the dowels after coating them lightly with glue. Apply glue to the mating

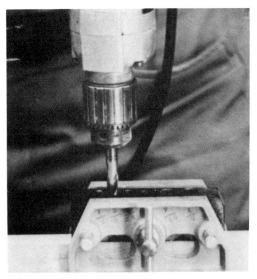

Fig. 36-1. Dowel holes must be accurately located and aligned. It's best to use a dowel jig for aligning and centering the holes.

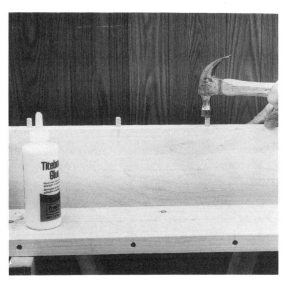

Fig. 36-2. Drive dowels so only one inch shows. If you're using smooth dowels, taper ends and cut grooves along dowel length.

Fig. 36-3. It will be necessary to cut dadoes in both the shelf and desk top sections with a router. Use a piece of wood as a guide.

Fig. 36-4. This view shows the spacer and desktop assembled. Note at the top of the picture, the thickened edge of the desktop.

surfaces then bring them together and clamp. After the glue has set, remove the clamps and trace the outline of the side. Be sure to mark the button hole centers. The two rear buttons conceal screw heads, the front two are dummies and used only for appearance. Cut the outline with a saber saw then sand smooth to remove all kerf marks. Next, drill the button holes—½ inch diameter and ¼ inch deep. At the rear location drill the ³⁄₁₆-inch screw-clearance holes. Round off edges with a router. Do not round off the inside bottoms.

The rear panel is also made up of glued stock. Again, use dowels and follow the procedure outlined above. In this case however, the location of the dowels is not critical.

After gluing the board, rip it to size, then cut the rabbet along the lower edge.

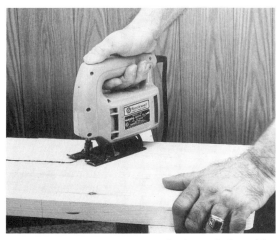

Fig. 36-5. Use a saber saw to cut out the diagonal edges of the side pieces for the desktop. Then round off and sand edges smooth.

Fig. 36-6. To locate pilot holes for the lag screws, arrange pieces as shown and adjust until you find alignment with apencil.

Fig. 36-7. The final assembly consists of fastening the pedestal section with glue and screws to the underside of the desk section.

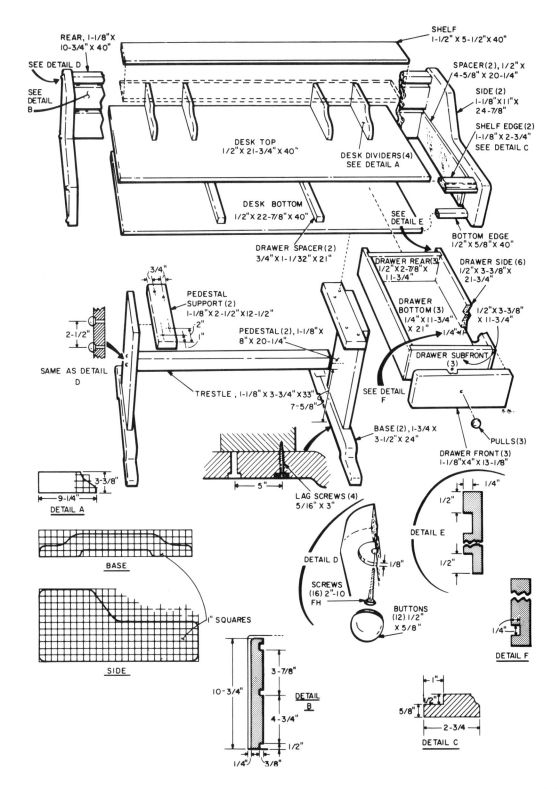

REAR, 1-1/8"X 10-3/4" X 40"

SEE DETAIL D

SEE DETAIL B

SHELF 1-1/2" X 5-1/2"X 40"

SPACER(2),1/2" X 4-5/8" X 20-1/4"

SIDE (2) 1-1/8"X11"X 24-7/8"

SHELF EDGE(2) 1-1/8"X 2-3/4" SEE DETAIL C

DESK TOP 1/2"X 21-3/4" X 40"

DESK DIVIDERS(4) SEE DETAIL A

DESK BOTTOM 1/2"X 22-7/8" X 40"

SEE DETAIL E

BOTTOM EDGE 1/2"X 5/8" X 40"

DRAWER SPACER(2) 3/4"X1-1/32" X 21"

DRAWER REAR(3) 1/2"X 2-7/8" X 11-3/4"

DRAWER SIDE (6) 1/2"X 3-3/8"X 21-3/4"

DRAWER BOTTOM(3) 1/4"X11-3/4" X 21"

1/2"X 3-3/8" X 11-3/4"

1/4"

3/4"

PEDESTAL SUPPORT (2) 1-1/8"X 2-1/2"X12-1/2"

2"

1"

2-1/2"

SAME AS DETAIL D

PEDESTAL(2),1-1/8"X 8"X 20-1/4"

DRAWER SUBFRONT (3)

TRESTLE , 1-1/8" X 3-3/4"X33"

7-5/8"

SEE DETAIL F

PULLS(3)

BASE(2),1-3/4"X 3-1/2" X 24"

DRAWER FRONT (3) 1-1/8"X4" X 13-1/8"

5"

LAG SCREWS (4) 5/16" X 3"

1/4"

1/2"

DETAIL E

1/2"

3-3/8"

9-1/4"

DETAIL A

BASE

SIDE

1" SQUARES

DETAIL D

SCREWS (16) 2"-10 FH

1/8"

BUTTONS (12) 1/2" X 5/8"

1/4"

DETAIL F

3-7/8"

10-3/4"

DETAIL B

4-3/4"

1/2"

1/4"

3/8"

1"

1/2"

5/8"

2-3/4"

DETAIL C

239

Do this on the table saw, making two passes, one with the board held vertically, the second with the board held horizontally. Set the depth and width of the cut for ½ inch. Cut the ½-inch grooves for the desktop and shelf also. Make a series of cuts on the table saw or use the router. Use the router to round off the top and outside bottom corners.

The shelf is made with ½-inch wood. The edge is thickened with a strip of 1⅛-inch stock. Rabbet the top edge of the strip to accept the ½-inch board. Shape the leading edge of the strip with a router. Use a rounding cutter for the lower edge and a beaded cutter for the top edge. Glue the strip to the board carefully. The joint should be tight so it will look like one piece. Repeat the procedure for the desktop. Because of the width, glue-up several pieces of ½-inch boards to obtain the required size.

The pedestals are cut next. These are straight-sided and do not require special treatment. Likewise, the trestle is straight. Cut these to the proper lengths, then rip to width. Round off the corners. Make up the two pedestal support blocks. These are cut to size, then drilled to accommodate the flat-head mounting screws. Countersink the holes for the screw heads. Also drill and counterbore the screw holes for the trestle.

Base pieces are cut from 1¾-inch stock. Make a layout on kraft paper, then cut and trace onto the lumber. The lumber should be 3½ inches wide so that only the shaped ends of the pieces need be cut with the saber saw. Sand the pieces after cutting and be sure to remove all saw marks.

Lay out the two lag screw mounting holes. Counterbore the holes to accept the washers.

Prior to assembling the sections, sand all surfaces smooth. Start with a medium-grit paper such as 80 then work with finer grits ending with 220.

The desk compartment top and bottom are glued to two spacers cut from ½-inch wood. These are butted and held in position with a few brads. Clamp securely. When the glue sets, add the rear panel and shelf. The sides are installed and fastened to the rear piece with flat-head screws. The spacers are also screwed to the side pieces. This will bring all members of the desk compartment together. The leading edge of the shelf is fastened to the sides with 10d finishing nails, one at each end. Sink the heads and fill.

Install the pedestal support blocks at the top of each pedestal. Use glue and nails. Invert the pedestal and mount the base pieces. Drill pilot holes to correspond to the lag screw holes drilled earlier in the base pieces. Use glue and join all pieces. Be sure to use washers under the lag screw heads.

Mount the crosspiece after both pedestals have been completed. Stand the pedestals on a flat surface while installing the crosspiece. Join with flat-head screws and glue. The pedestal assembly is now fastened to the underside of the desk compartment. Use 1¾-inch, No. 10 flat-head screws. Note: the screws will penetrate the ½-inch plywood bottom. Since the drawer bottoms are raised slightly, the points will clear the drawers. If smaller screws are used, they won't have the necessary holding power.

Drawers are made with 1⅛-inch fronts and ½-inch sides, rear and subfront. Joints are rabbeted at the front and dadoed at the rear. A groove at the lower edge holds the ¼-inch plywood bottoms. Cut the parts to

MATERIALS LIST

Note: Except where noted, all lumber is pine.

Purpose	Size	Description	Quantity
Sides	1⅛″ × 11″ × 24⅞″		2
Rear	1⅛″ × 10¾″ × 40″		1
Shelf	½″ × 5½″ × 10″		1
Shelf edge	1⅛″ × 2¾″ × 40″		2
Desktop	½″ × 21¾″ × 40″		1
Desk bottom	½″ × 22⅞″ × 40″	Plywood	1
Bottom edge	½″ × ⅝″ × 40″		1
Pedestal support	1⅛″ × 2½″ × 12½″		2
Pedestal	1⅛″ × 8″ × 20¼″		2
Trestle	1⅛″ × 3¾″ × 33″		1
Base	1¾″ × 3½″ × 24″		2
Spacer	½″ × 4⅝″ × 20¼″		2
Drawer spacer	¾″ × 1 1/32″ × 21″		2
Drawer side	½″ × 3⅜″ × 21¾″		6
Drawer rear	½″ × 2⅞″ × 11¾″		3
Drawer subfront	½″ × 3⅜″ × 11¾″		3
Drawer front	1⅛″ × 4″ × 13⅛″		3
Drawer bottom	¼″ × 11¾″ × 21″		3
Desk dividers	½″ × 9⅜″		4
Buttons	½″ × ⅝″		12
Pulls			3
Screws	2″—10 FH		16
Lag screws	5/16″ × 3″		4

size and dado as shown. The subfront must be drilled for the screw clearance before assembly. The drawer fronts are cut to size and the edges rounded with the router.

Assemble the drawers with glue and brads. Place the brads through the subfront, angling them slightly. The heads will be hidden when the fronts are installed. Note that the fronts are raised 1/16 inch above the drawer bottoms. Add the drawer spacers between the drawers.

Finally, cut the compartment dividers and install below the shelf. They are not held with nails or glue. Simply cut them so they slide in with a snug fit. Finish the desk with stain and gloss topcoat.

Note: the doweling jig is available at lumberyards. However, if you have difficulty locating a source, write to Armor Products, Box 445, East Northport, NY 11731.

Trestle Table and Benches

THESE EARLY AMERICAN trestle table and bench sets are almost as popular today as they were in the Colonial days. These furniture pieces are rugged rather than fragile, and beautiful in their simplicity. If you shop around in the furniture stores, you will find that these pieces are available in both 1⅛-inch stock and in 2-inch stock. The heavier 2-inch stock is the better, although more expensive, choice. Prices in the better furniture stores were five times higher for a set similar to the one constructed here.

When buying your lumber, choose boards that are fairly flat and be sure to avoid any that have sap streaks. If possible try to avoid boards that are not edge-dressed. Another thing to watch for are the knots. These should not be missing, loose, or chipped. With a little patience you can purchase wood that will be easier to work with and most important, will help you to turn out a choice piece of furniture.

If the board edges are not dressed, (sides are rough and uneven), the first step must be to even them up. The best way to do this is to draw a line with a straight edge then trim freehand with a saber saw or on the band saw. Trim one edge only, then rip both edges of the stock on the table saw. This will ensure that they are square and parallel. The boards for the tops of the table and benches should be left a few inches oversize in length. This will be trimmed off later after the boards are glued-up.

Dowels are used when gluing the top. This will make for a stronger joint and will greatly simplify the alignment of the boards when clamping. There are several methods of locating the dowels. A jig will work

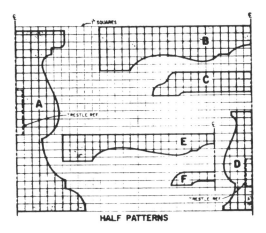

HALF PATTERNS

well. Simply clamp it in place and drill through the dowel-sized bushing. *Bushings* are small metal plugs with pointed centers. They are easy to use and inexpensive.

Arrange boards so the grain and knot patterns are to your liking, then mark them accordingly. Drill the necessary holes, then dab a little glue on one end of the fluted dowels and drive them home with a hammer. The glue used should be of the water-resistant type, especially for the tabletop. The benches and table bases may be assembled with white glue. Before applying the glue have your gluing area set up so that you will not waste time later. Have clamps open to proper size and have clamp pressure strips ready, as it will take considerable time to apply glue to all the edges of the boards and it is necessary to clamp the boards before the glue begins to set. Apply the glue with a small paint brush.

To prevent bowing of the top, the clamps should be alternated between top and bottom. After the glue sets, plane the surface joints so the top will be smooth and free of steps or bumps. The length may now be trimmed with a portable saw. Use a strip of wood as a guide to ensure a straight square cut.

The bench tops and ends are made of one-piece wide boards, however the table ends must be glued-up because of the width. Follow the same procedure used when making the top. If you can make the width with two boards, fine. If not, use as many boards as needed to make the width. Again make the length a little longer than the finished size to allow for trimming. Two inches in the overall should suffice.

After the glue has set, plane the joint. Then draw the outline of the design onto the board. Be sure to include the top and bottom lines. If you have a radial arm saw, trim the top and bottom lines, then cut the scroll design using a band saw or saber saw. After cutting, sand smooth, then round off all corners with a router.

The base and upper supports of the end panels are cut from 2-inch stock. After cutting and before assembling to the ends, sand smooth and round edges as done with the end sections. Assemble with glue and lag screws. Washers must be used under the lag screw heads.

The trestles are cut next. Note that these are "fakes" with ends added on. In olden days before glue and screws were so plentiful, cabinet makers had to use the mortise and tenon with peg to hold their work together, but thanks to progress, a difficult task becomes a very simple one.

Make up the ends as indicated, notching the "slot" for the peg. Add the peg using glue and nails. Two dowels hold the end to the table. Use glue when assembling. The benches are assembled in a similar manner.

To give the table a worn colonial look, the corner edges are well rounded with a plane or spokeshave. If you desire you can add a few gouges along the ends and sides.

The type of finish is a matter of

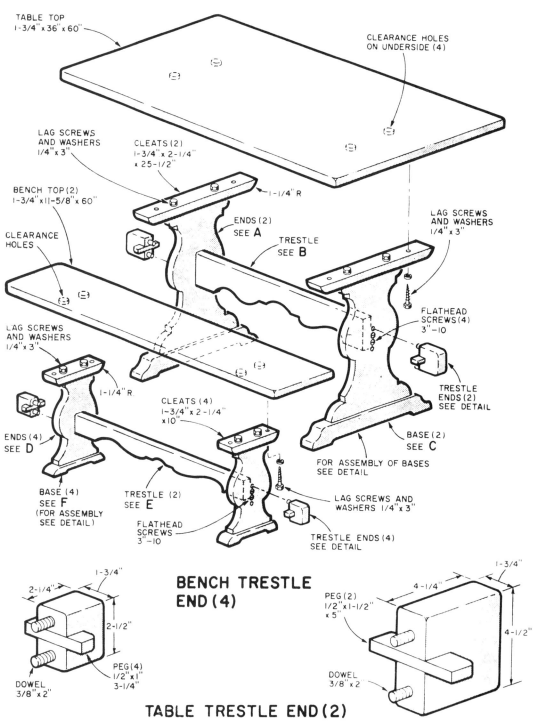

TABLE TOP
1-3/4" x 36" x 60"

CLEARANCE HOLES
ON UNDERSIDE (4)

LAG SCREWS
AND WASHERS
1/4" x 3"

CLEATS (2)
1-3/4" x 2-1/4"
x 25-1/2"

1-1/4" R

BENCH TOP (2)
1-3/4" x 11-5/8" x 60"

ENDS (2)
SEE A

TRESTLE
SEE B

LAG SCREWS
AND WASHERS
1/4" x 3"

CLEARANCE
HOLES

FLATHEAD
SCREWS (4)
3"-10

LAG SCREWS
AND WASHERS
1/4" x 3"

1-1/4" R

CLEATS (4)
1-3/4" x 2-1/4"
x 10"

TRESTLE
ENDS (2)
SEE DETAIL

BASE (2)
SEE C

ENDS (4)
SEE D

BASE (4)
SEE F
(FOR ASSEMBLY
SEE DETAIL)

TRESTLE (2)
SEE E

FOR ASSEMBLY OF BASES
SEE DETAIL

FLATHEAD
SCREWS
3"-10

LAG SCREWS AND
WASHERS 1/4" x 3"

TRESTLE ENDS (4)
SEE DETAIL

BENCH TRESTLE END (4)

2-1/4"

1-3/4"

2-1/2"

DOWEL
3/8" x 2"

PEG (4)
1/2" x 1"
3-1/4"

PEG (2)
1/2" x 1-1/2"
x 5"

1-3/4"

4-1/4"

4-1/2"

DOWEL
3/8" x 2"

TABLE TRESTLE END (2)

NOTE:
BE SURE DOWELS DO NOT INTERFERE
WITH SCREWS HOLDING TRESTLES

244

Fig. 37-1. The glue used on the top boards should be a water resistant type. When applying clamps, insert scrap wood between clamp and work which will prevent marring of the tabletop edges.

Fig. 37-2. After the glue sets, plane the surface joints of the tabletop so that the top will be smooth and free of steps and bumps. The length may now be trimmed with a portable saw.

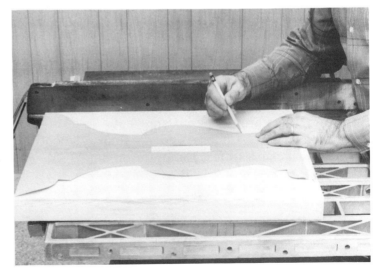

Fig. 37-3. Draw the outline of the support ends on a 2-inch board. Be sure to include the top and bottom lines. Cut out scroll design with band saw and end trim with radial or portable saw.

Fig. 37-4. Above are the two trestle ends. These have slots cut to hold the fake pegs. The dowels hold these ends to the table ends and simulate the old fashioned mortise and tenon with a peg.

Fig. 37-5. As shown, a special router cutting bit is used to round off the edges of the trestle supports for both the table and the benches.

preference, but generally a dark walnut stain is most suitable for this type of furniture. There are numerous stains and finishes available. Choose one to your liking and be sure to test the color on a piece of scrap wood before applying to your work. Prepare the surface by giving a thorough sanding until all work is smooth.

MATERIALS LIST

Purpose	Size	Description	Quantity
Tabletop	1¾″ × 36″ × 60″	Pine	1
Trestle	1¾″ × 5¾″ × 40″	Pine	1
Trestle ends	1¾″ × 4¼″ × 4½″	Pine	2
End	1¾″ × 18″ × 23½″	Pine	2
Base	2¼″ × 3⅛″ × 26¼″	Pine	2
Cleats	1¾″ × 2¼″ × 25½″	Pine	2
Pegs	½″ × 1½″ × 5″	Pine	2
Bench top	1¾″ × 11⅝″ × 60″	Pine	2
Trestle	1¾″ × 3½″ × 40″	Pine	2
Trestle ends	1¾″ × 2¼″ × 2½″	Pine	4
End	1¾″ × 7¾″ × 12⅞″	Pine	4
Base	1¾″ × 2¼″ × 11½″	Pine	4
Cleats	1¾″ × 2¼″ × 10″	Pine	4
Pegs	½″ × 1″ × 3¼″	Pine	4
Fluted dowels	⅜″ × 2″		24
Flat-head screws	3″—10		12
Lag screws	¼″ × 3″		36
Washers			
Glue			

Note: All lumber indicated as 2″ will measure approximately 1¾″. Table and bench tops and ends are listed above as one piece. These are glued-up from appropriate number of pieces. Four inch or six inch pieces may be used.

Two Shaving Bars

IF YOU FIND your shaving gear cramped for space in the medicine cabinet, build a wall-hung shaving bar. Here are two excellent models styled by a noted industrial designer. Each of these is easily constructed of cabinet wood, aluminum, glass and mosaic tile.

One model features a mirror that slides up for access to the interior of the cabinet, and a lower drop-front that doubles as a closure and shelf. This cabinet is made of ½-inch solid walnut, except for the hardboard back and plywood mirror panel.

Remember that the side pieces must be mirror images of each other, not exact duplicates. These are grooved at the rear to take the back panel, and at the front for

sliding mirror unit. Note that a supporting plywood panel, not the mirror itself, slides in the grooves. The mirror is simply cemented to the panel.

The panel is rabbeted at the top and bottom for long aluminum angle "irons" that serve as handles, and along the sides to fit into approximately 9/16-inch-wide grooves on the sides.

The mirror is held in the raised position by magnetic catches. Mount these catches onto the mirror backing and fit the mirror unit into place *before* you glue the sides of the cabinet into position.

The hot glue is used to bond the ceramic tile to the drop-front. An aluminum angle across the top provides a handle for

Fig. 38-1. A desk-lid-type arm supports the panel when it is in the open position and a magnetic catch keeps it closed. The mirror slides up and down, providing more storage space.

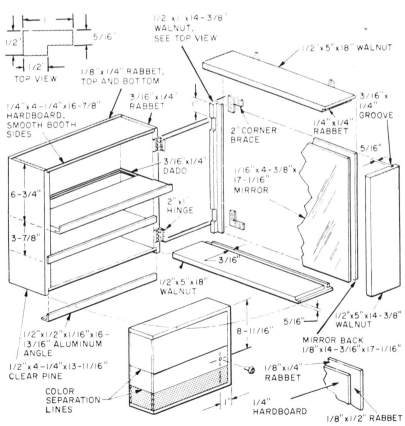

1/2"

5/16"

1/2"
TOP VIEW

1/8"x1/4" RABBET, TOP AND BOTTOM

1/2"x1"x14-3/8" WALNUT, SEE TOP VIEW

1/2"x5"x18" WALNUT

3/16"x1/4" RABBET

2"CORNER BRACE

3/16"x 1/4" GROOVE

1/4"x1/4" RABBET

5/16"

1/4"x4-1/4"x16-7/8" HARDBOARD, SMOOTH BOOTH SIDES

6-3/4"

3-7/8"

3/16"x1/4" DADO

2"x1" HINGE

1/16"x4-3/8"x 17-1/16" MIRROR

1/2"x5"x18" WALNUT

3/16"

1/2"x5"x14-3/8" WALNUT

1/2"x1/2"x1/16"x16-13/16" ALUMINUM ANGLE

1/2"x4-1/4"x13-11/16" CLEAR PINE

COLOR SEPARATION LINES

8-11/16"

5/16"

1"

MIRROR BACK
1/8"x14-3/16"x17-1/16"

1/8"x1/4" RABBET

1/4" HARDBOARD

1/8"x1/2" RABBET

Fig. 38-2. The hot glue is used to bond the ceramic tile to the drop-front. Also be sure to heat the aluminum strips, which are used in both bars, before applying to achieve a better bond.

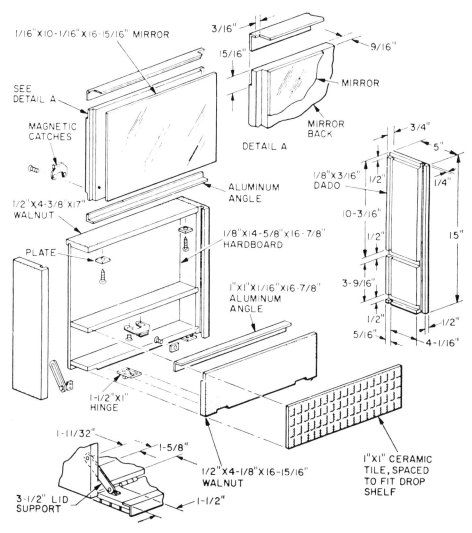

this door. Heat the aluminum (and those on the mirror panel) before applying the stick glue. A desk-lid type arm supports the panel in the open position; a magnetic catch keeps it closed.

The other model has a front that swings out. Study the diagrams carefully, and note that the front *nests* over the main part of the cabinet which is made of pine and a hardboard back panel. Retaining edges on the shelves consist of angle-aluminum cemented onto the rabbeted shelf edges.

The swinging front is a three-sided affair with a mirror on the inside. It is made of ½-inch solid walnut and a hardboard back. Metal corner braces are used on the right-hand hinge post for added strength.

Wall-Hung Sewing Center

THIS COLONIAL-STYLE wall-hung sewing center will store all things needed for a well-organized sewing room. By utilizing an unused wall area, it allows more floor space which is usually at a premium in most homes. Another added advantage is that the drawers and storage shelves are at eye level—therefore no stooping to find things.

The novel lift-out tray simplifies thread storage, and pegs hold the spools of thread so they are clearly visible. Small parts jars on the door as well as the scissor rack all add up to a tidy sewing center. Two large drawers for material and pattern storage, an odds-and-ends tray, two fair-sized shelves and a knickknack shelf topside, are also included.

Rip lumber to size, then lay out patterns for the scalloped top and side section. Make the layouts on kraft (wrapping) paper, then cut out with scissor or sharp knife. Transfer the outlines to the workpieces and then cut with a saber or jigsaw.

Next, rabbet the rear edges of the two side pieces as well as the top and bottom shelves. One-eighth-inch door skins were used. These are the same panels used on hollow doors. They're smooth, inexpensive, and most lumber dealers carry them.

Cut the rabbet to suit the thickness of the rear panel. The rabbets on the upper and lower shelf pieces run the full length but the sides are cut with stopped rabbets. This means that the rabbet will not run the full length to the edge. (See drawing).

If you have a vise, use it to hold the work while cutting the rabbets. If you do not have a vise, support the work with a clamp as shown.

The two vertical dividers are cut to match the rabbeted shelf pieces. This means they should measure ⅛ inch less than the upper and lower shelves.

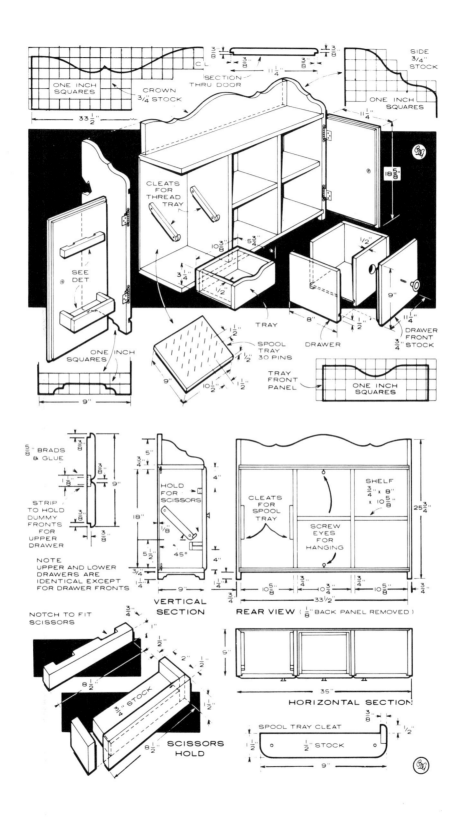

SECTION THRU DOOR

SIDE 3/4 STOCK

ONE INCH SQUARES

CROWN 3/4 STOCK

33 1/2"

ONE INCH SQUARES

11 1/4"

18 5/8"

CLEATS FOR THREAD TRAY

SEE DET

ONE INCH SQUARES

9"

10 3/8"   5 3/4"

3 1/4"

1/2"

1/2"

TRAY

1 1/2"

SPOOL TRAY 30 PINS

1/2"

9"   10 1/2"   1 1/2"

TRAY FRONT PANEL

1/2"

DRAWER

8"

1/2"

DRAWER FRONT 3/4 STOCK

9"   11 1/4"

ONE INCH SQUARES

5/8" BRADS & GLUE

3/8"

3/8"

1/8"

9"

3/8"

3/8"

STRIP TO HOLD DUMMY FRONTS FOR UPPER DRAWER

NOTE UPPER AND LOWER DRAWERS ARE IDENTICAL EXCEPT FOR DRAWER FRONTS

5"   3/4"

4"

HOLD FOR SCISSORS

18"

1/8"

5 1/2"   45°

4"

3/4"

1 1/4"

9"

VERTICAL SECTION

SHELF 3/4" x 8" x 10 5/8"

CLEATS FOR SPOOL TRAY

SCREW EYES FOR HANGING

25 3/4"

3/4"   10 5/8"   3/4"   10 3/4"   3/4"   10 5/8"   3/4"

1 1/4"   33 1/2"   3/4"

REAR VIEW (1/8" BACK PANEL REMOVED)

NOTCH TO FIT SCISSORS

3/4"   1"

1/2"

2"   1 1/2"

8 1/2"

3/4" STOCK

1/2"

8 1/2"

SCISSORS HOLD

5"

35"

HORIZONTAL SECTION

3/8"

1/2"

SPOOL TRAY CLEAT

1/2" STOCK

1/2"

9"

253

Fig. 39-1. Use a router to rabbet the rear edges of the two side pieces. Cut the rabbet to suit the thickness of the rear panel.

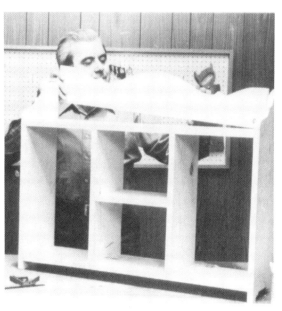

Fig. 39-2. Scalloped panel is fitted to the frame. The divider section should be narrower than sides in order to fit the rear panel.

Fig. 39-3. In order to get firm and even clamping pressure, save the cutout pieces from the scallop to fit in place under clamp.

Fig. 39-4. Cleats for the spool tray are installed at a 45-degree angle. To eliminate end grain, a small wood stop is added to the ends.

Cut the rear panel to size and round the corners so it will clear the rounds left by the router. If you're ambitious, you can leave the panel square and instead chisel out the corners left by the router. Either method is acceptable.

Set the rear piece aside and cut the center drawer divider next. Apply a thin coat of white glue to all the edge grain pieces and allow to dry. Apply more glue to each section as it is to be assembled. The assembly sequence is important.

Make up the H by assembling the two verticals and the center drawer divider. Use 2-inch finishing nails and be sure the assembly is square. Check with a T-square.

Fig. 39-5. Drawers are assembled with butt joints. Sides and subfront are dadoed to accept drawer bottoms cut from ⅛-inch plywood.

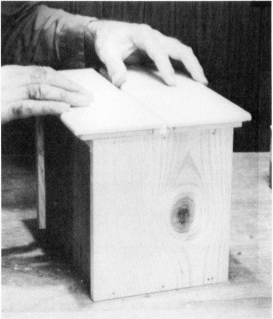

Fig. 39-6. The upper drawer has two dummy fronts to give the appearance of small drawers. A narrow wood strip joins them together.

Fig. 39-7. Cabinet nears completion with installation of spool tray and sliding tray. It is best to apply finish at this point.

MATERIALS LIST

All lumber ¾″ pine except where noted.

Purpose	Size	Quantity
Side	9½″ × 26″	2
Top shelf	9½″ × 33½″	1
Bottom shelf	9½″ × 33½″	1
Top scallop	6″ × 33½″	1
Vertical divider	9⅜″ × 18″	2
Horizontal divider	9⅜″ × 10¾″	1
Shelf	8″ × 10⅝″	1
Rear panel	⅛″ × 18¾″ × 34¼″	1
Cleat	½″ × 1½″ × 8¼″	2
Door	11¼″ × 18⅝″	2
Drawer front	9″ × 11¼″	1
Drawer front	4½″ × 9″	2
Drawer subfront	½″ × 8⅛″ × 9⅝″	2
Drawer side	½″ × 8″ × 8⅛″	4
Drawer rear	½″ × 7⅜″ × 9⅝″	2
Drawer bottom	⅛″ × 7¾″ × 10⅛″	2
Drawer dummy strip	⅜″ × 1⅛″ × 10¹¹⁄₁₆″	1
Tray side	½″ × 3¼″ × 4¾″	2
Tray front	½″ × 3¼″ × 10⅜″	1
Tray rear	½″ × 3¼″ × 10⅜″	1
Tray bottom	⅛″ × 5¼″ × 10″	1
Scissor rack	¾″ × 1″ × 8½″	1
Jar shelf front	½″ × 1½″ × 8½″	1
Jar shelf bottom	¾″ × 2″ × 7½″	1
Jar shelf side	½″ × 1½″ × 2″	2
Spool tray pulls	½″ × 9″ × 10½″	1
Hinges	No. 56306 (Sears)	5
Eye screws		2

Next, add the top and bottom shelves to the H section. Be sure to center the assembly on the upper and lower shelves. The use of a gauge block cut from scrap will help in this step.

Although not shown in the assembly photos, be sure to add the small shelf in the right compartment at this time. Sides should also be added now. The rear panel cut previously can be used as a guide to check squareness of the assembly. You can tack it in place temporarily after the sides have been installed. This will keep the "box" square. It will be installed permanently after the finish has been applied. It is much easier to get at the corners with a brush or even a spray gun with the rear panel removed.

The doors and drawers are made next, and all are cut with a ⅜-inch offset. Choose good flat pieces for the doors. If necessary, glue-up two or more pieces to obtain the proper width. Rabbet the rear edges with a straight cutter. Make the rabbet ⅜ inch wide and ⅜ inch deep. Follow with a rounding off bit to round the outside edges.

The upper drawer has two dummy fronts to give the appearance of two small drawers. Make two separate pieces as shown, then join them with a narrow strip. Use glue and small brads when assembling the strip.

The drawers are of butt-joint construction. Cut the pieces to size then dado them to accept the bottom panels. The easiest way to make the dadoes is on a table saw, using a blade with a ⅛-inch kerf. Set the blade height to ¼-inch, then adjust the fence accordingly. The sides, subfront and rear panels are cut from ½-inch lumber. The drawer fronts are cut from ¾-inch stock.

Cut out and assemble the door shelf and scissor rack. The scissor rack should be notched to fit your particular scissors. Assemble with glue and nails.

The cleats for the spool tray are cut from ½-inch wood. To eliminate end grain, a small piece is added to the ends as shown. Sand the cleats, round off the corners and install at a 45-degree angle. The spool holder consists of finishing nails, but you can use ⅛-inch dowels or lollipop sticks if you prefer.

The hinges for the doors are from Sears. If you substitute, be sure that the hinge is narrow enough so it does not protrude from the edge of the cabinet.

The top scallop is added to complete the project. Use nails, glue, and if possible, clamps. The scraps from cutting the scallops can be used under the clamps to spread the pressure and to protect the edge of the scallop.

Add the cabinet hardware, catches, and rear panel after applying the finish.

You can leave the wood natural, stain it, or apply one of the popular antique finishes. If left natural or stained, be sure to apply a clear topcoat of brushing lacquer or shellac.

As you will note after completion, the cabinet is quite heavy. Do not attempt to hang it through the ⅛-inch rear panel. This is not strong enough. Instead, use two eye screws behind the drawer compartments and fasten to the wall with lag screws.

Index

A

all-in-one entertainment
   center, 1-11
   swivel base for, 7
   cassette compartment for,
   4
aluminum angle stock, 248
antiquing, 77, 116, 150
   hardware, 12
Armor Products, 108, 145
Arvon Products, 150

B

band saws, 36
   sawing jig for, 40
banjo wall clock, 12-15
bar
   cabinet and, 88-92
   contemporary, 78-87
beading, 12, 46
beds

captain's trundle, 25-34
foldaway storage unit
   and, 138-145
bedside table, 16-17
benches
   picnic, 93-95
   trestle, 242-247
bevel trimmer bit, 155
bookcase/desk, corner,
   109-116
bookrack
   Colonial desk with, 72-77
   corner desk and, 109-116
   stool and, 69-71
   table and, 117-122
bookshelf/table, 117-122
brackets, 89
butcher block
   assembly of, 134
   light-and-dark, 53-55
   table of, 132-137
butler's tray table, 18-24

butt hinges, 218
butt joints, 149, 152

C

cabinet
   bar and, 88-92
   china, 192-201
   sports gear, 223-227
   storage, 192-201
cabinet/bar combo, 88-92
captain's trundle bed, 25-34
cart
   cheese and wine, 45-51
   mobile server, 182-191
cassette compartment, all-
   in-one entertainment
   center, 4
casters, 30, 145, 167
   concealed, 82
ceramic tiles, 228-235
   thermo-set glue for, 250

cheese and wine cart, 45-51
chessboard game table, 52-60
child's bookrack and stool, 69-71
child's footlocker, 61-68
china cabinet, 192-201
circular saw, 123
clamping, 103, 155, 211, 254
  edging, 196
cleating, 72, 73, 97, 118, 149
clock
  hall, 100
  movements for, 100, 108
  spice rack and, 207
  wall, banjo style, 12-15
Colonial desk with bookrack, 72-77
contemporary bar, 78-87
contoured edges, 46
corner bookcase/desk, 109-116
corners, rounding, 243
crosscutting, 219

D
dadoing, 2, 3, 28, 152, 237
  guide for, 194, 195
  Rockwell wobble head, 164
  stopped, 165
Deftco Danish Oil Finish, 11
desk
  Colonial, bookrack and, 72-77
  corner, bookcase and, 109-116
  divider unit with, 123-128
  home office unit, 161-170
  lightweight, 171-173
  trestle, 236-241
  writing, 96-99
distressed finishes, 243

divider unit with desk, 123-128
doors
  folding, 85
  glass, 192, 198, 201
  hanging, 144
  hinged, 105
  magnetic catch for, 107, 157
  piano hinges for, 169
  recessed, 189, 190
  revolving, 90
  sliding, 215
double-pointed nails, 6
dough box end table, 129-131
doweling, 78, 110, 111, 197, 236, 237
  jig for, 37, 47, 79, 102, 146, 148, 241, 242
  joints using, 79
  legs attached with, 113, 179
drawers, 11, 16, 25, 56, 62, 64, 77, 83, 116, 149, 150, 155, 156, 168, 183, 215, 240, 257
  dividers in, 185, 203
  false front for, 190, 255
  slide hardware for, 63, 82
  vertical, 5
drill press, 19
drilling, jig for, 58
drop leaf, hinges for, 185, 186

E
edging, clamps for, 196
enamel finish, 16
end table, dough box, 129-131
entertainment center, all-in-one, 1-11, 1

F
finials, 13
finishing
  antique, 77, 116
  distressed, 243
  French polish, 24
  glazed, 116, 150
  high gloss enamel, 16
  lacquer, 51, 108, 160
  linseed oil, 16
  non-toxic, 137
  oil, 11
  outdoor furniture, 93
  paint, 42
  paste wax, 99
  prefinished lumber vs., 117
  Satinlac gloss, 87
  shellac, 71
  stains, 16
  stenciling, 42, 44
  varnish, 145
  wood filler for, 11, 160, 169
fishing rod rack, 223-227
fluting, 174, 178, 180, 229, 231
foldaway bed/storage unit, 138-145
folding doors, 85
footlocker, 61-68
Forstner bit, mortising with, 137
framing, web-type, 182
framing panels, 62
French polish, 24

G
game table, chessboard, 52-60
glass doors, 11, 104, 192, 198, 201
  installation of, 107
glazed finish, 116, 150
gluing

jig for, 6
  sizing woodgrain with, 39
  thermo-set, 69, 207, 248
grain, glue sizing of, 39
grilles, metal, 122
grooving, 18, 19, 29, 102, 103
gun rack, 223-227

H

half-lap joints, 40
hall clock, 100-108
hardware
  antiquing, 12
  brackets, 89
  butt hinges, 218
  casters, 30, 82, 145, 167
  drawer pulls, 145
  drawer slides, 63, 82
  hinges, 86, 144
  hooks, 30
  knife hinges, 90
  magnetic catches, 107, 157
  metal grilles, 122
  piano hinges, 169
  self-closing hinges, 197
hinges, 144
  butt, 218
  door, 86
  glass door, 11
  knife, 90
  mortising, 20-22, 168
  mortising for, 168
  piano, 169
  self-closing, 197
hole sawing, 89
home office unit, 161-170
hooks, 30

J

jigsawing, 12, 13
jointer, 134, 148
joints

butt, 149, 152
doweled, 79
half-lap, 40

K

knife hinges, 90
knots (lumber), 72

L

lacquer finish, 51, 108, 145, 160
leatherette panels, 58
legs
  doweling to attach, 113, 179
  fluting, 174, 178, 229
  gluing stock for, 146
  ready-made grooved, 52
  ready-made turned, 47
  routing and grooving, 18
  solid stock, 137
  squaring and shaping, 228
  tapered, 174, 178, 229
lightweight desk, 171-173
linseed oil stain, 16
louvered panels, 141, 144

M

magazine table, 174-181
magnetic catches, 107, 157
metal grilles, 122
Michael-Reagan Company, 113
mirrors, 248
miter gauge, 53
mitering, 88, 110, 164, 165
mobile server, 182-191
molding, 13, 84, 152, 189
  cove, 88
  raised panel effect with, 155-157
mortising
  Forstner bit for, 137
  hinges, 20-22, 168
Murphy bed, 138-145

N

nails
  countersinking, 129
  double-pointed, 6
  filling holes from, 129
non-toxic finishes, 137
notching, 211, 219, 220

O

occasional table, 146-151
oil finishes, 11
outdoor furniture, 93-95

P

painting, 42
panels
  door, 85
  framing for, 62
  glass, 104
  louvered, 141, 144
  molding for raised-effect, 152, 155, 157
  prefinished, 88, 117
  spacing in, 220
paste wax, 99
patio unit, three-in-one, 218-222
pegboard tool rack, 210-217
piano hinges, 169
picnic table/benches, 93-95
pilot holes, screw, 26
pine rocking horse, 35-44
planter, Plexiglas, 235
planter table, tile-topped, 228-235
plastic laminates, 78, 83, 86
Plexiglas planter box, 235
plywood
  construction with, 61, 96, 153, 182
  edge finishing for, 142, 166
  oak veneer, 152, 161
  sawing, 3
pulls, drawer, 145

R

rabbeting, 3, 72, 102, 103, 152, 164, 252, 254
  filler blocks for, 102
radial arm saw, 119, 122
recessed doors, 189
revolving doors, 90
ripping, 19, 25, 132, 219
rocking horse, pine, 35-44
routing, 18, 19, 27, 28, 246
  contoured edges with, 46
  fluting by, 174, 178, 180
  truing edges with, 109

S

saber saws, 12, 27, 99
sanding, rounding corners by, 41
Sapolin stain, 51
Satinlac gloss finish, 87
sawhorse/toolbox, 202-206
scallops, 254
screws, pilot holes for, 26
sealer, 108
self-closing hinges, 197
server cart, 182-191
sewing center, wall-hung, 252-257
shaving bars, 248-251
shellac finishing, 71
shelves, 5
sizing woodgrain, 39, 85
sliding doors, 215
spice racks, 207-209
spool holder, 257
sports gear cabinet, 223-227
squaring assemblies, 184
staining, 51, 87
stenciling, 42, 44
stool, bookrack and, 69-71
stop gauge, 102

stopped dado, 165
storage unit
  cabinet-type, 192-201
  foldaway bed and, 138-145
  sports gear cabinet, 223-227
swivel base
  installation, 6, 10
  plan for, 7

T

table saw, 123
  plywood wide-slot insert for, 164
  support jig for, 164
tables
  avoiding warpage in, 45
  bedside, 16-17
  bookshelf and, 117-122
  butcher block, 132-137
  butler's tray, 18-24
  chessboard, 52-60
  dough box, 129-131
  magazine, 174-181
  occasional, 146-151
  picnic, 93-95
  three-in-one patio unit, 218-222
  tile-topped planter, 228-235
  trestle, with benches, 242-247
tapering legs, 174, 178, 229
templates, 27
tenoning, fake, 72, 74
thermo-set gluing, 69, 207, 248
three-in-one patio unit, 218-222
three-in-one sports gear

cabinet, 223-227
tile-topped planter table, 228-235
tool rack, pegboard, 210-217
toolbox/sawhorse, 202-206
toys, rocking horse, 35-44
tray table, 18-24
trestle desk, 236-241
trestle table and benches, 242-247
trundle bed, 25-34
turned stock, 61, 62, 64, 109, 112, 129, 189

U

U-Bild Enterprises, 131

V

varnish, 145
veneer tapes, 166, 167

W

wall clock, banjo, 12-15
wall-hung sewing center, 252-257
wardrobe, 152-160
warpage, board placement to avoid, 45
water putty, 188
web framing, 182
Weldwood panels, 117
wheels, 45, 47, 48, 51
wobble head, 164
wood filler, 11, 160, 169
workbench, 210-217
writing desk, 96-99

Other Bestsellers from TAB

☐ **MAKING ANTIQUE FURNITURE—Edited by Vic Taylor**

A collection of some of the finest furniture ever made is found within the pages of this project book designed for the intermediate- to advanced-level craftsman. Reproducing European period furniture pieces such as a Windsor chair, a Jacobean box stool, a Regency table, a Sheraton writing desk, a Lyre-end occasional table, and many traditional furnishings is sure to provide you with pleasure and satisfaction. Forty projects include materials lists and step-by-step instructions. 160 pp., Fully illustrated, 8 1/2″ × 11″.

Paper $15.95   **Hard $25.95**
Book No. 3056

☐ **DESIGNING AND BUILDING COLONIAL AND EARLY AMERICAN FURNITURE, WITH 47 PROJECTS—2nd Edition—Percy W. Blandford**

Original designs that allow plenty of room for creativity! This volume captures the spirit and challenge of authentic Early American and Colonial craftsmanship. Blandford, an internationally recognized expert in the field, provides first-rate illustrations and simple instructions on the art of reproducing fine furniture. Every project in this volume is an exquisite reproduction of centuries-old originals: drop-leaf tables, peasant chairs, swivel-top tables, firehouse arm-chair, ladderback chairs, tilt-top box tables, hexagonal candle stands, trestle dining tables, wagon seat benches, jackstands, dry sinks, love seats, and Welsh dressers. 192 pp., 188 illus.

Paper $12.95   **Hard $21.95**
Book No. 3014

☐ **MORE PROJECTS FROM PINE: 33 NEW PLANS FOR THE BEGINNING WOODWORKER—James A. Jacobson**

Make beautiful and functional gifts from pine—for your home, for your friends, for profit! This easy-to-follow guide offers 33 more woodworking projects . . . each requiring only a small investment of time and money. Detailed drawings and photographs make this the perfect resource for the novice woodworker, yet the material lends itself to skillful variations at all levels. Success with the simpler projects will give you the confidence to move on to the more advanced pieces. 192 pp., 131 illus.

Paper $10.95   **Hard $17.95**
Book No. 2971

☐ **101 KITCHEN PROJECTS FOR THE WOODWORKER—Percy W. Blandford**

These 101 practical as well as decorative projects for every level of woodworking ability are sure to provide pleasure and satisfaction for builder and cook alike! Included are bread and cheese boards, carving boards and butcher blocks, trays, cookbook stand and stacking vegetable bin, spatulas, forks, spring tongs, mug racks, pivoting and parallel towel rails, spice racks, tables, a hutch, and much, much more! 270 pp., 214 illus.

Paper $14.95   **Hard $23.95**
Book No. 2884

☐ **WOODWORKER'S 30 BEST PROJECTS—Editors of *Woodworker* Magazine**

A collection of some of the finest furniture ever made can be found within the pages of this project book. Designed for the woodworker who has already mastered the basics, the projects presented in this book are for the intermediate- to advanced-level craftsman. Each furniture project comes complete with detailed instructions, a materials list, exploded views of working diagrams, a series of step-by-step, black-and-white photos, and a photograph of the finished piece. 224 pp., 300 illus.

Paper $14.95   **Hard $23.95**
Book No. 3021

☐ **DESIGNING AND BUILDING OUTDOOR FURNITURE, WITH 47 PROJECTS—2nd Edition—Percy W. Blandford**

Imagine relaxing and enjoying all the comforts and beauty of well designed outdoor furniture and patio accessories you made yourself! Now you can do it easily and affordably—with these 47 do-it-yourself projects. There are step-by-step instructions, detailed two-color illustrations, and exploded working diagrams for each piece of furniture. Important tips on technique help you add those finishing touches that will give your outdoor furnishings that professional look. 224 pp., 158 illus.

Paper $12.95   **Hard $21.95**
Book No. 2984

☐ **COUNTRY FURNITURE—114 Traditional Projects—Percy W. Blandford**

Show off a house full of beautiful country furniture—you created! There is an undeniable attraction about hand-made furniture. Whether the craftsman is an amateur or professional, individually made furniture carries on the tradition of the first settlers and their ancestors. Blandford captures the rustic flavor in these traditional projects—and shows how you can too! Projects range from simple boxes to more elaborate cabinets and cupboards. 260 pp., 246 illus.

Paper $15.95   **Hard $24.95**
Book No. 2944

☐ **BUILD YOUR OWN KIT HOUSE—Jonathan Erickson**

Building a house from a kit is an affordable choice. Erickson makes it possible for you to buy and build a kit home of your own from scratch. It answers real-life questions potential kit homeowners should pose to lending institutions, contractors, dealers, and others. The pros and cons of time, cost, and quality are examined so that you can make decisions from a solid knowledge base. 272 pp., 153 illus.

Paper $14.95   **Hard $22.95**
Book No. 2873

Other Bestsellers from TAB

☐ **77 ONE-WEEKEND WOODWORKING PROJECTS—**
Percy W. Blandford

Let this guide put the fun back into your hobby! Over-flowing with step-by-step instructions, easy-to-follow illustrations, dimensioned drawings, and material lists, this indispensable guide includes plans for 77 projects: tables, racks and shelves, take-down book rack, low bookcase, corner shelves, magazine rack, portable magazine bin, shoe rack, vase stand, beds and cabinets, yard and garden projects, toys, games and puzzles, tools, and more. 304 pp., 226 illus.
Paper $14.95   **Book No. 2774**

☐ **BUILDING OUTDOOR PLAYTHINGS FOR KIDS,**
WITH PROJECT PLANS—Bill Barnes

Imagine the delight of your youngsters—children or grandchildren—when you build them their own special back-yard play area! Best of all, discover how you can make exciting, custom-designed play equipment at a fraction of the cost of ordinary, ready-made swing sets or sandbox units! It's all here in this step-by-step guide to planning and building safe, sturdy outdoor play equipment! 240 pp., 213 illus.
Paper $12.95   **Book No. 1971**

☐ **79 FURNITURE PROJECTS FOR EVERY ROOM—**
Percy W. Blandford

Just imagine your entire home filled with beautiful, hand-crafted furniture! Elegant chairs, tables, and sofas, a hand-finished corner cupboard, luxurious beds and chests, and more! With the hands-on instructions and step-by-step project plans included here, you'll be able to build beautiful furniture for any room . . . or every room in your home . . . at a fraction of the store-bought cost! 384 pp., 292 illus.
Paper $16.95   **Hard $24.95**
Book No. 2704

☐ **THE WOODTURNER'S BIBLE—2nd Edition—Percy**
W. Blandford

All the hands-on instruction and project plans you need are in this sourcebook that hobbyists and professional wood-crafters consider the most complete guide to woodturning tools and techniques available. Included are details on choosing the proper lathe and lathe accessories. Dozens of step-by-step project plans are illustrated throughout. 400 pp., 313 illus.
Paper $16.95   **Book No. 1954**

Send $1 for the new TAB Catalog describing over 1300 titles currently in print and receive a coupon worth $1 off on your next purchase from TAB.

(In PA, NY, and ME add applicable sales tax. Orders subject to credit approval. Orders outside U.S. must be prepaid with international money orders in U.S. dollars.)
***Prices subject to change without notice.**

To purchase these or any other books from TAB, visit your local bookstore, return this coupon, or call toll-free 1-800-233-1128 (In PA and AK call 1-717-794-2191).

Product No.	Hard or Paper	Title	Quantity	Price

☐ Check or money order enclosed made payable to TAB BOOKS Inc.

Charge my   ☐ VISA   ☐ MasterCard   ☐ American Express

Acct. No. _____ Exp. _____

Signature _____

Please Print
Name _____

Company _____

Address _____

City _____

State _____ Zip _____

Subtotal	
Postage/Handling ($5.00 outside U.S.A. and Canada)	$2.50
In PA, NY, and ME add applicable sales tax	
TOTAL	

Mail coupon to:

TAB BOOKS Inc.
Blue Ridge Summit
PA 17294-0840   BC